Independent Women in British Psychoanalysis

Independent Women in British Psychoanalysis celebrates the lives and work of female psychoanalysts whose significant contributions to the Independent Tradition have hitherto been overshadowed by their male counterparts.

The contributors in this volume look at seven female psychoanalysts who broke new ground with their contributions to theory and practice: Ella Freemen Sharpe, Marjorie Brierley, Paula Heimann, Marion Milner, Enid Balint, Nina Coltart and Pearl King. The chapters tell the individual stories of these psychoanalysts alongside their theories, showing how their personal lives embody and illustrate the essential universal developmental task of becoming oneself and finding one's own voice. The themes across the chapters include infant and child development with (m)other, trauma, constructive use of aggression, creativity, a theory of clinical technique, and independence of mind in a social world.

This book will be of interest and relevance to psychoanalysts and psychotherapists, developmental psychologists, sociologists, group analysts and historians of psychoanalysis, as well as those interested in feminism and women's position in society.

Elizabeth Wolf is a training and supervising analyst of the British Psychoanalytical Society and works full-time in psychoanalytic private practice. She contributes to the development and teaching of the Independent Tradition in psychoanalysis, in seminars for both psychoanalytic candidates and psychotherapists, in committee work at the Institute of Psychoanalysis, including co-chairing the Association of Independent Psychoanalysts for two terms, and in her writing.

Barbie Antonis is a Fellow of the British Psychoanalytic Society, teaches at the British Society and is co-Chair of the Winnicott Trust. For over twenty years she worked as a Consultant Psychotherapist in the NHS at Parkside Clinic in London. Now semi-retired from clinical practice, she continues to teach, supervise and write. She chaired the annual Cambridge Conference for ten years until 2012. Integral to her work and identity as a psychoanalyst, Barbie is a jazz singer and sings as a soloist, in a choir and with her quartet.

Psychoanalysis and Women Series

The *Women and Psychoanalysis Book Series* grew from the work of the International Psychoanalytical Association Committee on Women and Psychoanalysis (COWAP). Publications further the conversations on women, sexuality, gender, men, and psychoanalysis, and intersections with diversity and cross-cultural experience. We value written exchanges between psychoanalysis and related disciplines of gender studies, anthropology, sociology, politics, philosophy, arts and activism. We encourage contributions from all regions, allowing for global perspectives and different creativities on topics relating to women, gender and sexuality. The series editorial board is comprised of Paula Ellman (Editor-in-Chief, North America), Carolina Bacchi (North America) Sara Boffito (Italy), Lesley Caldwell (UK), Amrita Narayana (India), and Paula Escribens Pareja (Peru).

Series Editor: Paula Ellman (previously Frances Thomson-Salo)

Titles in the series:
Changing Sexualities and Parental Functions in the Twenty-First Century: Changing Sexualities, Changing Parental Functions By Candida Se Holovko

Psychoanalytic Explorations of What Women Want Today: Femininity, Desire and Agency By Margarita Cereijido, Paula L. Ellman and Nancy R. Goodman

The Desire and Passion to Have a Child: Psychoanalysis and Contemporary Reproductive Techniques By Patricia Alkolombre

Independent Women in British Psychoanalysis: Creativity and Authenticity at Work By Elizabeth Wolf and Barbie Antonis

For further information about this series please visit
https://www.routledge.com/Psychoanalysis-and-Women-Series/book-series/
KARNACPWS

Independent Women in British Psychoanalysis

Creativity and Authenticity at Work

Edited by
Elizabeth Wolf and Barbie Antonis

Routledge
Taylor & Francis Group

LONDON AND NEW YORK

Designed cover image: Untitled (2021) © Paola Somaini

First published 2024
by Routledge
4 Park Square, Milton Park, Abingdon, Oxon OX14 4RN

and by Routledge
605 Third Avenue, New York, NY 10158

Routledge is an imprint of the Taylor & Francis Group, an informa business

British Library Cataloguing-in-Publication Data
A catalogue record for this book is available from the British Library

ISBN: 978-1-032-28403-3 (hbk)
ISBN: 978-1-032-27999-2 (pbk)
ISBN: 978-1-003-29669-0 (ebk)

DOI: 10.4324/9781003296690

Typeset in Times New Roman
by Taylor & Francis Books

To all the significant 'others' who have been listening and responding throughout my journey, but especially to Stephen. EW

To my supervisees, whose company I have enjoyed so much, and to family members, who have supported me through the writing of this book. BA

Contents

Figures

Acknowledgements

We would like to thank all the candidates who took our course 'On the Contribution of Independent Women Psychoanalysts' at the Institute of Psychoanalysis. We found their enthusiasm invaluable in encouraging our ongoing development of the course and subsequently this book. We pay tribute to our own training analysts, teachers, supervisors and colleagues in the Independent Tradition with whom we have been in dialogue throughout our professional lives. Our special appreciation goes to our colleagues from the Winnicott Trust, particularly Angela Joyce and Amal Treacher Kabesh, who sadly died in 2022. It was Amal who helped us see that the idea of this book could take shape and come into being. We are also grateful to Paula Ellman, for focusing and guiding us in the process. We thank Giles Milner and the Institute for Psychoanalysis for permission to reproduce Marion Milner's artwork. We thank Paola Somaini for her permission to reproduce one of her paintings for the cover of our book.

Preface

The Women and Psychoanalysis Book Series grew from the work of the International Psychoanalytical Association Committee on Women and Psychoanalysis (COWAP). The IPA–Routledge series furthers global perspectives and different creativities on topics related to women, gender and sexuality, and psychoanalysis, considering intersections with diversity and cross-cultural experience.

This volume offers the insiders' look at female authors of British Independent Psychoanalysis, a tradition characterized by a focus on the process of being and becoming oneself, authenticity and creativity in the analytic process.

The authors of the chapters, dedicated to seven female analysts, are also analysts from that psychoanalytic culture, the majority women: Elizabeth Wolf, Barbie Antonis, Joan Raphael-Leff, Ken Robinson, Jan Abram, Emily Alster, Maia Kirchkheli, Paola Somaini, Jonathan Sklar. The book proposes a creative encounter between generations for the writers but also, we believe, for the interested reader.

The contributions of the writers represented here, Ella Freemen Sharpe, Marjorie Brierley, Paula Heimann, Marion Milner, Enid Balint, Nina Coltart, and Pearl King, were significant for the theory and practice of psychoanalysis at the time and they remain so. The volume leads us through the personal and clinical journeys of these women, as they found their voices as Independent psychoanalysts and created new ways of being with patients and practising psychoanalysis.

Independent Women in British Psychoanalysis: Creativity and Authenticity at Work embodies and illustrates the essential universal developmental task of becoming oneself and finding one's own voice as a central issue especially for women authors whose contributions are often at risk of being marginalized. This volume endows these analysts with the stature and eminence their creative ideas deserve. By making links between psychoanalytic theory and other disciplines, the editors and authors offer inspiration for further creative activity.

The *Women and Psychoanalysis Book Series* Editorial Board represents all regions of the IPA, with six editors collaborating as a team from Goa (India),

London, Lima, Milan, San Francisco and Washington DC. We are women writers and editors active in psychoanalysis both regionally and in the IPA. We encourage single author and multiple author book proposal submissions to our IPA–Routledge Book Series on topics of women, gender, femininity and masculinity. We offer our close-up consultation and guidance in the crafting of the book proposals, and throughout the writing and publishing process.

The Women and Psychoanalysis Book Series Editorial Board:
Carolina Bacchi
Sara Boffito
Lesley Caldwell
Paula Ellman (Editor-in-Chief)
Paula Escribens Pareja
Amrita Narayanan

Contributors

Emily Alster is a psychoanalyst with the British Psychoanalytical Society, and a member of the Association of Independent Psychoanalysts. She is in full-time Private Practice in London. She teaches at the Institute of Psychoanalysis and the Tavistock Clinic. She is a member of the Winnicott Trust and was Book Review Editor for the International Journal of Psychoanalysis.

Jan Abram is a Training and Supervising Analyst of the British Psycho-analytical Society. She was past Chair of the BPAS Scientific Committee and Chair of the Archives Committee. She is Vice President of the European Psychoanalytic Federation for the annual Conferences (2020–2024). She is Visiting Professor at University College London, where she teaches on the MSc Psychoanalytic Studies course. She was a member of the Paris Group (the IPA and EPF Research group on The Specificity of Psycho-analytic Treatment Today) and was its Chair between 2016 and 2019. Jan Abram has published several books and articles, notably: The Language of Winnicott (1st edition 1996; 2nd edition 2007) (ACRL Choice Outstanding Academic Book of the Year 1997); Donald Winnicott Today (2013); The Clinical Paradigms of Melanie Klein and Donald Winnicott: comparisons and dialogues (2018, with co-author R.D. Hinshelwood) and The Surviving Object: psychoanalytic clinical essays on psychic survival-of-the-object (2022) in the New Library of Psychoanalysis Series, Routledge (a collection of her clinical papers). Her forthcoming books are Donald Winnicott: A Con-temporary Introduction, Routledge, and, with R.D. Hinshelwood, The Clinical Paradigms of Donald Winnicott and Wilfred Bion: comparisons and dialogues, Routledge. She is Series Editor for The Routledge Clinical Paradigms Dialogues Series with R.D. Hinshelwood.

Joan Raphael-Leff, academic and clinician (Fellow, British Psychoanalytical Society) specialises in Reproductive and Early Parenting issues, acting as con-sultant to perinatal and women's projects worldwide. In 1998 she founded COWAP, the International Psychoanalytic Association's committee on Women and Psychoanalysis. Between 1997–2004 she was Professor of Psychoanalysis at the Centre for Psychoanalytic Studies at the University of Essex, UK, and was later appointed Head of University College London's MSc degree in Psycho-analytic Developmental Psychology. She currently leads the UCL/Anna Freud Centre's Academic Faculty for Psychoanalytic Research. Her 150+ peer-reviewed single-author publications, and 13 books include: The Marion Milner Tradition – Lines of Development. Evolution of Theory and Practice over the Decades. (M. Boyle Spelman & J. Raphael-Leff (eds)), Routledge, 2022; Dark Side of the Womb – pregnancy, parenting & persecutory anxieties, London: Anna Freud Centre, 2017; The Anna Freud Tradition – Lines of Development, Evolution of Theory and Practice over the Decades. (N.T. Malberg & J. Raphael-Leff (eds)), London: Karnac Books, 2012; Female Experience: Four Generations of British Women Psychoanalysts on Work with Women, (J. Raphael-Leff, & R. Jozef Perelberg (eds)). Routledge, 1997/2008.

Ken Robinson is a member of the British Psychoanalytical Society, Honorary Member of the Polish Psychoanalytic Psychotherapy Society, Visiting Pro-fessor of Psychoanalysis at Northumbria University, and formerly, like Pearl King, Honorary Archivist of the Institute of Psychoanalysis. Like Ella Sharpe, his first training was in English Literature which he taught at University before training as a psychoanalyst. He works in private practice in Newcastle upon Tyne and also joint-facilitates a Professional Doctorate in Psychoanalytic Psychotherapy at Northumbria University. Ken teaches and supervises nationally and in Europe. He has published widely on the history of psychoanalysis, clinical topics, and the nature of therapeutic action. His recent publications include the introduction to volume one of *The Collected Works of D.W. Winnicott* (2017, republished 2019), *The Contemporary Freudian Tradition: Past and Present*, jointly edited with Joan Schachter (2020) and, most recently, "'Too little and too lately known': the experience of mourning", (*Imago Budapest*, 2021), and "The End of Transference: One Contemporary Freudian View" (*Jahrbuch der Psychoanalyse*, 2022).

Maia Kirchkheli is a fellow of the British Psychoanalytical Society. She qua-lified and worked as a psychiatrist in a Drug and Substance Misuse Clinic in Georgia before emigrating to the United Kingdom. After completing an MA in Consultation and the Organisation: Psychoanalytic Approaches from The Tavistock and Portman NHS Foundation Trust, Maia trained as a psychoanalyst at The Institute of Psychoanalysis in London. She is currently in full-time private practice in London and teaches extensively on The Inde-pendent Tradition, Freud, Winnicott and the work of Milner in the Con-tributions from Independent Woman Analysts to BPAS candidates. She is a guest lecturer at UCL and the BPA. She won the Winnicott Essay Prize (Student Path) for her paper 'Beyond Words' in 2017, and the Rozsika Parker Prize (post-qualification path) for 'Holding and Visceral Attention, Bodily Concentration of an Analyst under Covid-19 Lockdown', published by the

Journal of British Psychotherapy in 2021, and in *The Marion Milner Tradition: Lines of Development – evolution of tradition, theory, and practice over the decades*, (Joan Raphael Leff & Margaret Spelman (eds)), Routledge, 2023. Her main area of interest is the overlap of Art and Psychoanalysis.

Jonathan Sklar, MBBS, FRCPsych is an Independent training and supervising psychoanalyst of the British Psychoanalytical Society. Originally trained in psychiatry at Friern and the Royal Free Hospitals, he later trained in adult psychotherapy at the Tavistock Clinic, London. For many years, he was consultant psychotherapist and head of the psychotherapy department at Addenbrooke's and Fulbourne hospitals in Cambridge.

He now works in analytic practice in London. He has lectured widely across the world, taught psychoanalysis annually in South Africa for over ten years, termly in Chicago for ten years until 2018, as well as regularly across Eastern Europe. From 2007 to 2011, he was vice president of the European Psychoanalytic Federation, with special responsibility for seminars for recently qualified analysts as well as new analytic groups in East Europe. He was a board member of the International Psychoanalytical Association 2015 to 2019. He is chair of the Independent Psychoanalytic Trust.

Paola Somaini is a psychoanalyst with the IPA. Originally from Italy, Paola studied first at the Tavistock Clinic and then trained at The Institute of Psychoanalysis. She qualified as a member of the BPAS in 2015 and has been on the Committee of the Association of Independent Psychoanalysts (AIP) since 2017. Paola is the author of a paper, 'The Eyes to See', published in *Infant Observation*, 2013, and is also the author and illustrator of a children's book written during the pandemic, *I Can See It With My Elephant Eye* (2020, Lulu Publishing and Amazon). She is currently in full-time private practice as a psychoanalyst and teaches on the Independent Tradition and the work of D.W. Winnicott at the Institute of Psychoanalysis, the BPF and the Caspari Foundation.

Part 1

Setting the Scene

Introduction

On becoming

Elizabeth Wolf and Barbie Antonis

The process of becoming a psychoanalyst takes time.

This book is the culmination of an ongoing dialogue between us about our development as Independent women psychoanalysts of the British Psycho-analytical Society. We have been thinking and talking about the growth of our own identity as analysts for over 20 years. How this book came to be is entwined with the evolution of the Independent Tradition in the British Society, from its emergence right up to the present. Though this is inevitably a personal story, the journey of finding one's voice, of becoming oneself as an analyst, will surely be recognized beyond these shores; it is the endeavour of each of us. This is at the core of an Independent identity and, as such, we hope relating our personal experience will resonate with others. We feel it is important that this story be told as we experienced it. At the heart of the Independent contribution to psychoanalysis is the process of becoming an authentic self with an other. Our story, and those of the women in this book, we hope are vivid illustrations of this.

The story starts with the beginnings of the British Society. We are grateful for Jonathan Sklar's scholarly examination of the early history of the group of analysts who became known as Independent psychoanalysts in the 1950s, and the Bloomsbury and Cambridge origins of their core principles of freedom and respect. Joan Raphael-Leff interrogates the distinctive qualities of the Independent Tradition. Her chapter elaborates what was developing in Independent psychoanalytic theory and clinical practice in the area of subjectivity and the creation of mind within the analytic relationship, as it does between mother and baby, as well as her critique of it.

Creative Independent work was flourishing in the 1980s and 1990s, as evidenced by the numerous day conferences open to the public on living psychoanalysts' work, which were oversubscribed. Gregorio Kohon, in *The British School of Psychoanalysis: The Independent Tradition*, which he edited in 1986, evokes the breadth and significance of the ideas Independents were working on, which expanded and challenged the prevailing current psychoanalytic orthodoxies.

DOI: 10.4324/9781003296690-2

The contributions made by Independent analysts emphasized the interrelations between the analysand's and the analyst's subjective experience. This emphasis on subjectivity caused the creation, development, and re-evaluation of theoretical concepts and clinical notions like: *countertransference*, as something of clinical relevance, not just a psychopathological interference; *acting out*, as a means of communicating something significant emerging from the history of the individual; the revision of the *criteria for the selection of cases*, enlarging the spectrum of patients considered suitable for analysis; a demand for *modifications in technique*, in order to adapt to the patient, not the patient to the technique; the consideration of the *influence of the early environment* in the creation of an illness, including the study of *uses of regression*, and the creation of a *facilitating environment* in the context of the psychoanalytic treatment (James, 1980).

(Kohon, 1986, 75, original emphasis)

It is not surprising that these day conferences were not meetings of the British Society, reflecting the impulse to move away from the stultifying climate which many Independents (and others) experienced in the twice-monthly scientific meetings. In those meetings, the atmosphere was hierarchical; novices sat at the back of the lecture room while the front rows were for senior analysts who did most of the talking. What was lost was the importance of respectful dialogue which had been facilitated by the Middle Group women during the Controversial Discussions[1]. In a sense, the three groups – Freudian, Kleinian and Independent – were living separately under one roof, not referencing the others' work in writing or in meetings[2], allowing candidates to qualify without exposure to the different psychoanalytical traditions (introductory courses on the three main traditions were not compulsory for all candidates, as they are now), and not necessarily encouraging candidates to go to analysts of different traditions for supervision. This continued until the turn of the millennium. As early as 1952, Independents, prompted by Pearl King and Paula Heimann, set up a group outside of the Society where they could speak freely. The 1952 Club was also a space especially welcoming for newly qualified Independent associate members.

Yet, even during the two decades of creative work, there was growing tension and anxiety about the survival of an Independent grouping within the British Society. From being the largest group in the Society in 1945, it was becoming clear that the group would eventually disappear if there were not sufficient numbers putting themselves forward to become training analysts. Was this decline in numbers only due to the open-minded or liberal characteristic of the 'group', who refused to be a group? Without a single unitary theory or clearly expressed group identity, the Group of Independent Analysts was not attempting to attract or recruit members to believe in or conform to certain ideas or theories, but rather to foster in those associated with it the desire to become independently-minded free thinkers – to become themselves as analysts. Michael Parsons observed the fundamentally different ways in which candidates develop their psychoanalytic identity within the British Society in his overview paper, 'From Founders to the Present: A British Psychoanalytic Odyssey', commissioned by Elizabeth, issue editor of the *Psychoanalytic Inquiry* volume on British Psychoanalysts[3]. Parsons contrasts the process of 'learning' to be an analyst from one's analyst, teachers and supervisors, as it were from the outside, where the encounter is with a psychoanalytic theory "conceived as a whole and that seeks to encompass psychoanalysis in totality" (Parsons 2009b, 237), with the other approach, in which the individual candidate/analyst is in an on-going open-ended process of developing their psychoanalytic identity from the interaction of their internal self-experience engaging with the many viewpoints, and "discovering what matters to her" (Parsons 2009b, 236). Liberal groups that operate like the Group of Independent analysts perhaps inevitably do less well in attracting new candidates than groups which could be characterized, as they often are, in similar terms to a religious sect where strictness and conformity to a doctrine are demanded from trainees. Mary Twyman, Chair of the organizing committee of the Group of Independent Analysts in the late 1990s, told us her experience of developing along the lines that Parsons describes:

> I remember having a meeting with one of my supervisors and I remember her saying, "I think it's about time that you went, now just go, you don't have any more supervision for at least a couple of years, so just go and do it on your own." And I did. I think it wasn't as scary as I thought it would be ... I felt good about the fact that I could go out there and learn for myself, I found it valuable.
>
> (personal communication)

Contrast that with the culture of postgraduate seminars continuing after qualification; newly qualified analysts joining a group with senior analysts became prevalent first in the Klein Group, but has been more widely adopted by the other two groups in recent years, in recognition that this can be a good way to grow and progress younger colleagues. Though there have been post-qualification groups run by Independent training analysts, they have sought to encourage creative development and finding one's own voice, and not to encourage a group identity, or necessarily encourage the continuation of the 'group'. Once the majority of analysts who did not take sides in the Controversial Discussions grew old and gradually died, there was no system to replace them by schooling candidates in a tradition; Independents were too independent for that, and such an idea runs contrary to what in principle it means to be an Independent. What shifted, eventually, was the refocusing of the group (now named the Association of Independent Psychoanalysts, the AIP) to have a clear objective of teaching and promoting the Independent Tradition. If the ideas are not taught, then individual analysts cannot develop them or themselves further in that way.

The decline in candidates may also have been accelerated by the critical atmosphere between the groups within the British Society. Candidates with an inclination to an Independent way of thinking were apprehensive about presenting in clinical seminars for fear of being judged as non-analytic for not making here-and-now transference interpretations, or not interpreting the patient's aggression or envy, i.e. not doing analysis according to the Kleinian orthodoxy. We both remember the anxiety in clinical seminars of reporting extra-transferential interpretations, reconstructions, or anything other than a strict here-and-now so-called transference interpretation, which was seen by the majority of other candidates (Kleinian, as was often the case) and some clinical seminar leaders as not doing proper analysis.

A similar atmosphere was also present in scientific meetings where qualified analysts were afraid to speak or put themselves forward for assessment in order to progress. Not many Independents applied to be considered for panel assessment to become a training analyst, without which the group was shrinking. Mary Twyman recalled discussing this with her peers and told us,

> [T]here was a group of women Independents … [who] had a meeting to talk about our feelings about being training analysts and why we had decided not to. A lot of us felt intimidated … most of us were very *very* intimidated about the idea of having to stand up at scientific meetings and defend, or whatever … It was a failure of courage on our parts individually and perhaps collectively, but that's how it felt.
>
> (personal communication)

We are struck how little had changed (or possibly got worse) since Charles Rycroft wrote in 1993 about his experience giving a paper in 1954:

> The so-called scientific meetings were all too often not discussions but collisions. I once read a paper to the Society about a woman who had dreamed that the moon fell out of the sky into a dustbin [Rycroft 1955]. During the discussion Melanie Klein expressed her regret that I had not had a sufficiently deep analysis; at the time I took this as an insult to Dr Payne [Dr Sylvia Payne, Dr Rycroft's analyst]. I heard later that some of the audience had construed my paper as a conscious, deliberate allegory about Klein; it wasn't, but it is a pleasing idea.
>
> (Lanyado & Horne 2006, 20)

There were too few Independent training analysts – 15 in 1999 – and they, too, had difficulties when putting themselves forward for key Society positions, e.g. Chair of Education and President. One Independent who put themselves forward for the Independents' nomination for President, found not a single Kleinian colleague who would risk stepping out of line from Kleinian politics at the time and endorse them. Another colleague who put themselves forward for Chair of Education was similarly frustrated. The internal political pressures were pernicious. Looking back now, we see this anxiety as a crisis point for the group. But there was anxiety, too, in the BPAS as a whole about the aging membership with too few new candidates to reverse rapidly diminishing numbers, leading to fears that the British Society might not survive, certainly not in its current vibrant form. In April 1999, the then President of BPAS, Irma Brenman Pick, along with the Board, announced the 'Launch of a Consultation Process on the Future of Psycho-analysis and the Role of the Society'. In the Board's letter to the Society it states:

> We are responding to widespread concerns expressed within and beyond the Society about the future of Psycho-analysis. Members report a decline in referrals for four or five times a week treatment other than for training purposes; the average age at the start of training has risen to 38, and the balance has changed with more women and fewer doctors. All this against a backdrop of almost constant uninformed hostility and suspicion towards psychoanalysis in the media.
> (Consultation Launch, 22 April 1999, British Psychoanalytical Society, in the archives of the British Psychoanalytic Society)

All members were asked to write in 500 words their vision for the development of psychoanalysis over the next 20 years. Another survey of how members "allocate their time as analysts at present" would be launched to update the 1997/8 survey which first alerted the Society to the aging membership and overall decline in numbers. The practice of psychoanalysis itself felt under threat. At this time, CBT as a treatment modality for anxiety and depression was acclaimed – it was short, quick and cheap – and psychoanalysis and Freud were under serious critique for both theories and clinical practice. The International Psychoanalytic community was becoming increasingly divided and pluralistic, with the threat of, as one British analyst put it, "anything goes". In London, there was a new Institute emerging which became the British Psychoanalytic Association; were those analysts to be rivals for the few patients left?

The dissolution of the Gentleman's Agreement[4] in 2005 sorely tested the commitment to pluralism in BPAS. The so-called 'transitional arrangements' were meant to be in place to ensure that the different 'voices' in psychoanalysis, particularly analysts working within all three main traditions, would be heard, represented and not be discriminated against within the Society. Many analysts were concerned and outraged by an article in *American Imago*, Fall 2006, by Hanna Segal in which her words were taken as an unethical critique against her colleagues' integrity as psychoanalysts. Elizabeth and Ruth McCall, at the time serving as co-Chairs for the Group of Independent Psychoanalysts organizing committee, were motivated to work with senior Independents to compose a letter in response. 50 BPAS analysts signed the letter to the editor, Peter Rudnytsky, which was published alongside another from other BPAS colleagues in the following year.

> We are not disputing her theoretical position but her defamatory remarks about our competence and integrity as psychoanalysts. It is Dr Segal's statement that the work of British Independent psychoanalysts is nonanalytic and that it promotes patients living in a lie through the analyst (allegedly) actively taking on the parental role that we object to the most.
> (Ruth McCall and Elizabeth Wolf, co-Chair, Group of Independent Psychoanalysts, 15 February 2007, letter to Peter Rudnytsky)

Peter's reply the same day informed us that Hanna Segal had just written to him that she "owes an apology to colleagues whom she may inadvertently have offended by the paragraph at issue in her paper" but he went on to express his own view of the situation:

> I believe I acted in the best Independent spirit by publishing Hanna Segal's article, and I hope I may even have aided the Independent cause. One thing you can be sure of: it is her genuine conviction, and probably that of the Klein group as a whole, that the Ferenczi – Winnicott – Kohut tradition is 'essentially non-analytic'. You have had to live with this insidious attitude on a daily basis for years or even decades. Rather than have it fester beneath the surface, I think it is far healthier to bring it out into the light of day where it can be seen for what it is and disinfected.
> (Peter Rudnytsky, letter to Group of Independent Psychoanalysts, 15 February 2007)

It was perhaps the case that some Kleinian colleagues believed that there were no longer any differences between the groups. An illustration from the world of child psychotherapy, where the different schools had different institutional homes, the Independents (and to some degree, the Anna Freudians) located at the BPF (British Psychotherapy Foundation) and the Kleinians predominating at the Tavistock Clinic, demonstrates how widely the polarization and animosity in the BPAS had permeated other institutions where our members also played important roles. Ann Horne writes,

> I am reminded of the Association of Child Psychotherapists conference in 2000 when, asked what has most aided the 'crossing of borders' between training schools of different theoretical orientations, a senior Kleinian training analyst proposed in all seriousness that it was the acceptance by all groups of the Kleinian concept of projective identification. One might – from an Independent point of view, of course – offer that the saving of psychoanalysis in 1944 in Britain was the refusal of the majority of the members of the British Psychoanalytic Society to follow any

charismatic leader or omnipotent theory, and so sanity lay in the formation of the Middle, later Independent Group.

(Horne 2006, 21)

In the early 1960s, 'Middle Group' Child and Adolescent Psychotherapy
trainees at the Tavistock were allowed to go to Middle Group supervisors,
hence Juliet Hopkins reporting her luck to be supervised by Donald Winnicott on one of her training cases. She remarked, "As far as I know, no
other student child psychotherapist ever shared this good fortune, since
doctrinal differences dictated that students should be supervised only by
the orthodox" (Horne 2006, 22). By the late 1960s, Kahr comments on the
worsening atmosphere:

> The Kleinian bitterness towards Winnicott and his burgeoning indepen-
> dence reached such proportions that during the late 1960s certain tutors on
> the Child psychotherapy course at the Tavistock Clinic … expressly forbade
> their students to attend Winnicott's public lectures … Mrs Frances Tustin
> (personal communication, 22 February 1994), a renowned child psy-
> chotherapist … confessed that 'I in my training was brought up not to read
> Winnicott'. Another of those trainees, now a seasoned professional, laughed
> as she recalled how she visited Winnicott in secret, as though he epitomized
> some dreadful subversive underground movement.
>
> (Kahr 1996, 77)

These anxieties about external threats ran parallel to internal Independent
Group ruminations about identity and survival.

The issue of identity for Independents is central and might seem a preoccupation but it parallels the process in our patients of finding themselves.
Mary Twyman spoke to us about identity in 2013 when recalling the origins
of what became the annual Independent Group meeting at Cambridge. The
group, financially secure with the proceeds of the successful day conferences,
took up the suggestion from Peter Hildebrandt, who said, "why don't we just
take ourselves out of London and away from what was in Mansfield House[5]
and just talk among ourselves and give some time and attention to considering who we are and what we are doing – the sort of thing that the Independents are often talking about, that is, what is our identity?" "You might be
able to define a Kleinian (and possibly a CF) [Contemporary Freudian] by his
theory, but can only define an Independent by his attitude," Eric Karas, a
committee member wrote at the time.[6] With hindsight, we see how a prevailing anxiety diminished the confidence in the significant body of theory on
which Independents draw. This book attests to the strength of the theoretical
framework underpinning Independent clinical work.

Our story, and the story of this book's inception, is the next part and begins
with Barbie's involvement in the Cambridge meetings of the Independent

Group, where we first worked together. Barbie qualified as an analyst in 1998, just in time to attend the first weekend meeting of the group in Cambridge[7], convened with the title 'Rethinking Independent Group Thinking'. Evaluating what was regarded as a very positive experience, the Independents' organizing committee noted that while there was "passion" at the meeting there was also "difficulty acknowledging aggression". One Committee member remarked, "there was a great deal about us as free thinkers and not enough about our common clinical identity"[8]. In his Chair's report at the AGM in May, Eric Rayner wrote that they would hold another conference the following year to continue the theme, while acknowledging without spelling out "some serious tensions within the group"[9]. In June, the organizing committee appointed another planning group to make the arrangements for the second meeting with the theme of 'Our common theoretical links'.[10] In the same meeting it was agreed to set up a Think Tank to look at both scientific and political issues in the group, headed by Paul Williams. Barbie was invited to hear about the Think Tank, a group of psychoanalysts who convened in 1999[11]. Setting up the Cambridge meetings can be seen as one response to the recognition of crisis in the group and in the Society. The Cambridge convention was also seen as an opportunity for clarifying and safeguarding the core tenets and clinical technique relevant to working as an Independent psychoanalyst[12]. The report of the Think Tank to the third convention in March 2001 succinctly described the internal conflict and dilemma for the group.

> [C]ontemporary Independents are a Group characterized by a struggle for an identity, rather than a group characterized by an apparently coherent theoretical framework (Kleinian) or one characterized by an allegiance to a particular metapsychology and its continuing evolution (Contemporary Freudians) ... Whatever else the struggle of the Independents involves, one additional factor of importance is that the Group does not possess a broadly shared alliance in respect of core clinical and theoretical concepts ... the idea emerged to try to encourage Independent analysts to contribute their different perspectives on important subjects as a way of beginning to identify the shape(s) of contemporary Independent thinking. The Cambridge Colloquium is obviously one way of doing this, and is a good basis for the presentation of ideas ...[13]
>
> (Final Think Tank report to the Cambridge colloquium, 2001)

The Think Tank's main recommendation was for Independents to write and publish, and included a substantive list of topics to address, a longer process that in time culminated in a new book on *Contemporary Independent Thinking* edited by Paul Williams, Sira Dermen and John Keene (2012). However, it was Cambridge that really took off, the conference designed as a place where Independents could meet and talk together. Initially, survival took the form of attacking the Kleinians, perhaps an avoidance of facing the internal conflict in the group. There was one critique which was justified, stirring up anger against the Klein Group. A topic that dominated the first Cambridge meeting was the information, a revelation, that candidates in training with a Kleinian training analyst were having their supervision paid for by the Melanie Klein Trust, provided that they went to a Kleinian supervisor. The Independent Committee later decided to write to the Education Committee[14] alerting them to their concerns about the apparent breach of the agreement between the groups that candidates not be formally aligned with any group prior to qualification. Barbie recalls that this news went through the assembled participants at Cambridge like a bolt. It felt like a blatant betrayal of truth; the secrecy felt like underhand practice. There has been a belief that if developing analysts were exposed to a range of ideas they could be freed from becoming analysts that were clones of their own analyst. This hidden arrangement for supervision fees meant that no candidates in analysis with a Kleinian went to an analyst of another group for supervision, at least not until a candidate in Elizabeth's year told his peer group that he was the first one to go outside the Klein group for supervision after a difficult experience with a Kleinian supervisor.

From her involvement behind the scenes, Barbie joined the Independent Committee, now chaired by John Tydeman, in July 2001 and immediately agreed to lead the new planning group for the 2002 Cambridge conference on 'Early Experience, Representation and Enactment'.[15] Barbie's tenure as Chair of the organizing group ushered in a period of stability for the meetings; she held the idea of Cambridge in mind, as well as carrying the main responsibility for organizing it. A new venue had to be found and Churchill College's Moller Centre became the home for the Cambridge convention, a setting which was comfortable and nurturing. Elizabeth qualified in 2001 and joined the Cambridge Committee the following year, and we soon discovered we had common interests and a working group in which to develop our ideas. Working together brought us close and initiated what has become an enduring friendship.

Following her election to Fellowship in 2002, Barbie put her energy into the Cambridge conference, creating an imaginative space for playing with ideas. The first of her titles for the fifth meeting in 2003, 'Levels of Listening', inaugurated a period of developing themes of particular interest to us. Between 2003 and 2011, Cambridge became for Independents an anticipated event in the calendar. In those years the topics explored differentiating core concepts of Independent theory, finding one's authentic voice as a psychoanalyst and how those ideas came into our daily practice in the analytic relationship in the consulting room. These were of personal interest in our development. The work of finding one's voice, which is exactly what we were doing, can be heard in the other conference titles: 'Becoming one's own analyst' (2004), 'Becoming the analyst the patient needs' (2005), 'The patient, the analyst, his language, her mind' (2006), 'Mindful of the body/Mind full of the body' (2007), and 'With couples in mind' (2008), Barbie's last as Chair. Elizabeth became a Fellow in 2008 and, along with Tamar Schonfeld and other colleagues, continued on the Committee organizing Cambridge along these themes – 'Identity and its vicissitudes' (2009), 'The creative unconscious' (2010), and 'Analytic love' (2011) – before handing on to other colleagues. There was tremendous motivation to make the Cambridge convention not only serious but fun, to make a place for substantial and interesting work. Looking back, we now see that the original anxiety about identity that initiated the meetings gave way to appreciating the exploration of what it means to be an Independent psychoanalyst: the ongoing process of becoming, and the development of identity. We must have developed from the experiences at Cambridge a sense of continuity and going on being to give us the confidence to write, speak and teach; we also discovered a shared commitment to valuing authenticity in the analytic relationship. The conference themes expressed our shared concerns and interests in finding our voices and our ongoing development as psychoanalysts, and was the foundation for our close partnership writing together. The trust we developed in our working process led to a deepening dialogue in which we freely try out ideas with each other. This dialogue has become the signature feature of our teaching to this day.

The noughties also saw a period of heightened questioning about identity in the wider group of Independent Psychoanalysts after the Gentleman's Agreement was dissolved. This was a fraught period during which Elizabeth co-Chaired the Group of Independent Psychoanalyst's organizing committee with Ruth McCall, undertaking a sounding of views and a reframing of the group's purpose towards articulating and developing the Independent Tradition.[16] The group of Independent Psychoanalysts, now without a political function, changed its name to the Association of Independent Psychoanalysts (AIP) and redefined its objectives. In 2016 the constitution adopted the new object of the Association which was ratified at the AGM: "The object of the Association is the communication, promotion and development of theory and clinical practice arising from the Independent Tradition in psychoanalysis" (Constitution of the AIP).[17]

There was an urgency, widely shared, to bring the work of Independents to the candidates, as courses had dropped off the curriculum.[18] We joined other analysts in trying to describe what was particular about the Independent Tradition in both theory and clinical technique by deciding to create a course on Independent Women with the support and encouragement of Rosine Perelberg, then Chair of the Curriculum Committee, which Elizabeth also joined in 2005. We wanted to highlight the women and their ideas that inspired and stimulated our development. We became confident at playing with ideas, feeling more equipped to teach, and in a particular way.[19] Cambridge was a catalyst for our wanting to provide a course where the candidates would feel free and safe to try out the ideas, much as we had at Cambridge.

At the invitation of Rosine Perelberg and Joan Raphael-Leff, we wrote a paper together for the second edition of their book on *Female Experience – Affect and Body: On the Contribution of Independent Women Psychoanalysts* – and presented it at the conference on Female Experience, 'Women working with women', organized by COWAP[20] in 2008. From this, we had the framework for our course. The course we designed takes into account the early women pioneers recognized for their independence of thought during the Controversial Discussions[21], and some of the most significant contributors to the Independent Tradition right up to the turn of the millennium. Teaching this course inspired us to research and write about the stories and contributions of some of these women; unfortunately, this book cannot include all of them. Our course has remained on the curriculum, evolving over 15 years. In 2019, we gave our paper on Enid Balint at the Independent Psychoanalysis Trust conference titled, 'Independent women psychoanalysts of the British Psychoanalytical Society', which inspired us to gather and commission papers on some of the women. As we prepared to hand over to the next generation of Independent women psychoanalysts, we invited Emily Alster, Maia Kirchkheli and Paola Somaini to teach with us and to contribute to this volume.

This book represents the life of these ideas.

Ken Robinson's opening chapter on Ella Freeman Sharpe introduces a psychoanalyst who became one of the foremost teachers in the BPAS during the 1920s and 1930s, sought after as a training analyst and supervisor. Recognized for her considerable knowledge of Shakespeare and English literature, she brought her ear for poetic diction and metaphor as she listened to her patients, enlivening psychoanalytic understanding of intimate unconscious communications. Sharpe's recommendations to candidates still stands: follow the patient's process, pace and tempo. Ella Freeman Sharpe wrote one of the significant Memoranda on technique during the Controversial Discussions. Important themes of the Independent Tradition, begun by Sándor Ferenczi, are clearly present in her work.

Jan Abram's chapter tells us more about psychoanalysis in England in the 1930s and 1940s and Marjorie Brierley's central role as a peacemaker. She is credited with preventing the Society from splitting, using her considerable capacity for mediation evidenced by her 'Armistice Letter' of 1942. Brierley's seminal paper on affects in 1937 pointed the way to a new clinical technique, which placed affect at the centre of all that the analyst is registering in the clinical encounter. The development of these ideas had enormous implications.

Emily Alster's chapter on Paula Heimann must stand out as telling the story of the first 'Independent psychoanalyst'. The pain Heimann courageously endured on her journey to own her authentic voice and ideas is inspirational; her life is a testament to the quintessential qualities of becoming an analyst of the Independent Tradition.

Maia Kirchkheli is an artist and a psychoanalyst and brings both of these sensitivities to her connection to Marion Milner. The creative beginnings in the development of self in Milner's work are taken further in this chapter by Maia's innovative elaboration of a theory of creativity.

In the next chapter, Ken Robinson, a supervisee of Pearl King, is writing from his first-hand knowledge of her. King's determination to bring positive development to the BPAS with her organizational skills and her work to ensure that the history of the Controversial Discussions would be known and preserved, both reflect the deep impact of the previous generations' trauma and the continuing efforts to repair.

Paola Somaini, also with an artist's eye, perceives how Nina Coltart transformed her traumatic past into one of the most generative and generous psychoanalytic careers.

Elizabeth Wolf and Barbie Antonis, in the final chapter of this book, take the reader right into Enid Balint's consulting room to experience Balint's process as she developed the theories and clinical technique that are now hallmarks of Independent psychoanalysis.

Notes

1   These were scientific meetings in the British Society between 1941 and 1945 to discuss and examine the theories of Melanie Klein and Anna Freud.
2   "… it is in theoretical work that the separations are – for some analysts – tightly maintained: they would never be found quoting from colleagues of any of the rival groups" (Kohon 1986, 45).
3   Volume 29, Number 3, 2009.
4   An informal agreement between the three groups whereby there had to be even representation in committees and rotation of important Society offices.
5   63 New Cavendish Street, London W1M, location of the Institute of Psychoanalysis at that time.
6   Eric Karas, email to Daryl Cohen, Eric Rayner and Patrick Casement on 4 March 1999.
7   Paul Williams, Ruth Robinson, Patrick Casement with the help of Sharon Stekelman, Hon. Sec of the Committee, organized the first Cambridge meeting in March 1999.
8   Minutes of the Committee of the Independent Group of Psychoanalysts, 22 April 1999.
9   Chair report for the Independent Group of Psychoanalysts AGM, 12 May 1999.
10 Daryl Cohen Chair, Wilhelmina Kraemer-Zurné, Ruth Robinson and Patrick Casement organized the second Cambridge meeting held in Spring 2000.
11 Final Think Tank report to the Cambridge colloquium (2001).
12 We take it as accepted that the core training include a thorough grounding in psychoanalytic theory.
13 Final Think Tank report to the Cambridge colloquium (2001), Margaret Arden, Bernard Barnett, Abe Brafman, Mario Marrone, David Riley, Judith Szekacs Weiss, Sharon Stekelman, Paul Williams.
14 "By far the biggest item of expenditure listed in the public accounts of the Melanie Klein Trust for the year ending September 1997, is the £12,472 for supervision (£9443 in 1996). While there is no indication of the identity of the Supervisors and Supervisees, it is an established fact that one undergraduate student in Psychoanalysis with a Kleinian Training Psychoanalyst was funded by this Trust to have

supervision with a Kleinian Training Supervisor. (Hearsay has it that this is by no means an isolated case.)", John Tydeman, Chair Group of Independent Psychoanalysts to Eglé Laufer, Chair of Education Committee, BPAS, 30 October 1999.

15 Barbie Antonis (Chair), Wilhelmina Kraemer-Zurné and Helen Taylor Robinson organized the fourth Cambridge meeting in Spring 2002.

16 From 2005, the constitution was revised only to remove the political function from the object of the group: "The object of the group is the promotion and development of Independent Psychoanalytic thinking."

17 The Independent committee at the time consisted of Ruth McCall, Elizabeth Wolf and Renée Danziger, October 2016. They wrote to the AIP membership: "Now that the old groups, since the dissolution of the Gentlemen's Agreement, have no role in nominating individual group members for roles in the Society ... we think that the role of the old groups is more in the area of promoting theoretical and clinical understanding ... It is our view that over the last 70 years since the old Middle Group was formed there is now a distinctive set of clinical and theoretical principles that are truly independent. We call this strand of psychoanalytic thinking and practice the Independent Tradition and it is this which we wish to promote the understanding and development of."

18 "When I became the Chair of the Curriculum Committee in 2004, I noticed that very few candidates attended the Contemporary Freudian Tradition and none had taken the course on the Independent Tradition in the previous years. I thought that both courses needed revision. I also thought that they should be taught not at the same time when there were many other options, so that I organised the curriculum in a way that at the time these courses were offered in the second and third year there were no other options for such years." Personal communication from Rosine Perelberg, 2022.

19 See also Barbie Antonis and Elizabeth Wolf, 'The Pliable Medium'. In: *The Marion Milner Tradition*, Margaret Boyle Spelman and Joan Raphael-Leff (eds), London: Routledge.

20 A major conference celebrating ten years since the founding of COWAP, the IPA's Committee on Women and Psychoanalysis, and launching the new edition of the book *Female Experience – Four Generations of British Women Psychoanalysts on Work with Women*, July 2008.

21 For a full description of the Controversial Discussions, the main text is Steiner and King (1991). See also Rosine Perelberg (2006), IJP, and Barbie Antonis (2015).

References

Antonis, B. & Wolf, E. (2008). 'Affect and Body: The Contributions of Independent Women Psychoanalysts'. In: J. Raphael-Leff & R. Josef Perelberg (eds), *Female Experience: Three Generations of British Women Psychoanalysts on Work with Women*, London: The Anna Freud Centre, 316–329.

Antonis, B. (2014). 'Listening, Technique, and All That Jazz'. In: *Women and Creativity: A Psychoanalytic Glimpse Through Art, Literature, and Social Structure*, London: Karnac, 21–35.

Antonis, B. (2015). 'Controversial Discussions: Independent Women Analysts and Thoughts About Listening to Experience', *British Journal of Psychotherapy*, 31 (1).

Antonis, B. & Wolf, E. (2022). 'The Pliable Medium'. In: Margaret Boyle Spelman & Joan Raphael-Leff (eds), *The Marion Milner Tradition – Lines of Development: Evolution of Theory, and Practice Over the Decades*, Lines of Development Series. London: Routledge, 2022.

Bollas, C. (1979). 'The Transformational Object'. In: Gregorio Kohon (ed.), *The British School of Psychoanalysis: The Independent Tradition*, London: Free Association Books, 1986, 83–100.

British Psychoanalytical Society Consultation Launch, 22 April 1999, British Psychoanalytical Society Archives.

Horne, A. (2006). 'The Independent position in psychoanalytic psychotherapy with children and adolescents, roots and implications'. In: Monica Lanyado & Ann Horne (eds), *A Question of Technique: Independent Psychoanalytic Approaches With Children and Adolescents*, London: Routledge.

Kahr, B. (1996). *D.W. Winnicott: A Biographical Portrait*, London: Karnac Books.

King, P. & Steiner, R. (eds) (1991). *The Freud-Klein Controversies 1941–45*. London: Routledge.

Kohon, G. (1986). 'Countertransference: An Independent View'. In: Gregorio Kohon (ed.), *The British School of Psychoanalysis: The Independent Tradition*, London: Free Association Books, 51–73.

Lanyado, M. & Horne, A. (eds) (2006). *A Question of Technique: Independent Psychoanalytic Approaches With Children and Adolescents*, London: Routledge.

McCall, R. & Wolf, E., Letter from the Group of Independent Psychoanalysts to Peter Rudnytsky, 15 February 2007, Association of Independent Psychoanalysts Archives.

Perelberg, R.J. (2006). 'The Controversial Discussions and après-coup', *International Journal of Psychoanalysis*, 87: 1199–1220.

Parsons, M. (2009a). 'An Independent theory of Clinical Technique'. In: *Living Psychoanalysis*, London and New York: Routledge, 2014, 184–204.

Parsons, M. (2009b). 'Becoming and Being an Analyst in the British Psychoanalytical Society', *Psychoanalytic Inquiry*, 29 (3): 236–246.

Parsons, M. & Sklar, J. (2011). 'The Life Cycle of the *Psychoanalyst*: Reflections on a Seminar for Newly Qualified Psychoanalysts'. In: *Landscapes of the Dark History, Trauma, Psychoanalysis*, London: Karnac.

Segal, H. (2006). 'Reflections on Truth, Tradition, and the Psychoanalytic Truth', *American Imago*, 63 (3): 283–292.

Rayner, E. (1991). *The Independent Mind in British Psychoanalysis*, London: Routledge.

Rudnysky, P. (2007). 'Après-Coup, Tradition and Truth', *American Imago*, 64 (1): 121–125.

Rydnysky, P., *Letter to Group of Independent Psychoanalysts*, 15 February 2007, Association of Independent Psychoanalysts Archives.

Twyman, M. (2013). Unpublished transcript of interview with Barbie Antonis and Elizabeth Wolf.

Williams, P., Keene, J. & Derman, S. (eds) (2012). *Independent Psychoanalysis Today*, London: Karnac.

Wolf, E. (issue ed.) (2009). 'From Founders to the Present: A British Psychoanalytic Odyssey', *Psychoanalytic Inquiry*, 29 (3).

Chapter 1

The core question

'What is mind?'

Joan Raphael-Leff

"What is mind? No matter", "What is Matter? Never mind" – so begins Marion Milner's poem *Mind the Gap.*[1]

"No matter" she says "Never mind" – yet to these women mind did matter greatly!

This book celebrates a particular model of the mind delineated by the early Independents. To them, mind was neither a psychic apparatus nor 'matter' but – *a process.*

As Marjorie Brierley stated, mind had ceased to be seen as a static structure or a substantial thing but had become *a dynamic entity* (in keeping with Freud's metapsychology) – "a nexus of activities and a sequence of adaptive responses" (Brierley, 1944, p. 97). Mind as location of the faculties of rational thought, perception, memory, reason, but also, especially for these contemplative Independent women – of imagination and unconsciously generated creativity.

As we shall see, eventually in this group Mind came to be regarded not only as a fluid and multi-facetted process, but originating in mind-to-mind dialogue, and subject to lifelong intersubjective influences.

The context

The first generations of the British Psychoanalytical Society were exceptionally creative. In this chapter I will try to capture the volatile excitement of that heady era of psychoanalysis-in-the-making. President Ernest Jones's reluctant but judicious acceptance of non-medically qualified candidates fostered an interdisciplinary cross-fertilisation in which unusually, female analysts held a prominent place. Furthermore, a social network of interlacing contacts connected these erudite privileged English women to both Cambridge University and to the Bloomsbury bohemia of whom Dorothy Parker quipped – "they lived in squares, painted in circles and loved in triangles."

From the 1920s onward, in the questioning spirit of that intellectual elite, female psychoanalysts embraced new ideas and produced a flurry of adventurous contributions on female issues of abortion, menstruation and periodicity; the

DOI: 10.4324/9781003296690-3

psychology of fashion; eating disorders; drug and alcohol addiction; stammering; and children's games and play.

In addition, they introduced ideas from abroad. Despite language barriers, until there were sufficient home-grown training analysts, most candidates spent months between the wars in Vienna, Berlin or Budapest for a personal analysis with Freud, Sachs or Abraham, or Ferenczi respectively. This was not only less costly than in London but reduced transferential complexities within the Institute. As Ella Sharpe put it succinctly, her generation "had the English Channel between themselves and their analysts" (King & Steiner, 1991, p. 646).

While they were being analysed by Karl Abraham in Berlin, Alix Strachey indulged in giddy diversions, often in fancy dress, with her 'analytic-sibling' Melanie Klein. Becoming intrigued by Klein's ideas, Alix translated the material and arranged for Klein to give a series of lectures in London on Child Analysis. Following these Klein was invited to remain in England. Her ideas found some support amid those already treating children, and resonated with Jones's chosen emphasis on innate vs. environmental pathogenic factors.[2] This turn of events raised Freud's concerns, as Klein's work was much at odds with his daughter's book (1927) on the technique of child analysis she had pioneered in Vienna. Eager to placate, Jones set up exchange-lectures in 1935/36 to debate theoretical differences on the treatment of children, female sexuality and early attachment to the mother. But when Anna Freud visited London she was openly criticised by Melanie Klein and her colleagues.

The Controversial Discussions

Tensions intensified with the Nazi threat to psychoanalysis, and the mass migration of analysts escaping rampant antisemitism in occupied Europe. Now under one roof rather than cities apart, ideological frictions further escalated between Klein and Anna Freud. Oedipal emotions rumbled below the surface, as the struggle for succession intensified after Freud's death in London in 1939. In true British spirit the suggestively dubbed 'Middle Group' of indigenous analysts took on the role of neutral self-appointed peacekeepers, concerned to avoid a potential split in the Society.[3] It is generally accepted that their intercession graciously channelled the acrimonious atmosphere into meetings designed to elucidate meta-psychological differences from Freud and from each other. However, when in 2006 Rosine Perelberg (BPAS President, 2019 to 2022) challenged this 'founding myth' of two warring groups held at bay by the moderate 'natives of the island', on closer examination it emerged that behind their well-mannered courtesy, the future Independents raised the most crucial criticisms – especially Ella Sharpe, Marjorie Brierley and Sylvia Payne (see the verbatim account of these extraordinary discussions in King & Steiner, 1991).

The meetings were eventually held from January 1943 to May 1944 but by this stage of the Second World War, most English analysts had scattered – some were conscripted to army psychiatric units or the Emergency Medical Service, while others secluded in their country homes or stayed with friends outside the capital (as did Klein). By contrast, the 'continental' analysts were confined to London – externally labelled 'enemy aliens' and internally tortured by angst, multiple losses and survivor guilt about dear ones left behind. Yet such were the stakes that many members and candidates made an effort to attend meetings at 96 Gloucester Place even as bombs fell outside. What an odd coming together – time and space suspended, treasuring and rescuing psychoanalysis from the burning pyre. Although Marion Milner painted them as two confrontational red hens fighting over Freud's egg, discussions between Anna Freud and Melanie Klein remained scientific, civilised and – chic. In fact, in the scene described to me by both Paula Heimann and Anne Hayman, positioned either side of the room, the main protagonists were flanked by women in competitively elaborate hats …

Mind over matter

Focused on so-called 'primitive' psychic life, the initial debates contrasted Melanie Klein's idea of innate unconscious phantasies with Anna Freud's notion of self-centred primary narcissism.

I argue that in the wake of these heroic discussions the Middle Group's distinctive ideas about Mind began to crystalise. Concentration on the early months of life stimulated their imaginations. Besides a 'one-person psychology' of innate creativity, in keeping with the notation John Rickman was to propose more than a decade later (1957) these Middle Groupers became intrigued by the two-person dynamic that preceded three-person Oedipal triangulation.

Their springboard was Marjorie Brierley's 1937 proposal (cited by Susan Isaacs during the first series of 'scientific controversies', and further elaborated by Brierley in 1951), of neonatal *affective* and *sensorial* mental process that gradually develop into *perceptual*, and later, *conceptual*, experience. Furthermore, in response to Paula Heimann's presentation during the sixth discussion, Sylvia Payne commented on the inevitable difficulty of formulating the prenatal "rudimentary psychical world which must be present". But she emphasised that ushered in by birth, both "psychical awareness" and body ego arise within the primary object *relationship* – initially through the sensations of maternal handling of the baby's body (King & Steiner, pp. 546–9).

To the 'Middle Group' then, the infant's inner world did not arise solipsistically but was constituted *dyadically*. By drawing a distinction between the Ego and the evolving Mind their focus was *inter-psychic*, diverging from the Kleinian *intra-psychic* viewpoint (an innate Ego, with internally generated unconscious phantasy and narcissistic projections). It also differed from an Anna Freudian emphasis on *inter-structural* forces (the evolution of the Ego to mediate between conflictual internal structures and accommodation to external ones).

To the future Independents, Mind as a process was seen to evolve through *emotional engagement* – initially within the mother-infant ongoing exchange, then expanding through a lifetime of mind-to-mind communication with others.

As they began to elaborate this paradigm of the inherently dyadic and dialogic origins of an infant's mind, the psychoanalytic goal of 'autonomy' was tacitly being replaced with a growing belief in lifelong human 'inter-dependency'.

Love – signpost to the object

Post-war theorising was influenced by Ian Suttie's concept of a basic attachment-need for mother (1935), and also by Ferenczi's notion of Primary Object-Love (conveyed by his analysands Alice and Michael Balint, newly arrived from Budapest). Scottish Ronald Fairbairn dispassionately theorised this by stating that from the start, libido was object, rather than pleasure-seeking.

Drawing on his vast experience in Paediatrics, Donald Winnicott proposed that becoming human necessitated environmental facilitation. Ironically, as he himself admitted later "It was only through analysis that I became gradually able to see a baby as a human being ..." (quoted in Abram, 2008, p. 1125). In a BBC Broadcast series called 'The Ordinary Devoted Mother and Her Baby' that ran through the war years until the 1970s, he spoke directly to two generations of mothers about feeding, holding and handling. Highlighting the importance of *mirroring* (now termed maternal 'biofeedback'), Winnicott pointed out that 'apperception' fails when the mother is too self-engaged, so it is *her* face that is perceived, rather than a reflection of the baby's self in it (Winnicott, 1967, pp. 112–3). If we humans come to know our own mind through the mind of a caring other, we develop a growing understanding of emotional states in both self and other, and thereby enhance our empathy, the basis of social interaction. This two-way process begins very early.[4]

Contemporary neonatal research provides good evidence that like other primates, due to 'mirror neurons', a human newborn can imitate, match and respond to communicative social signals (Simpson et al, 2014).

Today's sophisticated equipment (allowing micro-analysis of freeze-framed filmed observations) reveals the interdigitating complexity of the primal 'dance' between a carer and small baby. But mothers had long observed that after a natural birth the newborn crawls vigorously towards the nipple, listens intently to her voice, alertly watches and mimics her face. Studies now confirm innate relational capacities: from birth, the baby comes to discriminate the mother's bodily smell, identifies her face over the first days, and by the end of that week not only recognises her voice but coos responsively.

Within weeks of birth, the acclimatising baby can be shown to have developed expectancies based on postnatal experience and 'entrains' to the rhythm of the primary caregiver. Amazingly, neonates can even be shown to remember precise verbal cadences from *prenatal* experience! For instance, empirical research ascertains they can distinguish a specific Dr Seuss book read aloud by the mother in late pregnancy from similar books by the same author (see Music, 2016, for details of infant research). As Freud had presciently noted "[T]here is much more continuity between intra-uterine life and earliest infancy than the impressive caesura of the act of birth would have us believe" (Freud, 1926, p. 138).

So, there is now much research evidence confirming the future Independents' belief that the mind evolves within a primary *relationship*. But here's the rub – paradoxically the baby the Middle Group conceived was regarded simultaneously as innately sociable yet symbiotically 'fused' with the mother, who was conceptualised as 'instinctively' merged with her conjoined baby having 'identical interests' (Alice Balint, 1949).

Fusion and confusion

I have long puzzled over this contradiction within Middle Group theorising. Their idealisation is perplexing, especially given the clear-headed discernment and meticulous observation they demonstrated elsewhere. This was detrimental as it delayed recognition of the baby's remarkable initiative and influence from the start. Venturing a guess why this fanciful distortion occurred (and still persists as we cling to our precious notions of perfection and merger), I suggest that unconsciously, for these early theorists, this romanticised notion of a symbiotically merged nursing couple may have compensated for a lack in infancy.[5]

In time the revered concept of 'fusion' was seen by some critical Independents as manifestation of a temporary state of satiation in the cognisant baby, or a retrospective illusion of adults yearning for an 'oceanic feeling' or craving to rescue by proxy. While Fairbairn and Klein had designated such 'fusion' as pre-natal, Winnicott deemed it an 'illusion of oneness' and solved the paradox by suggesting that newborn babies were BOTH object and pleasure-seeking, as did Michael Balint. Ella Sharpe however, argued that maintaining this illusory union provides a shaky foundation for identity. But by then reification of 'fusion' had taken its toll.

I suggest that unconsciously, glorification of 'fusion' reflected a placental ideal, a postnatal extension of the imagined blissful exchange in the womb. Persistence of the idea of reciprocal 'merger' obscured the fundamental asymmetry of mother and baby. Idealisation hindered awareness of the fine-grained complexity of ordinary maternal care. And furthermore, these otherwise astute theoreticians neglected the input of father, siblings and others. More importantly, veneration of the 'perfect' primary exchange (despite

Winnicott's emphasis on 'good enough') negated recognition of the inevitable mismatches and emotional process of 'rupture and repair' (Tronick, 1989) that actually enhances the dyadic state of consciousness ripening through dialogue between infant and their carers. Even today, 70 years after Winnicott dispelled the myth, idealisation of the 'nursing couple' persists among many healthcare professionals, including psychoanalysts, with great resistance to the idea of 'healthy maternal ambivalence' (Raphael-Leff, 2010). We may wonder why we cling so tenaciously to this ideal.

Ordinary experience

Paradoxically, already in 1947 Winnicott had sacrilegiously enumerated 18 reasons why ordinary mothers hate their babies. By citing the mother's (hidden) feelings, Winnicott ameliorated the idea of perfect unconditional care. Antagonism was exacerbated by his commensurately applying it to analysts, as experiences of '[H]ate in the Countertransference' (Winnicott, 1947).

Nevertheless, once the analytic treatment process came to be seen as isomorphic with babycare, it meant that analysts too may have complex feelings regarding their patients.

Real engagement became a major constituent of Independent thinking. By contrast to the Kleinian emphasis on the baby's inner world populated by projections and reintrojections of self-generated inborn phantasy, to Middle Groupers internal representations were seen as derived from actual external experience.

Far from Klein's view of destructive, envious, even sadistic infantile tendencies, they focused instead on primary love. Having dispensed with 'instinct', and especially vicissitudes of the 'Death drive', aggression was seen as a response to real frustration and deprivation.[6]

Clearly, if an infant learns about minds by being held in mind, it is essential to stay in touch with the mind of the carer.

Having designated *separation anxiety* as the foremost infantile fear, Fairbairn assumed that desperate defensive strategies are necessary to keep the external carer good, despite her fallibility. He described 'stubborn' attempts made by very young children to maintain a positive connection, including savage self-blame to account for an unsatisfying experience, even and especially in the face of ongoing neglect, or abusive treatment (Fairbairn, 1943).

Furthermore, Fairbairn (who by now had instructed Klein to link the term 'schizoid' to her proposed 'paranoid position'), presented an alternative model of the formation of psychic structure. He delineated drastic (tripartite) splits that occur in the infant's own ego in the process of internalising the confusing exciting/rejecting mother coupled in tandem with 'libidinal' and 'antilibidinal' parts of the divided self.

The carer's culpability

This view of an externally instigated fracture of the pristine unitary ego contrasts markedly with Freud's idea of gradual cohering unintegrated ego-nuclei, or the Kleinian notion of a paranoid-schizoid ego eventually achieving depressive position integration. In today's terms, if repression is represented by a horizontal split, Fairbairn's internal splits may be depicted as repeated vertical fragmentations of the self into sub-systems of internalised self-object dyads. But importantly, like Freud's recognition of the creative process when working through separation anxiety (vide his grandson's 'fort-da' game), Winnicott, Milner, Balint and others acknowledged that for more secure babies, *growth occurs precisely in the 'gap'* – specifically due to inevitable maternal failure. In reliable facilitating environments, self-generated solutions (e.g. transitional objects) come into being during moments of (tolerable) failure, absence and lack, through identification with the reflective/reflecting/containing mind of the (m)other.

But once maternal sensitivity was regarded as crucial, her *insensitivity* was defined as a potential source of damage.

In 1951, John Bowlby (who like Marion Milner, had been in supervision with Ella Sharpe) further bolstered the case, noting enduring aftereffects of bad preverbal experience. He argued persuasively that *maternal 'deprivation'* (whether due to poor primary care or institutionalisation) decisively shaped long-term personality development. Ironically, in his sweeping statement advocating exclusive, continuous maternal care of the preverbal infant he made few distinctions regarding the quality of care or even the degree of basic security when postulating long-lasting scars or fundamental deficits.[7]

A year later, a heart-breaking film documented the drastic effects of even a temporary loss when the attachment figure is not allowed to stay in hospital with the child. Produced by James Robertson, an affiliate of the Independents, 'A Two-Year-Old Goes to Hospital' (1952), dramatically illustrated a well-loved child's vigorous protest, deep despair and final collapse into detachment following this short but significant separation. (This film contributed to new regulations, allowing parents' admission with an ill child.)

The divided self

The sixties in London were a particularly creative period for the newly named Independent Group. Often called the 'decade of change' it brought an explosion of ideas in culture and the arts, a revolutionary ideology questioning authority and received wisdom. And vociferous demands for civil rights for women, workers and people of colour. This new open-mindedness formed the backdrop to the Independents' experimentation with new ways of treating a breed of self-alienated patients who manifested 'as if' personalities, and enduring tension between an authentic, private identity and a phony persona presented to the world.

Winnicott (1960) attributed this 'false self' to early pathogenic causes. Simultaneously, Ronnie Laing (Paula Heimann's erstwhile patient, and Marion Milner's supervisee) defined a ubiquitous 'divided self' (Laing, 1960) ascribed to basic 'ontological insecurity' within the family. Masud Khan then formulated the role played in such 'schizoid' patients by progressively incremental 'cumulative trauma' due to a breakdown of the mother's capacity as 'protective shield' (1963). Building on Ferenczi's concept of an innate desire to be loved, Michael Balint (who later married Enid) metaphorised the damage caused by failure of the originary 'harmonious interpenetrating mixup' as a deep tectonic fissure, leaving a seemingly irreversible early 'basic fault'-line (Balint, 1968). In the same year Guntrip (analysed by both Fairbairn and Winnicott) hypothesised that preverbal traumata underlay the profoundly schizoid condition, reflecting the 'lost heart of the self' that re-seeks the pre-ambivalent state of womblike 'fusion'.

A period of innovative clinical exploration followed in which the Independents' cross-disciplinary approach played a crucial role in generating theoretical change. Aiming to reach the 'child within the adult' they altered their treatment techniques. In accordance with the developmental premise of dialogism, to them the crucial mutative factor was the psychoanalytic *relationship*.

Heavily influenced by R.D. Laing and his colleague David Cooper, an 'anti-psychiatry' social movement was fomenting. Transforming the way madness was perceived, it negated medical biological models of diagnosis, ECT and drug treatment for psychosis. Some psychoanalysts too, questioned the orthodox view that psychotic persons were unsuitable candidates for therapy. They began offering alternative psychosocial treatments built on a paradigm shift towards *collaborative* work with patients (such as Marion Milner's therapeutic use in analysis of patients' drawings). Unconventional treatment approaches pioneered in the post-war years by psychoanalysts Tom Main, Wilfred Bion, John Rickman and Heinz Foulkes became popular in therapeutic communities, group analysis and day hospitals, empowering a sense of personal and collective responsibility.[8]

Regression and the new beginning

Although mother-blaming proliferated among family therapists (e.g. the 'schizophrenogenic' mother and 'double-bind' communication), pessimism was mitigated by the idea that if therapy provided a better form of mothering a 'new beginning' could be generated. Independent psychoanalysts now took a further step.

Since borderline psychopathology was attributed to preverbal misalignments, they condoned 'benign' regression as a means of enabling emotional reexperience of early trauma to be overcome. So rather than avoiding patient dependency, they assumed that supervised regression could mitigate distrust, and usher in a shift from vigilant self-reliance to a form of mature 'interdependence'.

This necessitated further modifications in technique.

The budding Independents bravely explored a new treatment option, pro-posing that 'as if' patients needed carefully managed conditions: they advo-cated patience and provisional interpretation to facilitate the patient's own self-discovery. Through trust in 'negative capability' (as Keats called it) they painstakingly fostered 'self-curative forces' in their patients. (Milner's detailed case study of a 20-year long treatment of 'Susan' (Milner, 1969) illustrates the provision of time, space and empathy, necessitating humility in curbing analytic 'cleverness' (in Winnicott's terms).)

Furthermore, since classically the patient was regarded as a discrete entity with tensions arising internally and discharged from within a closed energy system of drives, free association could suffice. However, Michael Balint noted that with regression "words lost their reliability as a means of communication" (Balint, 1968, p. 85) especially for preverbal problems. Somatic expressions became significant. As Marion Milner phrased it in her poem, *Mind the Gap*: "… Body and mind were two sides of the same join". But as ever, it was Ella Sharpe who had the first word: "A subterranean passage between mind and body underlies all analogy" (Sharpe, 1940, p. 202).

It seems to me that the Independents preceded the French school's reunifi-cation of body-mind in the field of psychosomatics, and today's ideas about activation of subsymbolic, bodily and sensory components of the emotional schema in the consulting room (e.g. Bucci, 2002). Their budding interest in the analyst's unconscious perception of embodiment as nonverbal commu-nication of preverbal experience, and reliance on one's own sensual proprio-ception anticipated contemporary ideas of 'neurobiological synchrony' and 'inter-corporeal' resonance.

The analytic relationship

My point is that consolidation of their belief in a dialogical process in which mothers were to be held accountable, also necessitated the openminded com-mitment for therapists to examine *both* sides of the psychoanalytic 'inter-psychic' exchange. Paula Heimann now entered the scene, having declared the analyst's countertransferencial response a useful affective tool rather than an emotional interference (1950). Her acknowledging and making use of perso-nal arousal was at odds with the Kleinian view. But she was in good company within the Middle Group as, already in 1927, Ella Freeman Sharpe had written about utilising her own 'discomfort' in the clinical situation (another example of poor receptivity to ideas before their time). And Theodor Reik, Heimann's analyst from Berlin, had recently published his book on intuitive *Listening With The Third Ear* (Reik, 1948) to the unconsciously perceived communications.

Newly defected from her favoured position as Klein's successor, Paula Heimann was invited by Sylvia Payne to join the group she then named 'Independents'. She further interrogated the idea of countertransference within 'a relationship between two persons'.[9] Like maternal intuition, it was seen to provide a means of elucidating the interplay of feeling experiences of both (Heimann, 1950). This differed from a Kleinian view of countertransference as the patient's projection 'into' the analyst.

Moreover, the upshot of applying their hypotheses of a mind-to-mind developmental dialogue to the treatment situation entailed recognition that meaning in the consulting room is *co-created* within a 'dyadic unconscious', as well as the conscious exchange. (In fact, Milner retrospectively termed her patient Susan's illness a 'truly mutual creation'.)

Based on presumed isometry between couch and cradle, *intersubjectivity* in the consulting room was fast becoming the hallmark of the newly established Independent Group.

Growing awareness of two-way unconscious interaction within the consulting room was also primed by Ferenczi's stress on reciprocal unconscious influences between carer and child/analyst and patient in 'Confusion of Tongues' (Ferenczi, 1933, but only published in English in 1949).

Heimann also emphasised the analyst's 'naturalness', and in time, *authenticity* became a by-word with far reaching theoretical ramifications, with psychoanalysts such as Nina Coltart, and later Neville Symington and Christopher Bollas claiming their analytic freedom to be themselves.

Having emphasised the uniqueness of each patient-analyst pair, the Independents now also felt compelled to scrutinise the therapist arm of the equation, aware that the analyst's unresolved issues may be retriggered within the consulting room, with potential to retraumatise.

As Nina Coltart later asked: *What do our patients require of us? What do we require of ourselves?* (1992, p. 116).

The making of an Independent

Other chapters in this book provide more detail about the individual lives and ideas fomented by seven women analysts who excelled as theorists within the Independent Group: Ella Freemen Sharpe, Marjorie Brierley, Paula Heimann, Marion Milner, Enid Balint, Nina Coltart and Pearl King.

The rich diversity among these pioneers highlights their daring in applying an exploratory approach to generate a nutritive dyadic encounter that fosters change in the minds of *both* participants.

As it happens, I was familiar with most of them. I was supervised by three: Paula Heimann and Enid Balint[10] while in training (through two pregnancies and breastfeeding), and later by Pearl King (along with Isobel Menzies) during the Membership programme. I was grateful that despite the disparity of our experience and age, they maintained social contact long after I qualified, as did Nina Coltart who generously filled my practice with her referrals. I was close to Anne Hayman, and knew and admired Marion Milner (about whom I have recently co-edited a book).[11] Sadly, Ella Sharpe had died prematurely in 1947 and I never met Marjorie Brierley who had retired to the Lake District by the time I began my training in 1970.

Although I always 'self-identified' as Independent, in the course of my training choice of a Study Group or Clinical Seminar was no longer necessarily segregated by schools of thought. This change, instigated by demands of the student organisation we candidates had established, was ratified in 1973 by Pearl King, who acknowledged that her new Curriculum Committee were conceding to pressures from three sources – students, seminar leaders, and 'newer educational objectives and attitudes' in schools, universities, and postgraduate institutions.

Documents from my training show that my cohort was taught by an eclectic assortment of analysts across different psychoanalytic groups.[12] I also regularly encountered Anna Freud at the Hampstead Child Therapy Clinic, took my babies to her paediatrician Josefine Stross at the Well Baby Clinic, and much later was External Examiner for the Child-Analysts' training, Professorial Head of the joint UCL/AFC Master of Science degree in Psychoanalytic Psychology, and finally co-editor of a book about her tradition (Malberg & Raphael-Leff, 2012). Currently in my retirement, I lead the Anna Freud Centre's Academic Faculty for Psychoanalytic Research.

But already, when after my qualification in 1976, Joe Sandler invited me to the Wednesday afternoon Hampstead Index-Group meetings for what he called a 'weekly argument about concepts', we found that the Contemporary Freudian's overlap with the Independents felt greater than our differences (largely due to Sandler's 1976 notion of 'role responsiveness'). Now in its 70th year, the Anna Freud National Centre for Children and Families prioritises 'mentalization' based on longitudinal studies linking the quality of attachment to theory of mind.

Looking back, as a candidate in my twenties, exposure to this tripartite grouping of perspectives both enriched my thinking and confirmed my suspicion that explanatory models may foster biased self-fulfilling expectations, even in a seemingly objective field such as empirical observation.[13]

I postulated that the divergent melding of theory and practice evolved by each school rested on their conceptualisation of early developmental processes, with a tacit equation between baby-carer and patient-therapist. In turn, these dictated a corresponding anamnesis treatment model reflecting optimal mothering, and outcome goals of the analytic situation (Raphael-Leff, 1983).[14]

Simultaneously, during my training I was working as a clinical investigator in the Medical Research Council's Social Psychiatry Unit based at the Maudsley Hospital's Institute of Psychiatry. That very different approach generated my understanding that the nature of treatment also rests on an idea of reversal of the origins of the mind's ills as these are conceived to have arisen – whether driven by biological constitution, psychosocial mismatch, or undigested trauma.

Contagious arousal

Meanwhile, this third generation of Independents agreed that repeated maternal impingement results in defensive modes of relating (which neuroscience now suggests are inscribed in procedural memories and biological traces).[15] After qualification I proposed that if intrapsychic awareness was seen to be constituted inter-psychically between *two* minds, the maternal mind and subjectivity had to be examined transgenerationally.

From my vantage point as a mother, and my clinical specialisation and research findings in gender, reproduction and early parenting, I argued that babycare poses a particular threat to susceptible people whose own early emotional issues remain unprocessed (Raphael-Leff, 1980). Furthermore, I linked the noticeable rise in perinatal disturbances to *discrepancies between idealised expectations and the reality of caregiving.* I proposed that current socio-demographic conditions in stratified societies with small nuclear families and little social contact between age-groups grant adults few opportunities to process their own infantile feelings in the presence of a baby before becoming parents. Unrealistic media depictions of babies, and unachievable standards of mothering resulted in disillusionment and postnatal depressive and persecutory disorders. I advocated setting up perinatal service provision that included realistic preparation, home visits and better childcare provisions and therapeutic groups (Raphael-Leff, 1991).

Later I articulated the pathway by which babycare exacerbates painful residues of the adult's own preverbal era, suggesting that in susceptible carers, 'contagious' resonance is provoked not only by isolation and continuous exposure to raw infantile feelings, but by the evocative smell, sight and direct contact with primal substances. And that primary carers' defensive solutions to such revival of undigested past experience may range from over-identificatory indulgences to regulatory detachment, as projections skew early interactive patterns in the new family (Raphael-Leff, 2015).

Conversely, having consulted to many postnatal projects around the world it was clear that lay-practitioners and seasoned mothers can be trained to support new parents. By encouraging recognition of the newborn as a person with both feelings and a budding mind, a healthy form of conversation can arise, as each baby-carer pair unconsciously coordinates their exchange patterns of *corrective attunement* which serve as a template for future relations (Raphael-Leff, 2012; Bain et al., 2019).

Conclusion

Over the past century, metapsychology and consequently psychoanalytical training have undergone many modifications around the world. These are due to influences such as feminist critique, disciplined infant observation and neonatal research, findings from neuroscience as well as the burgeoning of psychological field theory, family systems theories and philosophical expositions on the multi-dimensional mind of the human subject. Once the majority of not only patients but psychoanalysts were female, early debates of female sexuality that had laid dormant for a generation were re-questioned, along with issues of erotic transference, and specificity of gendered treatment parameters within the first four British generations (Raphael-Leff & Perelberg, 1997/2008).

The Middle Group's belief in the interchange between two minds as foundational enabled their realisation that if mind is process, understanding in analysis is similarly co-constructed. Designating analysis as a relationship divested the analyst's authority as the one with the answers. This fundamental change of having to tolerate not-knowing and uncertainty has since gained momentum in diverse forms, among both Self- and Ego-Psychologists, Relational groups in the US, as well as neo-Kleinians and Contemporary Freudians in the UK and elsewhere. From spearheading self-scrutiny, it was but a short step to conceptualising the consulting room as a shared transformational space.

In sum, the British Independents' paradigmatic shift from object-relations to intersubjectivity enabled a further awareness of 'subject' relations (Raphael-Leff, 2013), appreciating the significance of a lifetime of mind-to-mind communication with others.

So, when all was said – Mind matters most!

It seems fitting to end with the closing of Marion Milner's poem with which this chapter opened:

> I minded when I did not mind
> That the matter did not matter any more
> But I do know that it is
> Out of the gaps
> That new things grow.[16]

Notes

1 Lines of the poem are reproduced here and at the chapter's end by kind permission of Giles Milner on behalf of Marion Milner's estate. Written by Marion Milner in her 95th year, as a tribute for her friend Pearl King's 80th birthday. Excerpt from Marion Milner's 'Mind the Gap', a 1995 tribute to Pearl King, in Spelman Boyle & Raphael-Leff, 2022.

2 The interest in the minds of children preceded Klein's visit in 1926. Between 1924–29 Susan Isaacs ran an experimental nursery in Cambridge based on radical ideas about developing independence through play. Analysts who worked therapeutically with children, like Mary Chadwick and Nina Searle, produced papers on pathological states of mind, child analysis and technique. Before training as a psychoanalyst Marion Milner had written a book describing her psychological study on adolescents for the Girls' Public Day School Trust (1938). Karin Stephen (who married a fellow analyst, Adrian, Virginia Woolf's brother) had studied Philosophy and Psychology at Newnham in Cambridge and later taught there on psychoanalysis.

3 We can assume there were also anxieties about the rapidly changing culture of the British Psychoanalytic Society. Until Klein's arrival in 1926 there were only two Jews among the 54 members. A great demographic shift occurred after the influx of Jewish psychoanalysts fleeing the Nazis (and later refugees of conscience from Apartheid South Africa, and the return of emigres from Europe to Latin America to escape the Holocaust and post-war anti-Semitism).

4 Today's empirical studies show that toddlers as young as 15 months old have acquired a 'theory of mind' – an awareness that others have a mind. This means they can attribute thoughts, desires and intentions to others, and better predict or understand their behaviour.

5 Around the turn of the century in the European elite's milieu wet-nursing was commonplace. For instance, all Freud's children were wet-nursed bar bottle-fed Anna (see Ludwig-Körner, 2022). Feeds were regulated to a strict four-hourly schedule. Hugs, sleep and bowel movements were subject to a regimen advocated by Truby King, generally supposed to build character by avoiding cuddling and undue attention. This persisted until the 1950s when Spock's and Winnicott's influence changed the ideology. In England, most families in the privileged social classes employed nursery-nurses and nannies; children were home-schooled by governesses or tutors, and even to this day, many sent off to boarding school at a young age.

6 Ironically, a catalyst to a more realistic view of mothers may have been Anna Freud and her colleague Dorothy Burlingham's (1942) about-turn finding among evacuated children in the War Nurseries. Memories of the mother's *specificity* was recognised as foundational to the infant's growing self-and-other awareness as opposed to Anna Freud's previous conception of an interchangeable anaclitic provider of food-and-satisfaction (and Klein's biologically determined preconceived part/object). The emotionally-barbed hostile attacks Melitta Schmideberg made publicly on her own mother, Melanie Klein, may have been a second influence.

7 Bowlby's 1951 WHO monograph was hotly contested by both unconvinced psychologists who disputed application of his work with young delinquents to the general population, and by mothers who resented the post-war push back into domesticity. Yet some positive changes eventually occurred, including maternity leave legislation (albeit only introduced in the UK in 1975 through the Employment Protection Act).

8 These were not without their difficulties as Tom Main (1990) recounted years later and I found in my new workplace, the first day hospital in the world (the Marlborough Day Hospital) between 1971–76.

9 "The analytic situation is a relationship between two persons. What distinguishes this relationship from others is not the presence of feelings in one partner, the patient, and their absence in the other, the analyst, but the degree of feeling the analyst experiences and the use he makes of his feelings, these factors being interdependent" (Heimann, 1960).

10 On 15 March 2013 I was honoured to be asked by the Tavistock Centre for Couple Relationships to deliver the 18th Annual Enid Balint Lecture, during which I gave a brief account of my supervision with her.

11 *The Marion Milner Tradition – Lines of Development: Evolution of Theory and Practice Over the Decades.* Margaret Boyle Spelman & Joan Raphael-Leff (eds), Lines of Development Series, London: Routledge, 2022.

12 Teachers included Wilfred Bion, John Bowlby, Nina Coltart, Eric Brenman, Ernst Freud, William Gilespie, Elliot Jacques, Masud Khan, John Klauber, Donald Meltzer, Isobel Menzies-Lyth, Edna O'Shaughnessy, John Padel, Dinora Pines, Herbert Rosenfeld, Anne-Marie Sandler, Joe Sandler, Hanna Segal, Henri Rey,

and others. My fellow candidates included Marion Burgner, Alan Cooklin, Rose Edgecumbe, John Bing-Hall, Alan Mawson, Anton Obholtzer, Priscilla Roth, Joan Symington and Jane Temperley, among others.

13 In fact, as Assistant Editor of the British Journal of Psychotherapy, I ran an ongoing feature of subjecting the same infant observation account to a variety of experienced Kleinian, Contemporary Freudian and Independent clinicians

14 For instance, Klein's baby, seen as instinctually driven by projected sadism and envy, was coupled with a (biologically determined) pre-conceived maternal object irrespective of her qualities. This differed from Anna Freud's baby's anaclitic love for transposable care-providers (a view she changed in the war nurseries), which differed again from Ferenczi's infant's primitive loving relatedness towards the 'found' real object (who will inevitably disappoint).

15 Contemporary neuro-scientific evidence indicates that negative experience between infants and their carers leaves lasting imprints in the brain's neural network itself, with pruning or atrophy due to neglect, or chronically high arousal states which ultimately influence the child's capacity for affect regulation and integration, low cortisol levels and epigenetically inherited stress responses.

16 Lines of the poem are reproduced here by kind permission of Giles Milner on behalf of Marion Milner's estate. Excerpt from Marion Milner's *Mind the Gap*, a 1995 tribute to Pearl King, in Spelman Boyle & Raphael-Leff, 2022.

References

Abram, J. (2008). 'Donald Woods Winnicott (1896–1971): A Brief Introduction', *International Journal of Psychoanalysis* 89: 1189–1217.

Bain, K., Landman, M., Frost, K., Raphael-Leff, J. & Baradon T. (2019). 'Lay Counselors: Thoughts on the Crossing of Ecological Frameworks and the Use of Lay Counselors in the Scale Up of Early Infant Mental Health Interventions', *Infant Mental Health Journal*.

Balint, A. (1949). 'Love for the mother and mother-love', *International Journal of Psychoanalysis*30: 251–259.

Balint, M. (1968). *The Basic Fault: Therapeutic Aspects of Regression*. London: Tavistock Publications.

Bollas, C. (1992). *Being a Character: Psychoanalysis and Self-Experience*, London: Routledge, 1993.

Bowlby, J. (1951). *Maternal Care and Mental Health*, WHO monograph.

Brierley, M. (1937). 'Affects in Theory and Practice'. *International Journal of Psychoanalysis* 18: 256–268.

Brierley, M. (1944). 'Notes on Metapsychology as Process Theory', *International Journal Psychoanalysis* 25: 97–106.

Brierley, M. (1951). *Trends in Psychoanalysis*. London: The Institute of Psychoanalysis and Hogarth Press.

Bucci, W. (2002). 'The Challenge of Diversity in Modern Psychoanalysis'. *Psychoanalytic Psychology* 19: 216–226.

Burlingham, D. & Freud, A. (1942). *Young Children in War Time: A Year's Work in a Residential Nursery*. London: George Allen & Unwin.

Coltart, N. (1991). *Slouching Towards Bethlehem – and Further Psychoanalytic Explorations*. London: Free Association Books.

Fairbairn, W.R.D. (1943). 'The Repression and the Return of Bad Objects'. In: *Psychoanalytic Studies of the Personality*, London: Routledge, 1986, 59–81.

Ferenczi, S. (1933). 'Confusion of the Tongues Between the Adults and the Child (the Language of Tenderness and of Passion)', *International Journal of Psycho-analysis* 30: 225–230, 1949.

Freud, A. (1927). Introduction to the Technique of Child Analysis (also called 'Four lectures'), in *The Writings of Anna Freud*, Vol.1, New York: International University Press, 1974, 3–69.

Freud, A. & Burlingham, D. (1943). 'Infants Without Families: The Case For and Against Residential Nurseries'. In: *Infants Without Families and Reports on the Hampstead Nurseries 1939–45*, London: Hogarth, 1974, 543–664.

Freud, S. (1912). 'Recommendations to Physicians Practising Psychoanalysis'. In: *The Standard Edition of the Complete Psychological Works of Sigmund Freud*, Volume XII, London: Hogarth Press, 109–120.

Freud, S. (1926). 'Inhibitions, Symptoms and Anxiety'. In: *The Standard Edition of the Complete Psychological Works of Sigmund Freud*, Volume XX, London: Hogarth Press, 75–176.

Guntrip, H. (1968). *Schizoid Phenomena, Object Relations and the Self*, London: Hogarth Press.

Hayman, A. (2013). *What Do Our Terms Mean? Explorations Using Psychoanalytic Theories and Concepts*, London: Karnac Books.

Heimann, P. (1950). 'On Countertransference', *International Journal of Psychoanalysis*, 31: 81–84.

Heimann, P. (1960). 'Countertransference', *British Journal of Medical Psychology*, 33: 9–15.

Khan, M.R. (1963). 'The Concept of Cumulative Trauma', *Psychoanalytic Study of the Child*, 18: 286–306.

King, P. & Steiner, R. (eds) (1991). *The Freud-Klein Controversies 1941–45*. London: Routledge.

Laing, R.D. (1960). *The Divided Self – An Existential Study in Sanity and Madness*, Penguin Modern Classics, London: Tavistock Publications, 2010.

Ludwig-Körner, C. (2017). 'Stillen im therapeutischen Setting', *Forum der Psychoanalyse*, Vol. 33, 4, 401–413.

Main, T. (1990). 'Knowledge, Learning, and Freedom from Thought'. *Psychoanalytic Psychotherapy*, 5: 59–74.

Malberg, N.T. & Raphael-Leff, J. (eds) (2012). *The Anna Freud Tradition – Lines of Development, Evolution of Theory and Practice over the Decades*, London: Karnac Books.

Milner, M. (1938). *The Human Problem in Schools: A Psychological Study Carried Out On Behalf of the Girls' Public Day Schools Trust*. London: Methuen & Co Ltd. Revival: Oxon & New York: Routledge, 2018.

Milner, M. (1969). *The Hands of the Living God*. London: Hogarth Press and the Institute of Psycho-Analysis. Reprinted New York: International Universal Press, INC, 2010.

Milner, M. (1995). 'Mind the Gap'. Poem in: Spelman Boyle, M. & Raphael-Leff, J. (eds), *The Marion Milner Tradition: Lines of Development – Evolution of Theory and Practice Over the Decades*, London & New York: Routledge, 2022. Also in: *Between Sessions and Beyond the Couch*, Raphael-Leff, J. (ed.), Colchester: CPS Psychoanalytic Publications, University of Essex, 2002.

Music, G. (2016). *Nurturing Natures: Attachment and Children's Emotional, Sociocultural and Brain Development*, London: Routledge.

Perelberg, R.J. (2006). 'The Controversial Discussions and Après Coup', *International Journal of Psychoanalysis*, 87: 1199–1220.

Raphael-Leff, J. (1980). 'Psychotherapy with Pregnant Women'. In: *Psychological Aspects of Pregnancy, Birthing and Bonding*, Blum, B. (ed.), New York: Human Science Press, 174–205.

Raphael-Leff, J. (1983). 'Facilitators and Regulators: Two Approaches to Mothering', *British Journal of Medical Psychology*, 56: 379–339.

Raphael-Leff, J. (1991). *Psychological Processes of Childbearing*, London: Chapman and Hall. Fourth Edition: Anna Freud Centre, 2005.

Raphael-Leff, J. (2010). 'Healthy Maternal Ambivalence', *Studies in the Maternal*, 2: 1–15, Open Library of the Humanities, http://www.mamsie.bbk.ac.uk/.

Raphael-Leff, J. (2012). *Working with Teenage Parents: Handbook of Theory & Practice*, London: Anna Freud Centre, 2012.

Raphael-Leff, J. (2013). "'The Intersubjective Matrix': Influences on the Independents' Growth from 'Object relations' to 'Subject relations'". In: *Contemporary Independent Psychoanalysis*, Dermen, S., Keen, J. & Williams, P., London: Karnac Books, 87–162.

Raphael-Leff, J. (2015). *Dark Side of the Womb*, London: Anna Freud Centre.

Raphael-Leff, J. & Perelberg, R.J. (1997). *Female Experience – Four Generations of British Women Psychoanalysts on Work with Women*, London: Routledge, New Edition: Anna Freud Centre, 2008.

Reik, T. (1948). *Listening with The Third Ear – The Inner Experience of a Psychoanalyst*, New York: Grove Press.

Rickman, J. (1957). 'Number and the Human Sciences (1951)', *Selected Contributions to Psycho-Analysis*, 52: 218–223.

Sandler, J. (1976). 'Countertransference and Role-Responsiveness', *International Review of Psychoanalysis*, 3: 43–47.

Sharpe, E.F. (1927). 'Contribution to a Symposium on Child Analysis', *International Journal of Psychoanalysis*, 8: 380–384.

Sharpe, E.F. (1940). 'Psycho-physical Problems Revealed in Language: An Examination of Metaphor', *International Journal of Psychoanalysis*, 21: 201–213.

Simpson, E.A., Murray, L., Paukner, A., Ferrari P.F. (2014). 'The Mirror Neurosystem as Revealed Through Neonatal Imitation: Presence from Birth, Predictive Power and Evidence of Plasticity', *Philosophical Transactions of the Royal Society*. B369: 20130289. http://dx.doi.org/10.1098/rstb.2013.0289.

Suttie, I. (1935). *The Origins of Love and Hate*, London: Free Association Book, 1988.

Symington, N. (1983). 'The Analyst's Act of Freedom as Agent of Therapeutic Change'. *International Journal of Psychoanalysis*, 10: 283–291.

Tronick, E. (1989). 'Emotions and Emotional Communication in Infants', *American Psychology*, 44: 112–119. [Also Chapter 4 in: *Parent-Infant Psychodynamics – Wild Things, Mirrors and Ghosts*, Raphael-Leff, J. (ed.), London: Whurr, 35–53.]

Winnicott, D.W. (1945). 'Primitive Emotional Development'. *International Journal of Psychoanalysis*, 26: 137–143.

Winnicott, D.W. (1947). 'Hate in the Countertransference'. In: *Through Paediatrics to Psychoanalysis*, London: Hogarth Press, 1982,

Winnicott, D.W. (1960). 'Ego Distortion in Terms of True and False Self'. In: *The Maturational Processes and the Facilitating Environment, Studies in the Theory of Emotional Development*, London: Hogarth Press and The Institute of Psycho-Analysis, 1965.

Winnicott, D.W. (1967). 'Mirror Role of Mother and Family in Child Development'. In: *The Predicament of the Family – a Psychoanalytical Symposium*, Lomas, P. (ed.), London: Hogarth Press, 1971.

Chapter 2

Bloomsbury and the early evolution of British psychoanalysis

Jonathan Sklar

I am going to examine some of the overlapping early groups to develop British psychoanalytic thinking. Whilst it begins with stories about academic men in Cambridge and Bloomsbury, two women, Alix Strachey and Karin Stephen, became important, independently minded female analysts alongside their husbands, James Strachey and Adrian Stephen. Bloomsbury values informed their independence and the importance of having freedom of mind. There were others, too, like John Rickman, Sylvia Payne and Ella Freeman Sharpe[1], who were not from the Bloomsbury Group, but were equally committed to Independent values. Bloomsbury members contrived their own legends by continuously writing about themselves in their intricate relationships with each other, and the part that several of them played in disseminating Freud and shaping the psychoanalytic profession is undeniably significant. Likewise, the Cambridge Group was one of many to stand against a prevailing Victorian orthodoxy but is of particular interest for, unusually, taking in Freud and his early ideas about the unconscious and dream life, and for being part of the development of psychoanalysis in Britain.

Beginnings

The London Psychoanalytic Society was founded in 1913 by Ernest Jones. It changed its name to the British Psychoanalytic Society in 1919, when Jones reformed what he described as the Jungian 'rump'.[2] In Cambridge, G.E. Moore, Arthur Tansley[3], Bertrand Russell, John Maynard Keynes, Leonard Woolf, and Lytton and James Strachey, were all friends and belonged to the long-established and invitation-only Cambridge Apostles Society, which met regularly to discuss truth, sex and ethics, amongst other topics. Freud's contributions on the importance of an unconscious life and understanding the roots of sexuality in the mind were regarded by many as polluting, yet this group was very taken with his ideas on psychoanalysis from about 1910, when those ideas began to be published.

Alongside the London Psychoanalytical Society, the Medico-Psychological Clinic, better known as the Brunswick Square Clinic, opened its doors

DOI: 10.4324/9781003296690-4

between 1913 and 1922 and developed the first training programme in Britain, as well as offering psychoanalysis to a range of patients, including shell-shocked soldiers in particular. As Suzanne Raitt writes:

> Nowadays the Clinic is almost forgotten: Ernest Jones, in his zeal to establish his own primacy as father of the British movement, fails to mention it in his published reminiscences, even though some of the leading lights of the British Psycho-Analytical society under his presidency including James Glover, Sylvia Payne, Ella Freeman Sharpe, Mary Chadwick, Nina Searl, Susan Isaacs, Iseult Grant-Duff and Marjorie Brierley, received their first analysis or training there.[4]

Post-war Cambridge and Bloomsbury

It was after the war that Cambridge/Bloomsbury became a major locus of interest in psychoanalysis. The Cambridge Group that met from 1925 included James Strachey, John Rickman, Arthur Tansley, Harold Jeffreys, Lionel Penrose and Frank Ramsey, who were dedicated to putting psychoanalysis on a scientific footing. Many of them were in or close to the Bloomsbury Group, which was by that time the major culture carrier of psychoanalysis both through private discussions within the group and by widely disseminating psychoanalytic ideas in their writings on topics such as economics (Keynes's *The Economic Consequences of Peace* (1919), and his 1936 *General Theory of Economics*[5]), history (Strachey's *Elizabeth and Essex*, and his various biographies containing psychoanalytic insights, including *Eminent Victorians*), philosophy and living an ethical life (Moore, Russell[6] and his student Wittgenstein), and sexuality. A bohemian group, many of them lived close to each other in houses around Gordon Square and always had various friends and scholars staying. The group was loyal to itself, members were often in love with other group members both hetero- as well as homo-erotically, and was at the centre of artistic and political life in England. It was an inside-outside group that was very well connected to society whilst rejecting Victorian morality and frankly confronting sexuality in its webs of relationships. These often contained complex shifts, with friends becoming lovers without concern for gender. Keynes described himself as an 'immoralist'. G.E. Moore was deeply concerned with individual experiences as well as an aesthetic life.

The Hogarth Press had been set up in 1917 by Leonard Woolf and his wife Virginia Woolf – also members of Bloomsbury – and was importantly at the forefront of bringing Freud and psychoanalysis to the English-speaking world through its many translations by the Stracheys. In 1952, it would begin the project to publish the *Standard Edition* of Freud in English, and with the editorship of James Strachey in collaboration with Anna Freud, assisted by Alix Strachey and Alan Tyson, the complete works were published in 1953–1974. It was different from the *Gesammelte Werke* as it contained critical footnotes by the editors.

James and Alix Strachey

James Strachey and Alix Sargent-Florence, a member of the Bloomsbury Group, had met in 1919. On 31 May 1920, James wrote to Freud asking to begin analysis, and received his acceptance on 4 June, the day that he and Alix married. In October, they both went to Vienna for James to start his analysis, which continued until June 1922.[7] They were both invited to translate Freud's works into English, along with John Rickman. Alix's first assignment was 'A child is being beaten'.

Alix stopped analysis with Freud in 1922, and by 1924 she had moved to Berlin to have analysis with Karl Abraham, until he became very ill in the autumn of 1925. It was in Berlin that Alix befriended Melanie Klein, who, following on from her first analysis in Budapest with Ferenczi, was now also in analysis with Abraham. The analytic vision that Bloomsbury brought to British psychoanalysis broadened when Alix invited Melanie Klein to lecture in London in 1925 to the Society, where she was warmly received. In 1926, following Karl Abraham's early death, meaning a disrupted analysis of only nine months, Klein moved permanently to London. Alix later translated Klein's *Psychoanalysis of Children*, published in 1932.

By 1929, James Strachey was a training analyst. He was, with Ella Freeman Sharpe, the most sought after training analyst of the entire inter-war period, with three candidates successfully qualifying (Sharpe had five, Klein had one, Rivière two, Glover two, Jones one).[8]

Adrian and Karin Stephen

Meanwhile, in 1914, Adrian Stephen, the younger brother of Virginia Woolf and Vanessa Bell, had married Karin Costelloe, a philosopher at Newnham College, Cambridge. He was a conscientious objector during World War One and wrote on pacifism. Conscription upset many in the Bloomsbury Group. Stephen's stance was in association with Bertrand Russell's high-profile views[9], and he was familiar with Quakerism from his wife's family. That tradition expected quietness until someone was moved to speak; perhaps it was an early experience of quiet dignity with the other – and the later postulate of the psychoanalysis of free association could also find here a ready atmosphere for analysis to develop (John Rickman was also a Quaker and a pacifist). Adrian Stephen did not object to those wanting to go to war but preferred not to be part of it himself. Towards the end of the war, both Adrian and Karin trained medically prior to training as psychoanalysts, at the request of Ernest Jones, who was trying to persuade the British Medical Association to regard psychoanalysis as scientific.[10] They were elected to associate membership in 1927, which was the year Sándor Ferenczi lectured to the Society and was made an honorary member.

In the 1930s, the four Bloomsbury analysts, Adrian and Karin Stephen, and James and Alix Strachey, all had analytic private practices whilst also translating Freud and others into English and writing themselves. D.W. Winnicott began analysis with James Strachey in 1924. In the same year, James wrote what became a classic paper on technique – 'The nature of the therapeutic action of psychoanalysis'. For Adrian Stephen, the aim of psychoanalysis was to enable more freedom in the patient's mind. Whilst freedom was a fundamental concept in analysis for Freud, Adrian Stephen further highlighted its centrality, resonating his Bloomsbury culture alongside psychoanalytic values, and it was to become a key component of Independent British analysis as the culture of the British Psychoanalytic Society from the early 1930s. Thus the goal of greater mental freedom, a liberal political position, transposed into a core idea of psychoanalysis in London.

In the Second World War, Adrian Stephen was so angered by Nazism and anti-Semitism that he abandoned his pacifist stance and, in 1939, volunteered to become an army psychoanalyst. He felt it important for reasons of transparency as well as fighting for a cause he saw as just. It was in his paper 'On defining psychoanalysis'[11] that Stephen argued for allowing more freedom of the analysand's own mind. He was active in promoting reforms of the BPAS, especially the idea of transparency of its rules as well as against the long control that had been wielded by Jones as its President.[12] Towards the end of the Controversial Discussions, he became the Society's Secretary (1944–47).

The Controversial Discussions, 1942–1944

James Strachey characterised the battle between Melanie Klein and Anna Freud in the Controversies in his own wry, sensible way.

> My own view is that Mrs. K. has made some highly important contributions ... but that it's absurd to make out (a) that they cover the whole subject or (b) that their validity is axiomatic. On the other hand, I think it is equally ludicrous for Miss F. to maintain that (Psychoanalysis) is a Game Reserve belonging to the F. Family.[13]

The four Bloomsbury analysts were on neither side of the Controversial Discussions and joined with Sylvia Payne, Ella Sharpe, Marjorie Brierley, William Gillespie, John Bowlby and Michael Balint in trying to find common ground for all of the Society.

This did not mean that the BPAS meetings could only be about the theoretical differences between the two women. Karin Stephen wrote rather than spoke[14] at an extraordinary Business Meeting to discuss the state of affairs in the Society about the entrenchment of power leading to resentment, intimidation and non-cooperation: 'We are now witnessing the second phase, open revolt and ill-will, which requires courage, independence and free exchange of ideas. Both are fatal to creative work.'[15] Here, she was arguing about the sense of resentment due to economic dependence on having referrals if they were deemed to be critical or 'even by vigorous indecent thinking'.[16] She went on to examine the problem of training analyses:

> It is unsatisfactory in the extreme that so many members should be in the patient-analyst relation with one another over periods of years and years. Straightforward adult equality relations, such as should hold between fellow scientists, are hardly possible in these circumstances ...[17]

Karin Stephen also wrote that members of the Society should vote 'in favour of altering our methods of election in such a way as to make it impossible in the future for any individual or group to capture power over the Society for more than a limited period'.[18] Ernest Jones, as president from 1913 with the first London Society and then the BPAS from 1919 – a period, by then, of 30 years – was chairing the debate, meaning that Karin had considerable courage to openly speak truth to power. She ended by stating:

> It is not good for human beings to wield unchecked power: they become dictatorial and arrogant and there is too much temptation for them to favour supporters and penalise opponents or rivals. And it is humiliating for those who allow themselves to be ruled in this way: either they become subservient, or they become aggressive, or they become depressed and apathetic.[19]

These statements from Karin Stephen demonstrate her capacity to pinpoint particular issues within groups, issues that were and are potentially available to be thought about in all analytic Societies, and in particular the BPAS, from that point until today.

One could argue that, despite these critiques, Strachey, with his liberal views, stood somewhere in the middle, and that the BPAS did invite important foreign analysts to give their theories and debate metapsychology. Following this argument, much of the prevailing culture derived from the Bloomsbury openness to think and the freedom to express views, especially on the unconscious and sexuality, made available as core values within the analytic Society.

During the Controversies, Strachey, in relation to the powers of the Training Committee, thought that psychoanalysis

> ... keeps close to the facts in its field of study, seeks to solve the immediate problems of observation, gropes its way forward by the help of experience, is always incomplete, and always ready to correct or modify its theories.[20]

Strachey was arguing that technique was not so closely aligned with theory and the Society's problems were insoluble because of theoretical differences, bound up in training due to unresolved webs of transference/countertransference around the groups. He fought for compromise in the Society in order to protect psychoanalysis from external political forces. Training candidates was not about teaching affiliation with one theory against another theory but

> ... [f]or the Candidate, in proportion as he has been freed from his unconscious prejudices, will be able to accept those of the analyst's views which can be confirmed, to supplement those which prove incomplete, and to correct or reject those which seem false.[21]

Here we can value Strachey's and Stephen's view that psychoanalysis is aimed at mental freedom, the same structure of their liberal political ideas and the template both before and after the Controversies of the position of the Independent Group, who took neither of the two sides.

Bloomsbury and the concept of freedom

John Forrester describes the Bloomsbury Group as providing a readymade atmosphere of a non-judgmental aesthetic. The Group was also very curious about the unconsciousness of relationships, one's individual history and its impact on sexual life, and in particular within an envelope of truth-seeking. It was this small group of friends, the Bloomsbury Group, which particularly took psychoanalysis into itself, using it across different disciplines to examine unconscious process in an atmosphere of freedom to think – freedom to free associate and to bring freedom to engage in life beyond the harsh realities and dictates of two World Wars. It has been remarked that the Bloomsbury Group lived in squares and loved in triangles.[22] They were also able to examine ideas about control and freedom of citizens and individuals through the prism of psychoanalysis. This was an unusual atmosphere given the context of the many strands of family life and intellectual pursuits coming out of Victorian Britain – the control of children, discipline and corporal punishment, the homosexuality of the British boarding school experience, the lives of women and even suffrage in the UK.[23] Unusually, the Bloomsbury set was alive to the thinking together of the men *and* women within the Group.

The British Psychoanalytic Society accepted women to train in psychoanalysis probably more than elsewhere in Europe. It is hard to understand how that came about alongside the prevailing British attitudes about women and the bitter fight for suffrage. It certainly did not happen by the sort of ongoing incremental progress that is a common trope to defend against the giving away of male privileges. Married women and women over the age of 30 obtained the vote in 1918 and equal adult suffrage, the so called 'flapper franchise', came in 1928. But what was the history of these complexities? The franchise to vote prior to 1918 was property-based. Between 1884 and 1918 about a third of adult males as well as the entirety of females were excluded.

However, suitably qualified women, which meant women who were ratepayers (predominantly women living independently such as spinsters or widows, plus married women who owned property independent of their husbands) could vote in municipal elections from 1869 and in county council elections from 1888, vote and stand as candidates in school board elections from 1870, and stand as candidates in county council elections from 1907.

It was also very difficult for women to go to university and have a professional life. It was not until 1876 that the UK Medical Act repealed the previous Medical Act in the United Kingdom and allowed the medical authorities to license all qualified applicants irrespective of gender. In 1877 an agreement was reached with the Royal Free Hospital that allowed students at the London School of Medicine for Women to complete their clinical studies there. The Royal Free Hospital was thus the first teaching hospital in London to admit women for training. The arrival of a teaching hospital for (initially) only women helped to enable the establishment of women doctors and in time for them to become specialists, yet the prejudice must have long continued.

It seems that there were fewer barriers to women pursuing a career in psychoanalysis. Maybe this was because of the analytic discussions around the Oedipus complex that accepted primitive states of mind for both men and women. Yet for a long time the prejudice persisted that the phallic was more 'important' and that women were the lesser and might have penis envy. And the respect to be found in Bloomsbury for intelligent women was also part of the picture. The early female analysts in the British Society, later joined by the powerful views of first Melanie Klein and then Anna Freud, secured a firm position for women who wanted to train in psychoanalysis in London.

The point to be made is the value of freedom for men and women, freedom for citizens, freedom to think and write about the unconscious mind, not only for psychoanalysts but for others, then bringing together analytic texts in Europe and beyond, translating the papers and publishing them in English, as well as the great project of the *Standard Edition* for the English-speaking world. These were all acts of freedom beyond one country or language. Keynes wrote decades later:

> We repudiated entirely morals, conventional wisdom. We were, that is to say, in the strictest sense of the word, immoralists. The consequences of being found out had, of course, to be considered for what they were worth. But we recognised no moral obligation on us, no inner sanction, to conform or obey. Before heaven we claimed to be our own judge in our own case ... It resulted in a general, widespread, though partly covert, suspicion affecting ourselves, our motives and our behaviour. This suspicion still persists to a certain extent, and it always will. It has deeply coloured the course of our lives in relation to the outside world. It is a justifiable suspicion. Yet so far as I am concerned, it is too late to change. I remain, and always will remain, an immoralist.[24]

Now put that description alongside that of psychoanalysis's dictum to speak one's mind to the analyst by putting aside one's distinction between good and bad values and behaviour and to put aside the listeners' (both analysand's and analyst's) prejudices. Morality was put aside and replaced by the hegemony of the personal and the aesthetic of what is the human experience. The requirement is for absolute honesty and a boundary-less confrontation with human passion and sexuality. Analytic listening without prejudice was the atmosphere of psychoanalysis in its early formation in the BPAS. This was before the eruption of the Controversial Discussions, which demanded the setting up of theoretical walls for the Kleinian and Anna Freudian trainings within the Society, and that atmosphere continued for the Independent Group, that was seemingly transposed to being in the *middle* of the warring pair. Adrian Stephen's trenchant position that psychoanalysis was to allow more freedom in the patient's mind kept the concept of freedom as the key value of the Independent Group in the British Psychoanalytical Society.

The name of the group

How might we understand some naming the group as 'Middle'? Change came about with the need to find a new political balance in the wake of the Controversial Discussions and was first described by Edward Glover as the so-called 'Middle Group'[25], or as the non-aligned or Independent British analysts. The new model, the Gentleman's Agreement[26], was of a Kleinian and Anna Freudian wing of analytic training, either side, as it were, of the original Independent matrix of the society, which was indeed perceived as being in the 'middle'. Those not inside the two new training formations had the freedom to sift through competing theories that worked for them and their patients without the burden of allegiance. The central political issue was who had control over training: training analysis, supervision and curriculum – and is still the central political issue today.

It is still a conundrum that the British Psychoanalytic Society had a determination to learn about all kinds of developing theories within Europe, then later in the United States and after that, South America. It welcomed colleagues to teach and to stay and develop theory and practice. The core of such an atmosphere was certainly taken from Bloomsbury and followed a somewhat incandescent idea of having the freedom to develop oneself, not just one's internal object relational system but within the open atmosphere of the early Society. John Rickman was curious enough to go to Vienna for analysis with Freud, then later to Budapest to have analysis with Ferenczi, and further took the opportunity to have analysis with Melanie Klein when she practised in London. Such attitudes were about being independently minded. The group invited into its midst Melanie Klein and later Anna Freud, who warred within the Society. But to push the original analysts of the Society into a position of being in the middle, between Klein and Anna Freud, was a political act.

Many years later, when some colleagues who had trained in the Independent group had a desire, for personal reasons, to have a second, Kleinian analysis, it was not uncommon for that theory to be imbibed too. This could lead to a theoretical dissonance unless one changed one's group. In the late 1990s this led to a schism in the Independent Training group, as those colleagues who were theoretically now functioning with a Kleinian theoretical approach were still members. Yet it was not at all clear if their candidates who wanted an Independent analysis knew this. When challenged, one training analyst spoke to ask where else could one have a home, as admission to the Klein group was barred, membership being only through one's primary training analysis. Here we meet another political act that caused much difficulty to Independent training.

And what of more modern times? Michael Parsons wrote in 2014,

> [The concept of] the Independent tradition does not coincide with the Independent Group. There is a large overlap, in that the majority of analysts who have exemplified and developed the tradition have been part of the Group. However, there are members of the Independent Group that do not stand within the Independent tradition. Conversely, the Independent tradition is not limited to the Group, or even the British Society.[27]

At the core of the old and current British Society is the Independent Group, continuing the atmosphere of enquiry and respect for differing theoretical views as well as respect for its own history and its core value of freedom of mind.

Acknowledgements

I am grateful to John Forrester's work with Laura Cameron: *Freud in Cambridge*; also for Ken Robinson's skill as a historian of British psychoanalysis. I am also grateful for cogent comments from Phillip Waller, Fellow and Tutor in Modern History, Merton College, Oxford.

JS, December 2021

Notes

1 Sharpe was interested in Froebel and Pestalozzi, whose work centred on the individual's freedom to grow.
2 R.A. Paskauskas (1993). *The Complete Correspondence of Sigmund Freud and Ernest Jones 1908–1939*. Cambridge, Mass.: Harvard University Press, p. 328.
3 Following analysis with Freud from 31 March to June 1922, and late 1923 to summer 1924, in 1925 Sir Arthur Tansley, the eminent Cambridge ecologist, became a psychoanalyst at the BPAS.

4 S. Raitt (2004). 'Early British Psychoanalysis and the Medico-Psychological Clinic', *History Workshop Journal,* Issue 58: 63–85. To be clear, much of the clinic's work was far from what we might recognise as psychoanalysis, although immediately post-World War One, knowledge of analytic technique was not very great either. The interest in war trauma does seem to be an important strand in analytic understanding.
5 In John Forrester's view, Keynes's 1936 work contained anxiety about the future rather than hope – an inversion leading to lack of trust in the future due to the aggression of two world wars.
6 Moore and Russell were Apostles, but not part of the Bloomsbury Group.
7 Between March and June 1922, 40% of Freud's patients were from Cambridge. This meant that Freud became an expert in Cambridge academe, especially science, the subject for which it was the leading university in the country. Not only did this lead to the seeding of psychoanalysis in the UK and the Empire, but it attached analytic insights to scientific endeavours. An example was Tansley's botany.
8 J. Forrester & L. Cameron (2017). 'Bloomsbury Analysts'. In: *Freud in Cambridge.* Cambridge: Cambridge University Press.
9 Russell argued that the genuine pacifist neither seeks peace for its own sake or order and security, nor for his own tranquillity or comfort. He strives for peace in order that all human lives may flourish freely, because what motivates a pacifist is the brotherhood of men.
10 Adrian and Karin Stephen were both in analysis with James Glover. When he died in 1926, Adrian went into analysis with Ella Freeman Sharpe. Karin continued with Edward Glover, then with Clara Thompson on her visit to the US in 1927, where she met Ferenczi and enjoyed his lectures, and finally went into analysis with Sylvia Payne. Karin's work as a philosopher was supervised by her uncle, Bertrand Russell. Karin wrote *Psychoanalysis and Medicine – A Study of the Wish to Fall Ill* (Cambridge: Cambridge University Press, 1933).
11 A. Stephen (1936). 'On defining psychoanalysis', *The Psychoanalytic Review* 23: 225.
12 Jones was President of the BPAS for the extraordinarily long period of 1919 to 1944.
13 L. Appignanesi & J. Forrester (1992). *Freud's Women.* London: Weidenfeld & Nicholson, pp. 298–9.
14 Karin Stephen's deafness may have meant that she preferred to make a written rather than verbal contribution. The vigour of her mind was a powerful counterpoint to her hearing difficulties. See Forrester & Cameron, p. 554.
15 Ibid., p. 571.
16 Ibid., p. 572.
17 Ibid., p. 572.
18 Ibid., p. 572.
19 Ibid., p. 573.
20 Freud (1923). 'Two Encyclopaedia Articles', which Strachey had just finished translating, publishing it in the *International Journal of Psycho-Analysis.*
21 Adrian Stephen, quoted in Forrester & Cameron, ibid., p. 588.
22 Ibid., p. 553.
23 Women only received the vote on the same terms as men, aged 21, in 1928.
24 M. Keynes (1972 [1938]). 'My Early Beliefs'. In: *Essays in Biography,* Vol X, London: Macmillan & Cambridge University Press for the Royal Economic Society, pp. 447–448.

25 Ricardo Steiner, in *The Freud-Klein Controversies 1941–45* (1991), P. King and R. Steiner (eds), London & New York: Tavistock/Routledge, p. 681.
26 Really, this was the 'Ladies' Agreement' between Melanie Klein and Anna Freud.
27 M. Parsons (2014). 'An Independent Theory of Clinical Technique'. In: *Living Psychoanalysis: From Theory to Experience*. London: Routledge, p. 187.

Part II

Independent Women

Chapter 3

Ella Sharpe

Being Independent, following Freud

Ken Robinson

In her 'Memorandum on … Technique' (November 1943), Ella Sharpe advised:

> One has to tread Freud's path after him, start as he started not where he left off. There is no short cut.
>
> (King & Steiner, 1991, p. 645)

This quotation distils not only the main themes of her writings on technique and practice but the essence of her Independence. She was one of those who had come to Freudian thinking before both the arrival of Melanie Klein on the British scene in 1926 and the emigration of the Freuds to London in 1938. Broadly speaking she worked within the framework of classical Freudian metapsychology, which allowed her the freedom to explore new observations and developments without having to declare allegiance to either the Kleinian or the Anna Freudian Groups as they emerged. In that sense she was a British Freudian (Robinson, 2011), in the Middle Group, which later, at Paula Heimann's suggestion, would be renamed the Independent Group. Sharpe held that as psychoanalysts we cannot simply immerse ourselves in Freud's (or any other analyst's) writings and apply them; instead, understanding through personal practice must always precede precept. She believed that, against the background of our own analysis and our knowledge of the existing psychoanalytic literature, we must develop our own precepts out of our own practice, and, having developed them, let them be challenged by further practice, as we find ways of working with different forms of disturbance and their unique nuances in each patient. This is how it was for Freud. We must find our own technique, in the spirit of Freud's recognition, quoted at the outset of Sharpe's 'Memorandum', that his own technique was the "only method suited to [his] individuality" and that "others quite differently constituted might … adopt a different attitude to [their] patients and to the task before [them]" (King & Steiner, 1991, p. 639). For Sharpe psychoanalysts must believe in psychic determinism, in the "process set going by the method of free association", and in the centrality of transference, but they should also be at liberty to find their own technique of handling them. It is a major part

DOI: 10.4324/9781003296690-6

of Sharpe's thinking on technique that she emphasises "process" and "pace", pace as "ultimately set by the individual psyche in question", to which the analyst must attune herself. As she put it: "a valid technique is not directed to finding support for any theory, it is directed to only one object, the investigation of the psychical problems of a given individual, without a priori assumptions" (Ibid.). It is also important for her that the analyst should recognise that she is not infallible, that she has her own limitations and blind spots, that some people cannot be helped, and that where there is success it is ultimately down to "what the patient emotionally realizes for himself". Sharpe marks out her own independence, but she also draws attention to its dependence on Freud's "vision, tolerance, and sanity" that is far-removed "from the fears and the necessity for complete certainty that beset … his followers". In other words, in Sharpe's view we have our analytic parents who have laid down a theory and practice and we should neither ablate them nor descend into inauthentic imitation of them (King & Steiner, 1991, pp. 639–647).

In her 'Memorandum', Sharpe was speaking four years after Freud's death. He had still been asking questions of his own theory right up to where he "left off" in his final writings, especially with respect to the function of denial; but after the publication of his final papers in 1940 there were no new departures for Sharpe and her contemporaries to take into account. It had been very different in the years of her formation as an analyst.

Ella Sharpe's path

We do not know when Sharpe began to read Freud, but she moved into a vaguely psychoanalytic milieu in London in 1917, and in the following years she would have been aware of the steady stream of Freud's papers that extended his thinking, especially 'Beyond the Pleasure Principle' (1920), 'The Ego and the Id' (1923), 'Inhibitions, Symptoms and Anxiety' (1926), and so on. All these she had to assimilate, finding her own way along his path as it emerged, but it is also important to be aware of Sharpe's own path of development before 1917.

Freud had started out as a neuroscientist. Ella Sharpe started out as a teacher, and, as Sylvia Payne recognised in her obituary for her friend and colleague, there was continuity between Sharpe's old and her new profession. According to those who knew her as a teacher, she had an exceptional capacity to enter into adolescent problems and an insatiable curiosity about the human mind. These qualities, along with her specialist knowledge of literature, poetry, and drama, dovetailed into her psychoanalytic training and experience (Payne, 1947).

Ella Agnes Freeman Sharpe was born in 1875 in Sudbury, Suffolk, to parents who worked as silk weavers at a period when the industry was in decline. By the time that she was six her parents had moved to Nottingham, along with her baby sister, Martha Daisy Grace, who was profoundly deaf. Other members of the wider family moved to Nottingham around the same time, and some slightly later. When Ella was 12, another sister was born, Marion (or May) Kathleen. Her parents may have moved to seek work in the lace industry in Nottingham only to find it undermined by economic depression in the 1880s. By 1881 her father was running a café and continued in that role until his death in 1910. After his death, her mother, Mary Ann, continued to run it. When Ella Sharpe finished elementary school at 13 (the leaving age in 1888), she entered a pupil teacher training school under a scheme where 13 to 18 year-olds furthered their education whilst at the same time learning to teach. Nottingham was "a centre for excellence in the field of pupil teacher training" in this period (Jones, 1998, p. 29). She was already showing herself to be an independent young woman.

She went on to be an English Mistress and ended up co-Principal of a pupil teachers training centre in Hucknall, Nottingham before moving to London in 1917. At some point whilst in Nottingham, she attended Nottingham University which as yet had no charter to confer its own degrees. Its students could register for external London University degrees, but Sharpe did not avail herself of the opportunity. There is a curious legend, promoted it seems by Sharpe herself and then by Sylvia Payne, that her opportunities were limited by her father's death as she approached puberty, leaving her with the responsibility of looking after her mother and two sisters, "rather as an eldest son might have done", so that she could not pursue further study in Oxford after Nottingham (Payne, 1947, p. 54). In fact, her father died when she was 34. Her mother survived him, but Sharpe and her sisters, who formed a tight unit, lived separately from her until, in her later years they cared for her.

Two influences are important in Sharpe's educational development in these years. The first is her love of literature. According to one of her biographers, it was fostered by her father from whom she inherited "an impassioned and almost encyclopaedic knowledge … of Shakespeare and of English Literature". It is said that one of her earliest memories was sitting at his feet while he read a Shakespeare play to the family (Wahl, 1966, p. 265). The other influence came from Nottingham being an educationally enlightened city that was alive to innovation, especially the thinking of Pestalozzi and Froebel whose works, intertwined with Wordsworth's poetry, echo through some of her papers. In her paper on 'Vocation' (Sharpe, 1924), for example, she refers to Pestalozzi and Froebel as teachers "allied to the artist … [with] an innate feeling for mind-processes" (p. 215). Her indebtedness led her to maintain contact with her roots and she maintained an interest in the relationship between psychoanalysis and education throughout her life. The Nottingham Froebel Society was open to psychoanalytic thinking: Ernest Jones spoke there in December 1916 on 'The Child's Unconscious', and it is likely that Sharpe would have been present. She herself addressed it on 'Psycho-Analysis' in 1923. Pestalozzi's methods were child-centred and based on individual differences, sense perception, and the child's self-activity. Add to this Froebel's emphasis on self-realisation through play in a natural environment and it is not difficult to see how something of their ideas found their way into Sharpe's writing on technique and how their thinking has similarities with what it is to be an Independent analyst. Her emphasis on practice preceding precept, for example, and on self-activity, resonate with Froebel.

Sharpe moved to London in 1917 to seek treatment, it seems, for depression prompted by "the dissolution of a long and close friendship and ... the death of many of her former pupils on the battlefields of WW1" (Wahl, 1966, pp. 265–66). It was, ironically, the year of the publication of Freud's 'Mourning and Melancholia'. She found help at the Medico-Psychological Clinic in Brunswick Square and stayed on to train as a psychotherapist at the training arm of the Clinic, which had developed in 1915. The Clinic was eclectic – and much frowned on by Ernest Jones – but it was influenced by psychoanalysis and as it happened played an important role in the development of psychoanalysis in England (Martindale, 2004; Raitt, 2004). It was a first staging post for several future psychoanalysts, especially female psychoanalysts, whom Sharpe met there. James Glover was associated with it (and tangentially his brother Edward). It is remarkable that all who went on to join the BPAS after training there were women who did not align themselves with either Klein or Anna Freud, except for Susan Isaacs who became a follower of Klein, though she shared an interest in Froebel's ideas which were later fundamental to the milieu of the Malting House School in Cambridge, which she ran from 1924 to 1927 (Graham, 2008). Together with Isaacs, Marjorie Brierley and Sylvia Payne, Sharpe was extremely influential in the British Psychoanalytical Society (BPAS). Brierley played a major part in the Controversial Discussions (1941–45), as did Payne who, as President from 1944, went on to steer the British Society through the troubled waters churned up by the trauma of the Discussions; and Isaacs delivered the first discussion paper. Not surprisingly perhaps, Sharpe was a central figure in training, and the most sought-after training analyst and supervisor following the introduction of formal training on the Eitingon model in 1926. Others included Iseult Grant-Duff, Ethilda Budget-Meakin Herford, Gwen Lewis, Mary Chadwick and Nina Searl. The Clinic played a significant part in increasing the number of women members of the BPAS after 1919. In 1919 17% of the membership was female; by 1930 that figure had risen to 40%, almost half of whom had started out at the Clinic.

Why did Sharpe choose to travel to London for help with depression? It may be that, given her literary interests, she knew of May Sinclair's involvement in the Brunswick Square Clinic and of her interest in psychoanalysis. She may have known too that women had a voice there for Sinclair shared with its Clinical Directors, Jessie Murray and Julia Turner, strong suffragette and feminist sympathies. Sharpe was there by September 1917.[1] In April it had opened an in-patient extension to accommodate soldiers suffering from war-shock, soldiers not unlike the young men whom she had taught and whose loss had played a part in her search for help. The Clinic was closely connected with what was going on at the front. For example, one of its Directors, Hector Monro, had set up an Ambulance Corps whose mission was to move wounded troops from the battlefield to hospitals in Flanders. Some of the workers from the Clinic, including May Sinclair, spent time with the Corps and similar units.

Sharpe entered therapy with Julia Turner[2] and, as a trainee, she would probably have treated a war-shocked soldier.[3] After the war, others like Sylvia Payne (who had been superintendent at the Red Cross Hospital in East-bourne) joined on the basis of their experiences of treating war casualties. By Autumn 1919, Sharpe had become, along with Julia Turner and James Glover, responsible for analysing the trainees, as well as Honorary Assistant Director of the training. By this point her sister, May (or Marion) had become Secretary to the Clinic. The accounts that we have of the Clinic speak of a closely-knit community of trainees amongst whom close bonds were established (Dexter, 1918). At various points Sharpe shared lodgings with Nina Searl, Mary Chadwick, and Gwen Lewis in Gordon Street. James Strachey referred to them as the 'Gordon Street ménage'. They all shared an interest in child analysis and when lectures from Melanie Klein were planned in London in 1925, they agreed that she could use their drawing room, only to find that numbers were too great to accommodate (Meisl & Kendrick, 1986, p. 258).

The Clinic, then, was where Sharpe took her first steps along Freud's path. It was eclectic, but this was not the only reason that the psychoanalytic practice she encountered was as yet unformed. Before 1919 there was very little understanding in Britain of what constituted a reasonably sophisticated psychoanalytic technique. Only Ernest Jones and David Eder amongst British analysts had first-hand experience of being analysed in anything like Freud's way – Jones with Ferenczi and Eder with Tausk, both in 1913 – and Freud's papers on technique were not available in English translation until 1924. Many relied simply on dream interpretation and/or used Jung's word asso-ciation tests. Some continued to use hypnotism, and others even used crystal-gazing. From 1919 a much more recognisable practice emerged. With the end of the war, Sharpe joined other British would-be analysts in travelling to Europe for analysis. Towards the end of 1920 she went to Berlin, following James Glover who entered analysis with Karl Abraham in Berlin, as did his brother Edward. Sharpe went to Hanns Sachs, whom she probably chose because of his interest in literature, film and the arts. Later, Mary Chadwick, Sylvia Payne and Nina Searl also entered analysis with Sachs and became her analytic siblings. David Forsyth and Sylvia Payne both described the marked differences in their experience of technique before and after their analyses after the war with Freud and Hanns Sachs respectively (Forsyth, 1913; Forsyth, 1922; and King & Steiner, 1991, p. 650). Like all those who travelled to Berlin for analysis, Sharpe was welcome to take part in the activities of the Berlin Society and she benefitted from acquaintance with Abraham and his work.

Payne (1967) did not rate Sachs highly, but Sharpe got enough out of her analysis to return to Sachs in vacations when she could. He thought well of her, and they shared an interest in art, creativity and technique. It seems that she did learn from him, because more than one of her analysands described her pulling together the threads of a session at its end, in much the way that Sachs did (Gillespie, 1990, p. 14; Robinson, 2008, p. 47; Wahl, 1966, p. 266).

The exposure of British analysts to the thoroughly Freudian world of the Berlin Society, especially to Karl Abraham, led to increasing dissatisfaction with the Clinic. When James Glover returned from Berlin in 1921, he began to close it down, despite fierce opposition from his fellow Director Julia Turner. This must have been a very difficult time for Sharpe whose loyalties were divided between her past therapist and James Glover, who was not only idolised at the Clinic (and beyond) but, it seems, had "a strong fixation" on her (Wittenberger & Tögel, 1999, 1: 142). She threw in her lot with Glover. Together they made sure that those in training could continue with regular seminars at Glover's home in Mecklenburgh Square, a stone's throw from the Clinic.

In the same year, 1921, Sharpe was elected as an Associate Member of the BPAS, becoming a Member in 1923. She soon became a valued analyst. Ernest Jones congratulated Sachs on his pupil, when in 1923 she read "a most excellent paper [at a Scientific Meeting of the BPAS] on the analysis of Frances Thompson, religious poet" (Wittenberger & Tögel, 2006). Jones was equally enthusiastic about her contribution, on 'Vocation', to a series of lectures to the Sociological Society, also in 1923: it was "much the best and was really excellent" (Wittenberger & Tögel, 2006, 4:140). Sharpe's reputation remained high amongst key figures in psychoanalysis. Freud himself reported that he had "heard good of her" (Friedman, 2002, p. 323).

Just as Sharpe had embraced pupil-centred educational development as a teacher, so she wished psychoanalytic training to be trainee-centred. Her own self-directed training left her cautious that institutionalised training might curtail the freedom of trainees to find their own way. As she put it:

> Most of us worked our way by acquiring what imperfect technique we possess by dealing directly and almost unaided with our problems. We learned first-hand by trial and error; we had the inestimable advantage of talking case material over with friends and contemporaries. There was no leader and no led; we were independent. Help was reciprocal. We met on a common footing and had a common zest. I attribute some of the freedom we took for granted, the freedom we felt, to the fact that we were separated from our own analysts by the English Channel, an important bulwark of independence in so many ways … We did not gather round one person, neither one nor another as the source and fountain of

truth … I do not advocate that our students should have no more help than *we* had, but help can be given at the cost of independence if students continue too long moving in the orbits of their analysts instead of their own.

(King & Steiner, 1991, p. 646)

The freedom of self-realisation was threatened in the BPAS not only by for-malised training but by the atmosphere in the war years when warring camps emerged – the Anna Freudians and the Melanie Kleinians – leading to the Controversial Discussions. Each camp felt that it had the right way, "the Alpha and Omega of human development", as Sharpe put it (King & Steiner, 1991, p. 805). In the middle were those who remained independent and non-aligned, a more heterogeneous group precisely because they were indepen-dent. The impact of the battle over the Curriculum on students' learning experience was easily forgotten. It was Sharpe who was most attuned to their plight as well as to what sort of training environment would best facilitate their development.

Ella Sharpe in the Controversial Discussions (1941–45)

Sharpe had known Melanie Klein and her work from her Berlin days, and she remained an admirer of her gift of "insight into the unconscious phantasy life" of both children and adults, although she did not appreciate her "for-mulations" (King & Steiner, 1991, p. 644), especially her concept of the depressive position and its radical departure from Freud's thinking. She was not alone in this: many British Freudians were disturbed by Klein's evolving theories from 1933/4. When she contributed in the Discussions to the debate around Klein's concept of a depressive position, Sharpe questioned Klein's claim "that the loss of the breast has the same determining significance for all children, i.e., a 'depressive' significance", arguing that whether it takes on that significance depends on quantitative factors (Ibid., 1991, p. 404). She pre-ferred Freud's understanding of unfolding danger situations, regarding wean-ing as simply one stage in the child's "slow painful descent from the omnipotence of godhead to his own small weak stature and helplessness concerning his massive emotions", as "almost the last of the external physical birth throes" (Ibid., p. 339). Although she acknowledged many times how great a contribution Klein had made to recognising the nature of those "massive emotions", the emphasis for her was on successive developmental experiences of potentially traumatic helplessness, and narcissistic defence against it. Depres-sion, she argued, comes with "refusal to face … painful reality", with a pre-ference for the "'status quo' resistance to change" which "is really narcissism" (Ibid., 1991, pp. 806 and 813). This anti-progressive "status quo" resistance, is, for Sharpe, closer to the defensive backward pull to primary narcissism descri-bed in Freud's 'On Narcissism' than to his description of the death instinct in 'Beyond the Pleasure Principle'.

Despite Sharpe's independence, both factions in the Discussions tried to enlist her when battle lines were being drawn in the heat of debate. Susan Isaacs visited her on Klein's behalf to sound out where she stood, reporting back that Sharpe was "very firm and unmodifiable by us", that she had "closely identified herself, in her own mind, with Anna Freud", and that, like Bowlby, she "opposed us ... [on] the relative importance of the environment v. inner factors". Isaacs concluded: "She insists that in the scientific work, she is not concerned to 'prove' anything – but only to find out" (Isaacs, 1942). In other words, she is determined to go her own way entirely and do only such things as establish her independence and originality – and, doubtless, allegiance to Freud.

From the other side, Edward Glover also assessed her allegiances, con-cluding that her "position is uncertain, but she is much more Freudian than Kleinian. Nevertheless I think she should still be called a Middle Grouper" (Mühlleitner & Reichmayr, 1988, p. 496). But Ella Sharpe was neither given to being a disciple nor likely to get into a fight: the only position that she took up was open-mindedness and suspicion of any claims to infallibility.

This was the spirit that she brought to her comments on Susan Isaac's paper on 'Unconscious Phantasy' in the Discussions (King & Steiner, 1991, pp. 337–339). Rather than be pulled into a battle between opposing views, she tried to state "as clearly as possible" her own views in keeping with Freud's honesty about the "uncertainties of our knowledge".

Sharpe accepted that unconscious phantasy exists from infancy, though not from the start. She found this consistent with Freud's view on the infantile roots of dreams and with his recognition, in her words, that objects "forsaken by libido ... are retained to some degree in the conceptions of phantasy". Grounding her argument in Freud, she concentrated on the development of the earliest phantasies. Infantile hallucinatory wishful psychosis, she argued, "*command[s] entire belief*" (original emphasis) so that at the most rudimen-tary level the infant believes that he actually "possesses the real tangible breast", first on the outside, and then on the inside "as in pre-natal days". This wishful psychosis gives way to reality, to an awareness that it is a phan-tasy; "the capacity for mental imagery" emerges and with it "acceptance of a symbol" in place of the "concrete realisation" of perceptual identity. How-ever, infantile wishes for concrete realisation persevere beneath the surface, so that if "reality satisfaction fails", there remains a potential to revert through topographical regression to perceptual identity; but what was an appropriate developmental illusion in the infant is in regression psychotic. As Sharpe put it, the belief in an object within, whether good or bad, "preserves the illusions of non-bodily separation". Beyond infancy it is "an ultimate psychotic belief". Developmentally, "our troubles start with reality, with separation": the unfolding stages of the child's detachment from his mother require a process of mourning if the child is to develop. In Sharpe's view Klein's early Oedipus setting threatens to bypass the reality of separation because it has a psychotic quality: it entails "the delusion of the incorporation of the actual pregnant mother and the father together with the belief that the new baby is magically the child's own" so that the whole world is inside rather than separate.

This was in 1943, in the midst of war. Sharpe, who contributed to a short-wave series to North America, organised by Edward Glover, on *Inside the Nazi Mind* (Roazen, 2000, p. 173), was well aware that the Discussions were taking place in the context of war with Hitler and involved colleagues who had fled the Nazi regime: they were not simply about scientific differences but also about democracy, and freedom of thought (Whelan, 2000, p. 22). The most primitive illusion, the belief in the actual incorporated object, she argued, can have far-reaching consequences beyond infancy. She associated it with the Fascist belief in an idealised good object that had allowed the rise of Hitler, and with the narcissistic complacency of "pipe-smoking optimists ... who say 'God's in His Heaven, all's right with the world'".[4]

It is significant in this context that, in her response to Isaacs, Sharpe puts the final emphasis not on theory but on "practical analysis", on "*psychical delivery*" (original emphasis), from illusions about ourselves and others which facilitated facing reality and growth to "the stature of an individual separate existence" (King & Steiner, 1991, p. 340).

Sharpe's infant

The terms of the debates in the Discussions and Sharpe's strategy of indicating what she agrees with in Klein in relation to her understanding of Freud's metapsychology, tended to limit her freedom to pursue her own course, except when she was commenting on technique. In her work more generally, there is a more distinctly personal, poetic vision of the infant's development, a vision more in keeping with her belief that "children must be allowed to develop their own momentum of sensual pleasure in themselves and their own environment and to find their own goals" (Sharpe, 1936, p. 11). She first spelled it out in her paper on 'Vocation" (1924), so admired by Jones. In her lectures on dreams delivered between 1934 and 1936, Sharpe remarked on John Livingstone Lowes's work on Coleridge's *The Rime of the Ancient Mariner*. Lowes had recreated the workshop of Coleridge's mind, tracing what he had unified, from the books that he had read, through "the psychical mechanism of condensation, obedient to the magnet of unconscious interest, the source of all intellectual activity" (Sharpe, 1937a, p. 43). If there were space it would be possible to show what is condensed into Sharpe's 'Vocation', but I shall here comment simply on how her psychoanalytic understanding of development is deeply influenced by Froebel and Wordsworth (with Pestalozzi in the background). The three were commonly linked in the period when Sharpe was teaching (see, for example, Bowen, 1892, Fotheringham, 1899 and Hayward, 1904). I quote her:

The infant comes screaming and protesting at its expulsion from Nirvana. Through the gateways of the five senses he finds himself and the world around him. For him there is no taboo concerning seeing, touching, hearing, smelling, tasting. His initial interest is his own body. His initial curiosity is himself. His first powers are his own bodily functionings. The first phantasies are concerned with these things, until they take a wider range and concern others ... Outward discipline eliminates many and the slow incorporation of the ego-ideal represses the interest in them to the unconscious. Yet,

> Those first affections,
> Those shadowy recollections,
> Which be they what they may,
> Are yet the fountain light of all our day.

There at the hidden root of us lie the primal impulses to see, feel, touch, smell, taste, the curiosity and phantasies of all we experienced in the earliest infancy.

(Sharpe, 1924, pp. 209–210)

It is not difficult to hear Wordsworth in Sharpe's mind, not least because she quotes from his *Ode: Intimations of Immortality from Recollections of Early Childhood*. Equally, it is not difficult to be aware of the presence of Froebel's ideas: his belief, shared with Pestalozzi, in "the 'natural goodness' of all children in contrast to the doctrine of original sin" (Brehony, 1988, p. 54); his conviction that children will flourish like plants if they are appropriately nurtured (which she would use more explicitly in her paper on leaving home [Sharpe, 1935a]); his emphasis on sensory learning from first-hand experience; and on a natural order and rhythm. Sharpe did not have to buy into the pantheism of Froebel and Wordsworth to accommodate their account of infancy to her own vision. She draws on their recognition of the power of maternal holding and the role of the mother as primary educator (taken up again particularly in 'Feminine Development: Is Co-Education a Help or a Hindrance?' [1937b]). Like Wordsworth she understood how the infant "Drinks in the feelings of his Mother's eye" and "by intercourse of touch [holds] mute dialogues with [his] Mother's heart" (Wordsworth, 1950, p. 505); she also incorporates his, and Froebel's, awareness that such experience creates the conditions under which the infant can invest the world with life, meaning and joy. At the same time, she condenses Wordsworth's sensitivity to loss and grief as the child develops, as "Shades of the prison-house begin to close/ Upon the growing Boy" (p. 460) and his internal and external worlds threaten to destroy his creativity. Perhaps the most remarkable nuance that the magnet of Sharpe's unconscious interest picks up, however, is Wordsworth's sense that this danger is mitigated by the enduring nature of "the primal sympathy/ Which having been must ever be" (p. 462). Loss does not only bring "soothing thoughts that spring/ Out of human suffering" (p. 462) but it can co-exist with the "first creative sensibility" (p. 507), the recollected pleasure of being alive with "the five senses", in Nature, "the nurse,/ The guide, the guardian of my heart" (p. 165). This perseverance of "primal sympathy" becomes in Sharpe something akin to primary narcissism, not as a defence but as an enduring memory of good experience which can later exist side by side with, and bind, the hostility that comes with its loss (and the introjection of an associated parental imago), and which can fuel positive, creative investment in the world.

Although Sharpe held that "frustration and subsequent anxiety due to aggression" bring the deep-seated aggressive phantasies of the sort that Klein had described, she also emphasised the ongoing importance of "an infant's actual experiences of milk received and fæces given in non-anxiety periods":

> There are pleasurable bodily states of rhythmic functioning when what was taken and incorporated was good, bodily and psychically, and what the child produced was pleasing and acceptable. This is a pattern of infantile bodily and psychical well-being in reality ...
>
> (Sharpe, 1935b, p. 192)

In the Discussions Sharpe stayed close to the version of primary narcissism that Freud advanced in *Civilization and its Discontents* (1930), clarifying that such experiences, which are prolonged in the infant's hallucination of feeding, belong to a time before the reality of separation brings frustration, self-preservative hostility, and the capacity for "mental imagery" (King & Steiner, 1991, p. 338).[5]

These primal patterns of experience, when "recollected in tranquillity", like Wordsworth's "spots of time", have a "renovating virtue"; but they are not reparative in Klein's sense. They are simply re-experienced with a sense of loss but without depressive anxiety, and they bind hostility. As Sharpe sees it, the infant is born innocent, it loses "the primal narcissism of the garden of Eden" (King & Steiner, 1991, p. 812), but despite this loss (and its defensive desire to return to the status quo), its primal powers and pleasures can live on and be freshly channelled if all goes well enough and its fall from paradise is mourned. It might well be that when they are re-channelled the experience is marked not so much by loss as by ecstasy, as in Wordsworth, or as in Freud's account of Leonardo who "was overcome by emotion, and in ecstatic language praised the splendour of the part of creation that he had studied, or—in religious phraseology—the greatness of his Creator" (Freud, 1910a, p. 75). It is important that Sharpe does not present such joy as defensive idealisation.

On this basis, Sharpe believed, like Froebel, that the infant came into the world as "a unique individual who has the power and vocation to express the divine principle within him by his own creative activities in his own distinctive mode" (Lawrence, 1952, p. 188). Vocations, she writes (again echoing Wordsworth), are made in Heaven, the Heaven that lies about us in our infancy ... a person who finds a real vocation has carried the maximum amount of energy that was invested in ... early infantile pleasures up through successive stages of development ... from the very roots of primitive life.

(Sharpe, 1924, p. 209)

This is her Romantic version of Freud in the 'Five Lectures' (1910b). When this happens, she suggests, repression has worked in the interest of sublimation:

[T]he thing tabooed is repressed, but the vital charge of energy with which it was invested has been switched off at just the psychological moment to something that is *not* tabooed, and yet which is capable of taking the energy charge.

(Sharpe, 1924, p. 211)

Sublimation, she held, is synonymous with the development of "innate personal talents" (Sharpe, 1937b, p. 110).

One calling is being an artist, and in her 1935 paper 'Similar and Divergent Unconscious Determinants Underlying the Sublimations of Pure Art and Pure Science', Sharpe located the roots of the artist's capacity for sublimation in this infantile period, in the pattern of pleasurable rhythm in infancy. She believed "that creative art is at least one way of re-experiencing those experiences which are the basis of normal physical and psychical health" (Sharpe, 1935b, p. 192). The artist not only projects the rhythm of his infantile world into his work but gives expression to preverbal emotional experience. "Crooning, gurgling, crying, screaming, ... urinating, defaecating" give way to "manipulation of sound, gesture, water, paint, words ... to the end of a creation of harmony and design". In this way "the deepest phantasies of the infantile pleasure life" (Sharpe, 1924, p. 217) – life at the level of the pleasure principle – are sublimated in a form acceptable to the ego.

Sublimation and art

Sublimation is central to Sharpe's theory in general and to her aesthetic theory in particular. Freud had left the concept of sublimation relatively under-developed, and Sharpe, seeped in his work, gave it her own imprint. Drawing on Freud, she brought together what she found useful from Klein on early phantasies and from Sachs on the artist's guilt (Sharpe, 1924), with her own Romantic account of development, to present art as a triumph of Eros. "Balance, synthesis, and unity, characteristic of all great art", are, for her, the province of Eros (Sharpe, 1932, p. 378).

There are two aspects to Sharpe's account of sublimation: the *capacity* for sublimation and the *process* of sublimation. For sublimation to be possible the artist must be able to tap into the experience of infancy "when primal identification and object-love were united, when self-preservation and libidinal gratification were inseparable" (Ibid., p. 194). At the heart of this state for Sharpe is what she terms "a control rhythm … the production of the rise and fall of tensions that are rhythmical and pleasurable" (Ibid., p. 193), re-experiencing the self-preservative rhythm of the intake of milk and breath, the rhythm of the heartbeat and the pleasure of evacuation. She believed that the artist was able to use this rhythm creatively, in touch with reality, to redress the impact of infantile frustration that came with the fall from "the primal narcissism of the garden of Eden" (King & Steiner, 1991, p. 812). She saw in Van Gogh's late work a loss of rhythm, as hatred and aggression brought chaos to his life, and he lost contact with reality. Someone like Van Gogh who could not access this rhythm would need the *"psychical delivery"* (original emphasis) of analysis before sublimation proper could be possible.

Freud's view of the process of sublimation involved withdrawal of libido from objects on to the ego to become narcissistic libido, which was desexualised, and then available to be directed onto higher or cultural ends. Only late in life did he begin to turn his mind to how the aggressive drive might be sublimated. Sublimated energy for Freud served the purpose of Eros, and so it did for Sharpe too, but Sharpe also held that narcissism played its part in a different way. She held that in the experience of the primary narcissistic state, "physically the good experience meant life for the infant and life for the mother" (p. 195), and if, psychically, that has survived well enough in the form of a good imago with which the artist can identify "omnipotently", he can project the bad introjected experience of "hate and fear" onto his artwork, and give form to it. Art represents a "triumph over aggression" achieved not though repression or reaction-formation but through sublimated energy and the experience of rhythm acting as forms of Eros that bind hostility from within, so that the artist finds a way of "saving, preserving, restoring" threatened loved objects (p. 193), harnessing the omnipotence of the infant's earliest experience and "libidinal and self-preservative impulses" in such a way that "a delusion of omnipotence finds a reality channel" (Sharpe, 1930, p. 15).

Sharpe proposed a dialectical relationship between loss, sublimation and art. In 'Certain Aspects of Sublimation and Delusion' (Sharpe, 1930), for example, she views art as at root self-preservative in the face of death. Drawing on G. Elliot Smith's work,[6] she argues that the ancient cave-artist draws the animals he kills in a magical attempt to ensure that there will be more to kill; and he draws himself in an animal mask as if the animal were still alive in him, in a form of mastery over death. In this way, she thought, he temporarily escapes "from a world of apprehension and anxiety, a world of temporal things, of vicissitudes and death … In those few moments of conviction, immortality is ours" (p. 14). These first art forms spring from "problems of food (life) and death" (p. 13), but later the artist confronts the same problems intrapsychically. Where that involves hostile parental introjects, the safety of the ego depends on its capacity to deal with them. Sharpe contrasts the ways that identifications are handled by the artist and the melancholic. The deadly identification at the heart of melancholia brings the threat that "super-ego sadism, reinforced by id sadism, may destroy the ego" (p. 22), even to the point of embracing a phantasy of reunion in the concrete act of suicide. The artist, on the other hand, rather than being at the prey of the introjected object, has the power to externalise the internal situation into an art form, "moulding, shaping it, ... [and] re-creating symbolically the very image that hostility has destroyed" (p. 22). The distinction is important because it is a reminder that artistic creativity is fundamentally self-preservative even if it has secondary reparative qualities. So as Sharpe saw it, Shakespeare, in *King Lear,* for example, "made articulate and explicit in terms of the old man, the massive emotions of hate and love and terror of a tiny child" (Sharpe, 1934, p. 480) which otherwise would have been overwhelming, or worse. "Instead of taking the stage for a world, [Shakespeare] might have taken the world for his stage, as Hitler did" (Sharpe, 1946, p. 30). The alternative lies behind Sharpe's ecstatic celebration of the triumph of artistic creativity: "this art form is an omnipotent life-giving, a restoration, milk, water, semen, a child" (p. 17).

It is true that, as Susan Isaacs pointed out, both Sharpe and Klein are concerned with the artist's externalisation of a hostile internal situation, (King & Steiner, 1991, p. 457), but, in the larger context of Sharpe's contributions on infancy and sublimation, it is clear from these emphases that her thinking is distinct.[7] Despite Klein's claim that they had come to the same conclusions about art and reparation, Sharpe did not see art as reparative in Klein's sense (Klein, 1933, p. 254n). She had already drawn on Sachs's idea (Sachs, 1924) that the artist escapes his "especially sensitive" severe superego through his work, but she came increasingly to think that "sin and repentance are not the dynamic powers which initiate and maintain sublimation. The dynamic power is [genital] libido" (Sharpe, 1948, p. 108). Here, she built on Freud's ideas about the vicissitudes of the infantile wishful impulses stemming from the component instincts with the inception of genital organisation. As she understood it:

> ... [T]he repression of the Oedipal drives tends to endow the component impulses of pre-genital sexuality with something of the creative purpose of genitality. Creation, in its true sense, is inseparable from genital libido ... The ego, if it adapts successfully, takes over whatever is available to carry out its thwarted purposes in some alternative way ... This is in effect what sublimation is. It is the creation of analogy.
>
> (p. 108)

Technique

Sharpe's discussions of technique, which, as I have argued, mark her out unmistakeably as Independent, are second to none. They are characterised by remarkable sensitivity to the uniqueness of each patient, and to the process and tempo appropriate to each. She was especially alive to the importance of tact (or touch), which cannot be taught, and to listening with the unconscious, with empathy, and with the analyst's own affective responses. She emphasised the analysand's developmental potential, the internal and external obstacles to realising it, and "the interaction between internal psychological conflicts and events in the external world" (Sharpe 1935a, p. 337). Her own sublimated maternal capacities are manifest in her accounts of clinical work: the rhythm of her prose speaks of a deep empathic engagement with her patient as if she were the patient. The same quality shows itself in her teaching where she is attuned to the process of learning, and down-to-earth about practical problems like fees, questions asked by patients, reassurance and so on. It is very difficult to do justice to her clinical acumen in a short space, but since the concept of sublimation is as central to her practice as it is to her aesthetics, I shall focus on her sense of its role in an analysis. "An adequate analysis," she writes, "has the following result. The indestructible infantile wishes of the unconscious are canalized in sublimations which are symbolical of those wishes" (Sharpe, 1930, p. 362). One of her major concerns clinically is how to access those wishes (and the patient's infantile experience more generally) on the way to the patient representing them through sublimation or adapting them to reality. Here her literary skills came to the fore.

Throughout her writings on technique, she emphasises the importance of being able to draw on literature, biography, history, fiction, poetry and drama, as well as on children's literature and nursery rhymes, as an aide to the essential reconstruction of childhood in the analysis of adults. Indeed, she suggests that children's literature, fairy tales, Greek myths and Shakespeare should be compulsory reading during training, with an examination in, amongst other texts, *Three Blind Mice* (pp. 12–15). In each of the three major routes to uncover infantile experience – transference, dreams, and metaphor – her own literary expertise plays its part. Transference for Freud was a playground; for Sharpe it is a theatre, its drama requiring the analyst to accept being cast in the role of significant figures from the past and to be responsive to thoughts and feelings that come with these roles. In Sharpe's terms she must work through and exhaust, via herself, the roles that she is cast in without losing the analytic attitude that allows her to be simultaneously both in and outside them (Sharpe, 1930b, p. 266). As she puts it, "we accept the rôles in order to analyse them, but we cannot analyse them if unconsciously any rôle becomes psychically our own" (p. 378). Her work is a reminder that analysts used their affective responses to understand the patient before they came to be regarded as "countertransference". She also stressed how complex transference is:

> Not only are the *actual* parental figures going to be projected on to the analyst, but the phantastic and inhuman infantile primal figures will be

imposed on the analyst. Nor is this the whole of the drama. In the patient's personality there are the conflicts of the id, ego, and super-ego, and these roles will be distributed too. The analyst will represent id as against the super-ego of the patient; at other times, super-ego against the patient's id; sometimes the analyst will figure as the patient's ego. Patient and analyst will sometimes be in alliance against parental figures, or one parent will be in opposition to another. Transference is this ever-shifting interchange of roles in the present or past life of reality or the phantasy-life of super-ego, ego, id, played out with the analyst on whom some one of these roles is constantly being thrust.

(Sharpe, 1930c, p. 377)

It is in this arena that the whole gamut of the patient's development can be traced back through the developmental stages to the earliest experiences, introjections and identifications.

In her work on dreams, she draws on literary devices, including simile, metonymy and synecdoche as "spring[ing] from the same unconscious sources" as the mechanisms that govern the formation of dreams. Both are "the product of the closest co-operation between preconscious and unconscious activity" (Sharpe, 1937a, p. 19). She shows, for example, how displacement is achieved by means of synecdoche and metonymy. (It is sometimes said that in this respect her work prefigures Lacan's.) And in her essay 'An Examination of Metaphor' (1940), she harnesses another aspect of her literary skill, what one of her analysands described as "her great sensitiveness to the nuances of verbal and nonverbal expression and particularly to the implications hidden in the use of words and phrases which characterise most clichés" (Wahl, 1966, p. 266). Metaphor served her interest in the repetition of infantile experiences in different phases of life. In her view, it "fuses sense experience and thought in language" (Sharpe, 1950, p. 155). It evolves, she argues, with sphincter control over anus and urethra, at a time when language becomes a substitute for bodily substances. Metaphor opens up "a subterranean passage between mind and body" (p. 156). When a patient says "there's no point to anything right now" he may well be speaking unknowingly of preverbal experiences laid down in memory traces in which, for whatever reason, he felt hopeless in a feeding situation where the nipple felt absent. If another says, "I keep on searching but I just can't find what I'm looking for, but I know it's there" he too is uttering (or "outering") memories of a feeding situation, this time of an experience of nuzzling and searching to no avail. In the consulting room it might be possible to understand more from these clues, for example about the availability or non-availability of the mother, or about what bit of current life had stirred this now-verbalised memory. And so on.

It is characteristic of Sharpe's work that she was alert to and curious about particular nuances of language at particular times in particular patients. Just as in Freud's work, this alertness went beyond phrases and clichés to the phonetics of words and the patient's *phonetic* associations – to ambiguity, puns, homophones and so on – which offer a road to "the unconscious storehouse of our past ... [in] the concrete significance the words possessed when we first heard them" (Sharpe, 1937a, p. 28). Let me give a brief example from my own recent practice. A patient dreamed of making a cake for her birth family, or at least of trying to make a cake because one ingredient was missing: butter. My patient grew up feeling that she had to look after her anxious mother and as a result she herself was anxious that to assert herself would be destructive. As she talked about the circumstances that led to her dream, the day's residue, I found myself alert to the affective charge of the word "butter"; I suddenly realised that my patient had been able to dream what was missing from the family recipe: a capacity to be a *butter*, to say "*but what about me*", to plosively butt up against, butt them, or at another level to let rip with her butt-sphincter instead of exercising good-girl control over explosive feelings, especially aggressive feelings. Here she was, in her dream, making a cake to please people, but unconsciously she wanted to be a *butter*. In Sharpe's terms, aliveness to the language of the dream gave the dream "a twofold value", as "the key to the understanding of unconscious phantasy and ... the key to the storehouse of memory and experience" (Sharpe, 1937a, p. 38). "*Butter*" was "a psychical discharge which in infancy and early childhood would have been accompanied by a bodily one", if that had been permitted.

I end this all too brief account of technique with a reminder. Although Sharpe writes with great clarity about many aspects of technique with a multitude of examples, nevertheless she was keen, echoing Freud, to stress that in the consulting room analysis "does not start out from a few sharply defined fundamental concepts, seeking to grasp the whole universe with the help of these ... [but] gropes its way forward by the help of experience" (King & Steiner, 1991, p. 645). She was always careful not to claim too much either for analysis or the analyst. For the patient no less than the student or child, Froebel's "vital principle" remained true for her: "all true development and consequently all true education is a self-directed process" (Froebel, 1912, p. 17).

Ella Sharpe in action

I shall finish with a very brief pen-portrait of Ella Sharpe by Sylvia Payne who describes her in full flight at the Oxford Congress of 1928, delivering 'Certain Aspects of Sublimation and Delusion':

> Ella Sharpe's appearance and personality could not be separated from the paper which she was presenting. She was capable of being a great actress if other things had not interfered. On this particular occasion she wore a soft brick-red dress; her dark hair and dark eyes, and rather dark complexion were thrown into relief by the warm colour. She was tense,

because the paper was not an intellectual communication but a living thing to which she was giving birth. Her hands which were mobile and slender at that time, were alive as if electrified. I have known members of an audience to be disturbed by Ella Sharpe's delivery of a paper because her whole personality and body were involved in the presentation. She had no self-consciousness, although a casual observer might say she was nervous. The apparent nervousness belonged to the tension aroused by the importance to her of the event which was taking place, and not to fear of criticism or lack of belief in the content of her paper.

(Payne, 1947, p. 55)

Reading Payne's description of her as it were giving birth, I am reminded of Sharpe's idea that the artist has the power to externalise the internal situation into an art form, "and this art form is an omnipotent life-giving, a restoration, milk, water, semen, a child" (Sharpe, 1930, p. 17). Sharpe was the psychoanalyst as artist. I wonder if we might take a leaf out of her book and ask, as she did for the dancer and singer, what unconscious phantasy might lie beneath the sublimation of her performance? What was it that she was giving order and shape to, not just in her paper, but more generally? Could it be that the idealisation of her father handed down by Sylvia Payne, together with the puzzling fiction of his death as she approached puberty, is itself a sublimation? Did he in some way fall badly short of her normative account of "what the father means to a child" (Sharpe, 1945)? There is some evidence that he might have been estranged from the family for at least some time when Sharpe was 15, even though ten years later he was living in the family home.[8] And just over a year before his death Daisy told Helen Keller in a letter that "home [was] beset by trouble & pain on every hand" (6 November, 1909, Helen Keller Archive). He died in a hospital for the poor, probably from alcohol-related liver disease (cirrhosis of the liver, jaundice and exhaustion are cited on the death certificate). Ella Sharpe is named as reporting his death, but perhaps he had become psychically dead to his daughter, leaving her in a destructive fury towards him (and perhaps her internal representation of her parental couple) that could only be managed through a restorative act of mythic recreation? We shall probably never know.

Notes

1 Sharpe's copy of Freud's *Interpretation of Dreams* (1916), in the Institute of Psychoanalysis is dated 'Sept. 1917. 30 Brunswick Sq. WC1'.
2 Some accounts give Jessie Murray as her therapist, but I have chosen to accept the testimony of Laura Price who was at the Clinic at the same time. (University of Pennsylvania, Kislak Center for Special Collections, Ms. Coll. 184, VII Research of Theophilus Boll.)
3 For an inside account of the Clinic see Dexter, 1918.
4 In 1941 Sharpe contributed to a series of radio broadcasts edited by Glover, *Inside the Nazi Mind* (Roazen, 2000, p. 173).

5 Stonebridge (1999) argues something similar, but there are also differences in our understanding which there is not space here to detail.
6 Sharpe possessed a copy of Elliot Smith's *The Evolution of the Dragon* which she annotated heavily. It is now in the Archives of the Institute of Psychoanalysis.
7 Isaacs suggested that Sharpe had drawn on Klein's 'Infantile Anxiety-Situations Reflected in a Work of Art and in the Creative Impulse' (1929), "illuminatingly" (King & Steiner, 1991, p. 457), in her 1930 paper, but the dates of their papers suggest that this is unlikely. Klein read her paper before the British Psycho-Analytical Society on 15 May 1929, and Sharpe gave her paper just over two months later, on 3 July, at the Eleventh International Congress of Psycho-Analysis, Oxford.
8 In the 1891 Census Frank Sharpe is listed at two addresses: the family home, and another. The sole occupants of the latter are Sharpe and a young female housekeeper. By 1901 he was listed at only his home address and that address is given on his death certificate. He died 11 January 11 1910, and Ella Sharpe's name is given as 'informant' on the certificate.

References

Bowen, H.C. (1892). *Froebel and Education by Self-Activity.* New York: Charles Scribner.

Brehony, K.J. (1988). *The Froebel Movement and State Schooling 1880–1914: A study in educational ideology.* PhD thesis, The Open University.

Dexter, M. (1918). *In the Soldier's Service: War experiences of Mary Dexter: England, Belgium, France, 1914–1918.* Boston: Houghton Mifflin Company.

Forsyth, D. (1913). 'Psychoanalysis', *British Medical Journal*, 2: 13–17.

Forsyth, D. (1922). *The Technique of Psychoanalysis.* London: Kegan Paul, Trench, Trubner & Co.

Freud, S. (1910a). 'Leonardo Da Vinci and a Memory of his Childhood'. In: *The Standard Edition of the Complete Psychological Works of Sigmund Freud*, Volume XI, London: Hogarth Press, 57–138.

Freud, S. (1910b). 'Five Lectures on Psycho-Analysis'. In: *The Standard Edition of the Complete Psychological Works of Sigmund Freud*, Volume XI, London: Hogarth Press, 1–56.

Freud, S. (1923). 'The Ego and the Id'. In: *The Standard Edition of the Complete Psychological Works of Sigmund Freud*, Volume XIX, London: Hogarth Press, 1–66.

Fotheringham, J. (1899). *Wordsworth's Prelude as a Study of Education.* London: Horace, Marshall and Son.

Friedman, S.T. (ed.) (2002). *Analyzing Freud: Letters of H.D., Bryher and Their Circle.* New York: New Directions.

Froebel, F. (1912). *Froebel's Chief Writings on Education.* Translated and edited by S. S.F. Fletcher and J. Welton. London: Edward Arnold.

Gillespie, W. (1980). 'Klein'. *International Journal of Psycho-Analysis*, 61: 85–88.

Gillespie, W. (1990). 'Reminiscences'. *International Review of Psycho-Analysis*, 17: 11–22.

Graham, P. (2008). 'Susan Isaacs and the Malting House School'. *Journal of Child Psychotherapy*, 34: 5–22.

Hayward, F.H. (1904). *The Educational Ideas of Pestalozzi and Froebel.* London: Ralph Holland and Co.

Sharpe, D., (1908). Letter from Daisy Sharpe to Helen Keller, 6 November 1908. Helen Keller Archive, American Foundation for the Blind, Louisville.

Isaacs, S. (1942). Confidential Notes and Comments on Talk with E.S., 6 July 1942, Melanie Klein Archive, the Wellcome Institute, London.

Jones, W. (1998). 'The Education of Girls and Women in Nottingham Between 1870 and 1914: With special reference to domestic ideology and middle-class influence'. https://hdl.handle.net/2134/33162.

King, P.H.M. and Steiner, R. (eds) (1991). *The Freud-Klein Controversies 1941–1945*. The New Library of Psychoanalysis. London: The Institute of Psychoanalysis and Routledge.

Klein, M. (1933). The Early Development of Conscience in the Child. In: *Love, Guilt and Reparation and Other Works 1921–1945*. London: Karnac Books and The Institute of Psychoanalysis.

Lawrence, E. (ed.) (1952). *Friedrich Froebel and English Education*. London: University of London Press.

Martindale, P. (2004). '"Against All Hushing up and Stamping Down": The Medico-Psychological Clinic of London and the Novelist May Sinclair'. *Psychoanalysis and History*, 6: 177–200.

Meisl, P. and Kendrick, W. (eds) (1986). *Bloomsbury Freud: The Letters of James and Alix Strachey 1924–1925*. London: Chatto & Windus.

Mühlleitner, E. and Reichmayr, J. (eds) (1988). *Otto Fenichel 119 Rundbriefe 1934–1945*. Frankfurt am Main: Stroemfeld Verlag.

Payne, S.M. (1947). 'Ella Freeman Sharpe—An Appreciation'. *International Journal of Psycho-Analysis*, 28: 54–56.

Payne, S. (1967). Letter to Masud Khan, 11 June 1967. Institute of Psychoanalysis Archives, London.

Raitt, S. (2004). 'Early British Psychoanalysis and the Medico-Psychological Clinic'. *History Workshop Journal*, 58: 63–85.

Roazen, P. (2000). 'The Correspondence of Edward Glover and Lawrence S. Kubie'. *Psychoanalysis and History*, 2(2): 162–188.

Robinson, K. (2008). 'Der Einfluss der Psychanalyse in Berlin während der Zwischenkriegszeit auf die Entwicklung der Theorie und klinischen Praxis in Grossbritannien'. *Jahrbuch der Psychanalyse*, 57: 41–55.

Robinson, K. (2011). 'A Brief History of the British Psychoanalytical Society'. In: *100 Years of the IPA: The Centenary History of the International Psychoanalytical Association 1910–2010, Evolution and Change*, Peter Loewenberg and Nellie Thompson (eds), London: IPA and Karnac Books, pp. 196–227.

Sachs, H. (1924). 'Gemeinsamer Tagträume'. Translated as *The Community of Daydreams*. In: *The Creative Unconscious. Studies in the Psychoanalysis of Art*. Cambridge, Mass.: Sci-Art Publishers, 1942.

Sharpe, E.F. (1924). 'Vocation'. In: *Social Aspects of Psychoanalysis*, E. Jones (ed.). London: Williams and Norgate, pp. 209–240.

Sharpe, E. (1930a). 'Certain Aspects of Sublimation and Delusion', *International Journal of Psycho-Analysis*, 11: 12–23.

Sharpe, E.F. (1930b). 'The Technique of Psycho-Analysis'. *International Journal of Psycho-Analysis*, 11: 251–277.

Sharpe, E.F. (1930c). 'The Technique of Psycho-Analysis'. *International Journal of Psycho-Analysis*, 11: 361–386.

Sharpe, E.F. (1932). 'The Defeat of Baudelaire'. *International Journal of Psycho-Analysis*, 13: 375–378.

Sharpe, E. (1934). 'The Tragedy of King Lear'. *International Journal of Psycho-Analysis*, 15: 478–480.

Sharpe, E.F. (1935a). 'Die Loslösung aus dem Familienkreis'. *Zeitschrift für psychoanalytische Pädagogik*, 9: 329–341.

Sharpe, E.F. (1935b). 'Similar and Divergent Unconscious Determinants Underlying the Sublimations of Pure Art and Pure Science'. *International Journal of Psycho-Analysis*, 16: 186–202.

Sharpe, E.F. (1936). 'Planning for Stability'. In: *On the Bringing up of Children*, J. Rickman (ed.). London: Kegan Paul, Trench, Trubner & Co.

Sharpe, E.F. (1937a). *Dream Analysis. A Practical Handbook for Psycho-Analysts*. London: Hogarth Press.

Sharpe, E.F. (1937b). 'Feminine Development: Is Co-Education a Help or a Hindrance?', *New Era*, 18: 109–111.

Sharpe, E.F. (1940). 'Psycho-Physical Problems Revealed in Language: An Examination of Metaphor'. *International Journal of Psycho-Analysis*, 21: 201–213.

Sharpe, E.F. (1945). 'What the Father means to a Child', *New Era*, 26: 149–153.

Sharpe, E.F. (1946). 'From *King Lear* to *The Tempest*', *International Journal of Psycho-Analysis*, 27: 19–30.

Sharpe, E.F. (1948). 'An Unfinished Paper on *Hamlet: Prince of Denmark*', *International Journal of Psycho-Analysis*, 29: 98–109.

Sharpe, E.F. (1950). *Collected Papers on Psycho-Analysis*. London: Hogarth Press.

Stonebridge, L. (1999). *The Destructive Element. British Psychoanalysis and Modernism*. London: Routledge.

Wahl, C.W. (1966). 'Ella Sharpe: The Search for Empathy'. In: Alexander, F., Eisenstein, S. and Grotjahn, M. (eds). *Psychoanalytic Pioneers*, New York: Basic Books, 265–271.

Whelan, M. (ed.) (2000). *Mistress of Her Own Thoughts: Ella Freeman Sharpe and the Practice of Psychoanalysis*. London: Rebus Press.

Wittenberger, G. and Tögel, C. (eds) (1999–2006). *Die Rundbriefe des "Geheimen Komitees"*, 4 vols. Tübingen: Edition Diskord.

Wordsworth, W. (1950). *The Poetical Works of Wordsworth*. de Selincourt, E. (ed.). London: Oxford University Press.

Chapter 4

The exceptional contributions of Marjorie Brierley

Affects, mediation and countertransference

Jan Abram

Marjorie Brierley is one of the original British female psychoanalysts of the British Psychoanalytical Society whose contributions to psychoanalysis are exceptional and exemplary. In this chapter the author will examine Marjorie Brierley's trajectory with special reference to her work on affects and her role during the Controversial Discussions (1942–45). Following André Green and David Rapaport, the author will argue that Brierley's seminal 1937 paper sowed the seeds for the concept of countertransference. The author concludes that Brierley's work, although mostly unknown and unrecognised, mostly uncelebrated, continues to reverberate today and makes her one of the founding leaders of what it means to be an Independent Woman of the British Psychoanalytical Society today.

Prelude

Marjorie Brierley's psychoanalytic work for the British Psychoanalytical Society spanned the period from 1929 to 1984. However, from 1945, when she retired from clinical practice, until her death, her contributions were exclusively writing reviews for the International Journal of Psychoanalysis (Thompson 2020 in Birksted-Breen 2021: 175–190).

This chapter focuses on two main areas of Marjorie Brierley's work. First Brierley's rigorous scientific approach is highlighted to illustrate how it led her to seek a scientific solution to the potential split of the British Psychoanalytical Society (BPAS) in order to calm the heated scientific exchanges between Melanie Klein and her followers and the classical Freudians during the 1930s. In 1942, Melanie Klein was almost at the point of resigning from the Society when Marjorie Brierley intervened by writing her well-known 'Armistice' letter, on 21 May 1942. In the letter Brierley proposed that the Society should pass an 'Armistice Resolution' in order to carry out the important scientific discussions (King & Steiner 1991: 164). The response to Brierley's initiative led to the setting up of what has become known as the Controversial Discussions of the British Psychoanalytical Society, which took place between 1942 and 1945 (King & Steiner 1991). In this way Brierley was

DOI: 10.4324/9781003296690-7

able to demonstrate a particular capacity to mediate on an organisational and analytic level. Without that key intervention, alongside her persistent and consistent call for open theoretical examination, it is quite possible that the history of the British Society may have been entirely different. Secondly, Brierley's scientific work, rarely referred to in the contemporary literature, is examined with a special focus on her 1937 paper, 'Affects in Theory and Practice'. This paper, presented at an International Psychoanalytic Conference in 1936, embodies a particular turning point in psychoanalytic theory in that it inaugurates the shift in ideas that lead to our contemporary concept of countertransference.

The aim of this chapter is to highlight that the work of Marjorie Brierley exemplifies both the usefulness of the notion of mediation analytically/clinically, theoretically and organisationally, and the essential affective attunement needed by analysts in their daily work. These are characteristics and qualities all psychoanalysts can aspire to, whatever theoretical orientation they are aligned to and whether they are in the consulting room or working in applied psychoanalysis.

Marjorie Brierley (1893–1984): a brief survey of her scientific trajectory

Marjorie Brierley was one of the early female psychoanalysts of the British Psychoanalytical Society who was, therefore, like all analysts of her day, pioneering the practice and theory of psychoanalysis in the UK. She started training in 1927, which was only a year after the start of the official training.[1] She had received a 1st class honours degree in psychology before training in medicine when she qualified in 1928. From 1922 to 1927, she was in analysis with J.C. Flügel for two years and for a further two years with Edward Glover.[2] Melanie Klein had just settled in London in 1926, having been invited to London by Ernest Jones. Initially, most analysts of the Society had welcomed Melanie Klein, including Edward Glover, who publicly appreciated her innovations.

In 1929 Brierley was passed for practice and so joined the House Committee of the London Clinic of Psychoanalysis while completing her training. She became a Full Member of the British Society in 1930 and by 1933, she was a Training Analyst, a Control Analyst (the term used for a Supervising Analyst), and taught clinical and theoretical seminars for candidates following the training. By this time, she was 40 years old (King & Steiner 1991: 1–6; Hayman 1986: 383–392).

Between 1932 and 1947, while she was a practising analyst, Brierley presented 13 papers to the Society, 11 of which were later published in the International Journal of Psychoanalysis (IJP). Between 1932 and 1978, she additionally wrote 57 book reviews and 24 abstracts for the IJP (Hayman 1986). Her published papers and other writings were selected and elaborated for a collection she entitled *Trends in Psychoanalysis,* published in 1951. In the introduction to that book (no. 39 of the International Psychoanalytical Library, which in 1987 became the New Library of Psychoanalysis), Brierley writes, "No science can remain alive if it ceases to grow and, if the theory of psychoanalysis does not continue to develop, pa will degenerate into a stereotyped cult" (Brierley 1951: 15). Brierley aligns herself with the basic principles as set out by Freud but emphasises that theory is: "a series of working-hypotheses, which and should be modified as knowledge advances, and not a creed to be espoused". In the spirit of this approach, she declares her aim that adheres to the aims of the BPAS, i.e. "the furtherance of the science of psychoanalysis". For Brierley, the "relativity of scientific knowledge is axiomatic" (Brierley 1951: 16).

This aim illustrates her approach to the development of psychoanalysis and at the same time suggests her concern that new theories do not become a "creed to be espoused". It seems clear from her essays during the Controversial Discussions that it was the quality of proselytising that she criticised above all concerning some of the adherents of Melanie Klein.

Thomas Kuhn's revolutionary book, *The Structure of Scientific Revolutions,* first published in 1962, pointed out that when the previous paradigm of a given scientific discipline fails to function for the practicing scientist, it will lead to a scientific crisis (Kuhn 1962). The application of Kuhn's theory offers a way of viewing the conflicts in the BPAS that led to the Controversial Discussions of 1942. This moment constituted a Kuhnian "scientific crisis" in psychoanalysis that coincided with a crisis in the organisation of psychoanalysis in London. Judith Hughes argued that Melanie Klein's innovations "reshaped the psychoanalytic domain" (Hughes 1989: 1–26). This could be seen as emanating from her Kuhnian scientific crisis when the classical Freudian model did not accord with her clinical experience. For example, Klein proposed, through her clinical findings, that the Oedipus complex started much earlier than the age of four or five (Abram 2013: 1–3). But the increasing crisis in the BPAS during the 1930s came to a head when Sigmund Freud and Anna Freud were obliged to move to London just before the outbreak of World War Two, in early 1938. The inclusion of many new analysts from Berlin and Vienna into an Institute in which Melanie Klein and her ideas had been blossoming for almost a decade, caused such major disruption in the scientific meetings there was almost a split in the Society. This painful historical moment has been very well documented (King & Steiner 1991: 1–27).[3] And, as Winnicott famously noted, the concurrent air raids over London taking place during some of the Controversial Discussions were hardly noticed.

Marjorie Brierley served on many committees, including the Board, the Council, and the Training Committee. In 1938, she resigned her position on the Training Committee so that Anna Freud could take her place when she moved to London. This respectful and generous action gives an indication of

Marjorie Brierley's character. According to John Bowlby, who was interviewed by Pearl King for the book she edited on the Controversial Discussions with Riccardo Steiner, Marjorie Brierley was "small and slight, with an
extremely lined face. She spoke in a small and hesitant voice. Her mind was
acute ... and she probably had a better grasp of scientific principles than
anyone else" (King & Steiner 1991: x). The photograph of Marjorie Brierley
in the BPAS archives illustrates her beauty and seriousness. There is also a
hint of dreaminess with a faraway expression in the photo.

It is interesting to note the friendships Marjorie Brierley forged with her
fellow pioneering female analysts so as to offer a picture of how Melanie
Klein's innovations affected relationships. For example, Marjorie was for
some time a good friend of Susan Isaacs and Ella Sharpe, both of whom were
older. Up to the beginning of the Controversial Discussions, Susan Isaacs
became increasingly aligned to Melanie Klein and was one of her strongest
supporters. Her key paper 'The Nature and Function of Phantasy' (Isaacs
1948 in King & Steiner 1991: 264–321), was the first paper of the Controversial Discussions in which she set out Klein's argument on innate phantasy. Interestingly, Isaacs had been in analysis with Flügel in the 1920s,
possibly at the same time as Marjorie Brierley. Moreover, not only were Brierley
and Isaacs analytic siblings but curiously Professor Brierley, a professor of
Botany at Reading University, was the first husband of Susan Isaacs. After their
divorce he married Marjorie in late 1922 and they moved to live in Reading. As
far as can be ascertained Marjorie Brierley had not been married before and had
no children. So not only had Susan Isaacs and Marjorie Brierley shared the same
analyst they also married the same man. It is difficult to know what effect this
had on their professional relationship up to and during the Controversial Discussions, but from a letter written to Melanie Klein from Susan Isaacs in May
1942, it would seem that Isaacs was turning against Marjorie Brierley's position
and, by the tone of the letter, seems to be increasingly aligned with Melanie
Klein. Nevertheless, in that same letter to Klein, Isaacs concedes that in Scientific Meetings of the previous years she (Isaacs) may have had too much "pride
of possession" regarding new Kleinian theory, and had showed "too much dis-
play, without appreciating what rivalry and antagonism this would inevitably
arise" (New York Archives, 28 May 1942).[4]

My impression is that this is precisely what Brierley had described as a
particular attitude amongst the followers of Melanie Klein in her Armistice
letter when she writes "your own attitude and that of your friends, towards
your work, has been felt by many members to be a difficulty in the way of
getting to grips with the work itself" (King & Steiner 1991: 164–165).[5] This is
reinforced by Brierley's statement on technique when she writes under section
'8. Misgivings' (Ibid.: 624–628). After declaring that she has always been
"greatly interested" in Mrs Klein's work, finding it both illuminating and
useful, she adds that she also found that it "lacked perspective" was too
"prone to over-simplification and to over-emphasis". She continues: "The

main root of my own misgivings has always been the direct first-hand impression that neither Mrs Klein nor her closest adherents are sufficiently realistic about her work" (King & Steiner 1991: 625). In that statement on technique Brierley moves on to say how in 1939 she had proposed a series of symposia as a way of addressing differences in a scientific way and that the present enquiries, while constituting an exercise to address differences, also "represents an attempt to deal with our crises in a democratic way."[6]

Her friendship with Ella Sharpe, distinct from her friendship with Susan Isaacs, seems to have strengthened during the Controversial Discussions. Sharpe was more aligned with Anna Freud and was also regarded as an English Freudian. She had been analysed by Hanns Sachs in Berlin in 1920, and was elected a Member of the British Society in 1923. She is well-known for her lectures on technique and, according to Bowlby, her clinical seminars were "excellent", as we can read about in Chapter 3 of this book. Thus, at the start of the Controversial Discussions, Marjorie Brierley's effort to take a position of scientific neutrality presumably had an effect on her friendships. While it is likely the friendship with Ella Sharpe was strengthened, it is also very likely Brierley would have been seen by the followers of Melanie Klein to be aligned with Edward Glover; not just because he had been her Training Analyst, but also because she refers to his work in her own papers, as she acknowledges in her book (Brierley 1951).

However, the fact that Glover had become quite antagonistic towards Melanie Klein while he was simultaneously analysing her daughter, Melitta Schmideberg, must have disconcerted Brierley, to say the least. Perhaps this was why she found herself very much *in between* the warring factions. She emphasised a scientific (i.e. neutral) approach, and her appreciation of both Kleinian developments and Freudian principles meant that she also represented those original psychoanalysts who were in the majority at that time, all of whom were trying hard to avoid siding with either the Klein Group or the classical Freud Group. During the Controversial Discussions, Edward Glover had rather disparagingly called those members (who in fact were not an organised group) the 'Middle Group'. It was not until many years later in 1968 that many of these analysts (but not all) came together under the leadership of William Gillespie and called themselves The Group of Independent Analysts. This designated them as a group of analysts who, while recognising common ground, actively wished to separate themselves from what was increasingly becoming two groups – either the Klein or the Freud group. Winnicott, widely seen as the leader of the so-called 'Independent Group', in fact declined to join any group, even the Group of Independent Psychoanalysts led by his friend and colleague William Gillespie. He wished to maintain his identity as a psychoanalyst i.e. non-aligned with any group![7]

It is clear that Marjorie Brierley has come to represent one of the original and truly non-aligned analysts. I have not come across any documentation about what she thought about William Gillespie's initiative in 1968 and whether, had she been living and working in London, she would have joined. Nevertheless, recently, along with Ella Sharpe and Sylvia Payne, Brierley has been described as one of the architects of the Independent Tradition and it is her 'Memorandum on Technique' that particularly defines her as an Independent analyst (Antonis 2014). At that point in history, there was no such thing as an 'Independent' analyst with a capital 'I', but several contemporary analysts might concur with this view (cf. Kohon 1986; Parsons 2014). This chapter is included in this book because Marjorie Brierley's approach exemplifies the tenets of Independent psychoanalysis as set out by the editors, Elizabeth Wolf and Barbie Antonis (see Introduction).

Riccardo Steiner has recently praised Brierley's 1943 'Memorandum on Technique' as one of the "hidden gems of the Controversies" (Steiner 2014: 15). This memorandum illustrates Marjorie Brierley's capacity to incorporate all perspectives while at the same time focusing on the patient's unconscious transmission of their affects. As Steiner highlights, Brierley had "an extremely flexible approach" to the clinical situation by declaring how she made use of different techniques and theories for each patient related to the patient's particular pathology. But, while she agreed with some of the Kleinian developments based on clinical facts, as we have seen, she was not afraid of also criticising Klein for a lack of theoretical rigour (King & Steiner 1991: 617). In addition, she commented on what she perceived as an "idealisation" of Melanie Klein by her adherents, as mentioned above.

While Marjorie Brierley's scientific trajectory from the 1920s was rigorous and blossoming with an obvious commitment to psychoanalysis and its development, scientifically and organisationally, it is sad to note that once the Controversial Discussions had concluded she retreated from being an active member of the Society. This happened shortly after the resignation of Edward Glover in 1944, when Marjorie Brierley retired with her husband, Professor Brierley, to the Lake District in England. As far as can be ascertained, she did not practice as a psychoanalyst again.

Anne Hayman, a well-known Independent psychoanalyst of the British Psychoanalytical Society, wrote a Memorial Lecture on Marjorie Brierley that she presented to the Society in 1986. Brierley had died in 1984, and hardly anybody had noticed in the Society. The lecture was subsequently published in the International Review of Psychoanalysis in 1986. There are several contemporary British analytic authors who cite Brierley's work (see Raphael-Leff & Perelberg 1997; 2008). More recently, Barbie Antonis and Elizabeth Wolf, the editors of this book and members of the Association of Independent Psychoanalysts[8] of the British Psychoanalytical Society, have written on her work amongst other early female analysts. In 2014, Andrea Huppke, a German psychotherapist, gave a paper on Marjorie Brierley's work in celebration of Ulrike May's birthday. It is informative and stimulating but has only been published in German to date (Huppke 2014). Through these publications and the teaching of her work, Brierley's contributions will not be entirely forgotten; indeed it is hoped they will be studied and developed.

Before turning to the concept of affect, let me briefly refer to some of the themes Brierley had been writing about up until the beginning of the Controversial Discussions. The first one, in 1932, was on 'Some Problems of Integration in Women', followed by 'Specific Determinants in Feminine Development' (1936). For these papers, Brierley cites several papers of Melanie Klein's and it is clear that she found Klein's work especially helpful in relation to clinical work. Brierley's most celebrated paper, 'Affects in Theory and Practice' was published in 1937, a year after she presented it at the International Psychoanalytic Congress.

In 1939, the year she suggests a series of scientific discussions to address the developing scientific differences (mostly between Vienna and London), she published 'On Internalized Objects and Depression', followed by 'Internal Objects and Theory' (1942), 'Theory, Practice and Public Relations' (1943), 'Notes on Metapsychology as Process Theory' (1944) and 'Further Notes on the Implications of Psychoanalysis: Metapsychology and Personology' (1945). These papers, all written during the course of the Controversial Discussions, clearly show how Brierley was tackling Klein's conceptual developments that for the classical Freudians were increasingly seen as controversial.

In 1947, two years after she had stopped practising as a psychoanalyst, she wrote 'Notes on Psychoanalysis and Integrative Living'. Her final paper was published 22 years later in 1969 when Joseph Sandler, who had recently been appointed Editor of the International Journal of Psychoanalysis, invited her to write a paper for its 50th Anniversary Edition. Her title was 'Hardy Perennials and Psychoanalysis'. She writes about feeling privileged to be invited to offer a contribution:

> I have read manuscripts for later Editors for quite a number of years and have watched the Journal grow from strength to strength. I trust it will not be out of place for an old, if minor, hand to express her sincerest appreciation of the work of all those, past and present, who have borne the major burden and to wish today's Editor continuing success.
>
> (Brierley 1969: 447)

This paper is really her last word on psychoanalysis. While it is beyond the scope of this chapter to develop an in-depth appraisal of all of Brierley's scientific contributions, as can be seen from the titles of her papers, she was very interested in new developments in psychoanalysis and much influenced by Klein along with Glover and Jones. From the Lake District she continued to be engaged with the literature and made important contributions for the International Journal of Psychoanalysis through her perceptive reviews of important books – not least Strachey's *Standard Edition* of Freud's work. Nellie Thompson has recently published her appraisal of Marjorie Brierley's many reviews for the International Journal of Psychoanalysis (Thompson 2020 in Birksted-Breen 2021).

For this chapter, let us turn to her most cited paper on affects, remembering that both David Rapaport and André Green paid tribute to the "revolutionary nature" of Brierley's conceptualisations in this paper.

'Affects in Theory and Practice', 1936

This paper was read at the 14th International Psychoanalytic Congress held in 1936 at Marienbad, Austria, and published in the International Journal of Psychoanalysis the following year (Brierley 1937: 256–268). It was re-published as Chapter 2 of her book in 1951 where she creates four main sections: 1. The relative neglect of affect in theory, 2. Affect and instinct; problems of definition and classification, 3. Affect and ego development, 4. Significance of affects for psychoanalytic technique and therapy.

In 1953 David Rapaport traces the evolutionary phases of affect as a concept in psychoanalysis and notes that "Brierley's was the first attempt to state the ego-theory of affects … partly by stressing the role of affects in the interplay between internal and external reality, and partly by insisting that affects are tension, rather than discharge, phenomena" (Rapaport 1953: 177–198). To clarify this point he cites Brierley: "The conception of affects as tension-phenomena is, of course, in line with Freud's earliest formulations of the working of the psychic apparatus and the pleasure-pain principle (The Interpretation of Dreams)" (Brierley 1937: 259). Rapaport states that Brierley's emphasis on affects as tension-phenomena, "*is certainly in keeping with the general conception of ego-psychology: the ego, the secondary process, strives on the one hand to bind mobile cathexes, and on the other to control and delay their discharge*" (Rapaport 1953: 188, my emphasis). Pointing out that the concept of affect "played a leading role" in the development of psychoanalysis, Brierley states that the "modern concept" of the threefold structure, Freud's 1923 structural model, demonstrates that the "*development of mind is a progressive organisation, adaptation, and modification of instinct*" (Brierley 1937: 256, my emphasis). All patients in clinical practice, she emphasises, are concerned about their feelings and how analysis can help them control their emotions. She then starts to develop what will be radical for that era:

> In practice we find our way only by following the Ariadne thread of transference affect, and go astray if we lose contact with this. It is time that we restore affects to a place in theory more consonant with their importance in practice. This paper is an attempt to clear the ground by reviewing briefly some of the cardinal problems of affect.
>
> (Brierley 1937: 257)

Let me emphasise this elegant phrase, "Ariadne thread of transference affect", which for contemporary analysts seems familiar as a description of the analyst's finely tuned capacity to receive the transference affects that amount to feeling the patient's affects at the interpsychic-intrapsychic layers of experience within the transference-countertransference matrix of the analytic relationship.

While Brierley shows her allegiance to Freud's earliest formulations and her careful following of Glover's thinking on differentiating between tension-phenomena and discharge-phenomena, the whole thrust of her argument is radical in that it brings into play the crucial importance of object relationships concerning the analyst's emotional responses to the patient and how that impacts on technique by following the Ariadne thread of transference affect that in turn will create a "rapport" between analyst and patient. In the final parts of the paper Brierley emphasises that "Analysis cannot proceed unless there is established between analyst and patient that mysterious affective contact which we call 'rapport'" (Ibid. 1937: 266). For Brierley, rapport comes about through the analyst's capacity to empathise: "It is only by empathy that we can be certain what the patient is feeling". The task of the analyst is to "register and interpret affect in impulse-object terms" as well as analysing the affects themselves (Ibid.: 267). Through this process, she continues, the analyst will find a piece of developmental history. "We cannot only trace history; we can see history in the making. We can watch the process of affect modification going on under our eyes" (Ibid.: 267). In the final sentences of her paper, Brierley anticipates important aspects of what we would now refer to as the analyst's countertransference. She writes that while the analytic process aims to modify the patient's super-ego (an aim that the ego psychologists emphasise), modification in the psyche comes about by enabling the patient to "re-feel the feelings he originally entertained about the objects he has introjected". The story of super-ego modification, Brierley asserts, is the "libidinization of transference hate" (Ibid.: 267). The analyst who cannot tolerate her patients' overwhelming feelings will not be able to facilitate the process of super-ego modification. Following the Ariadne thread of transference affects anticipates the notion of countertransference and, in Brierley's words, "we do not work with theory, we work with living impulses and feelings" (Ibid.: 267). The living impulses and feelings emanating from the patient that impacts on our affects in the course of each session, and our understanding of this process, is now central to any analysis.

In 1970, André Green presented his report to the Congrès des Psychanalystes de Langue Française (CPLF) on the topic of affects, which later became a book in 1973 and was subsequently translated into English in 1999 for the New Library of Psychoanalysis (Green 1999). For the 1977 IPA Congress held in Jerusalem, André Green again presented on the theme of affect in his paper 'Conceptions of Affect'. In that paper he affirms that "with Brierley affect found its best advocate" based on the fact that she underlines the inadequacy of the quantitative standpoint and that "cathexis precedes differentiation and cognitive discrimination" (Green 1977: 144). 12 years after Brierley's paper on affects, Paula Heimann will emphasise the notion of affect as an instrument of the analyst in her 1949 paper 'On Countertransference', as seen in Chapter 5 (cf. Holmes 2014).[9] Green applauds Brierley's formula for the psychoanalyst when she says that the necessary qualities for analytic practice are a "combination of intelligent insight and affective comprehension" (Brierley 1937; Green 1977: 144).

While Brierley, to some extent can be seen to clear the way for others to follow, as she had intended in her paper, Green shows how Melanie Klein's work also played a part in the validation of early psychic development related to affects and technique. Green follows this acknowledgement by asserting that it was really Winnicott who brought the concept of affect into the arena of object relations through his 1947 paper, 'Hate in the Countertransference', two years before Paula Heimann's paper, (cf. Holmes 2014). From Winnicott's paper onwards, Green suggests, affect cannot "exclude the mother's affects and her capacity to tolerate, sustain and relay the affective messages to the baby, in a form which can be integrated by his self" (Ibid.: 145). Thus, the concept of affect is completely changed with Winnicott, due to the emphasis on the early psychic relationship. Green concludes affect can no longer be seen as an isolated phenomenon.

Now we can see how affect, and therefore Freud's economic theory, is essentially about communication between subject and object. In fact, affect is the *only way* in which the subject communicates to begin with. The object, or better to say the living and feeling mother/analyst, must therefore, be able to receive the communications. Winnicott's concept of holding and Bion's concept of container-contained, must have their roots in the concept of affect as relational (Bion 1962; Winnicott 1960).

Marjorie Brierley's last word on affects

In her paper, 'Hardy Perennials and Psychoanalysis', Brierley affirms much of her previously published work and, indeed, starts the paper by saying that she does not have much new to say. She offers her general impressions of how psychoanalysis has been developing and once more emphasises the role of relationship and the analyst's need for empathy:

> The analytic situation is one of mutual relationship between the two partners. To my mind the basic condition for progress in this relationship, through all the varying phases of transference, is sound empathy in the analyst. It is only attunement to his patient that will give him the sympathetic understanding of when and how to interpret. Perfect attunement is an ideal.
>
> (Brierley 1969: 448)

Interestingly, she notes how psychoanalysis is moving towards an emphasis on the person – the 'I' – and refers to her early idea of calling this kind of psychoanalysis 'personology'.[10] For Brierley, personology was distinct from metapsychology, and analysts should recognise the difference. Subjective language is the language of the consulting room and belongs to technique. Metapsychology is the language of theory and the language of clinical seminars and discussions between colleagues about the patient. This seems to hint at her approval of some of the new developments emerging from, especially, Winnicott (about whose work she has little to say), Fairbairn and Guntrip. In her final paper, Brierley focuses more on Guntrip's work than that of Winnicott or Fairbairn. She goes on to note that many authors (presumably those three), were negating instinct theory from their developments. While she seems to acknowledge the importance of stressing individual experience, she says she cannot see how instincts are not relevant to experience. However, without arguing on the side of instinct theory, and especially steering clear of her view on the notion of the death instinct, she finishes her final paper by commenting on the subject of aggression. She recognises that every human being has a problem with aggression to a more or less extent and concludes by turning to Hinduism.

> Speakers and writers today often insist publicly that real civilization must provide adequate constructive outlets for aggression. The Hindu trinity of Creator, Preserver and Destroyer is an apt description of the forces at work in human beings. Control of aggression by finding uses for it is more rewarding than panic suppression.
>
> (Brierley 1969: 452)

Summary and conclusions

As I hope to have made clear, my reasons for wishing to celebrate the work of one of the early female pioneers of British psychoanalysis are that Marjorie Brierley stands out as exemplary. She aimed at fostering scientific discussion in an atmosphere of openness, always asserting that psychoanalysis should be a living and evolving discipline. The need to address different interpretations of psychoanalytic theory that emerge from the clinical encounter contributes to such an evolution. This is an approach to be espoused for all psychoanalysts. Moreover, because of her previous attempts to create a structure for open dialogue, followed by her timely intervention when she wrote the Armistice letter to Melanie Klein, she demonstrated her special capacity to mediate on an interpersonal and organisational level. This is a quality also to be espoused in our Societies and international conferences.

Let us remember that psychoanalysis emerged as a therapeutic method for the hysteric who suffered from too much affect caused by trauma. Contemporary psychoanalysis attests to the view that the hysteric's symptoms arose, not because of a mental deficiency to mediate affects, but rather, because of not enough empathic and good enough holding by the mother at the earliest stages of development. In our practices today, we witness that a sense of being over-whelmed with emotion is one of the most common symptoms that bring people to seek analysis, as Marjorie Brierley asserted. And although each patient's nar-rative is unique, contemporary analysts expect to hear about an early psychic environment that was deficient in offering a consistent psychic reception of the infant's raw emotions. Deficiency at the earliest stages of psychic development causes traumata, and this will be re-vivified in the analysing situation; the ana-lytic process mobilises the re-vivification. But the patient will have to take responsibility for their intrapsychic attack on the self and that phenomenon is, perhaps, the most difficult of all analytic tasks for both analyst and analysand.

Post-1945, the evolution of psychoanalysis in the British Society across the different orientations tends, in general, to be seen as British Object Relations. But it is true to say that a Kleinian Object Relations is different from an Inde-pendent Object Relations because each is based on different clinical paradigms (see Abram & Hinshelwood 2018). Today, the majority of British analysts, regardless of which school they identify with, would concur that it is impossible to conceptualise the infant without a mother and therefore a modern concept of affect will always include the primary relationship. This is our common ground. Therefore, the patient's emotional suffering, due to *too much* unmediated affect and *not enough* holding and containing through good enough maternal and paternal functioning, is rooted in early infancy. It would be a great error to conclude that therefore all British trained analysts have the same theoretical base. Indeed, it is essential to recognise that despite the common ground and many shared concepts there are crucial distinctions to be made concerning the basic principles of each theoretical orientation that include interpretations of practice. Moreover, many questions remain concerning the compatibility of the distinct evolutions of theory since 1945. This is why there is an on-going need for a dialogue on different approaches in our scientific meetings. This plea has been recently discussed by Riccardo Steiner, following Strachey's idea for an Open Forum, who states: "I am convinced that today … psychoanalysis is strong enough … for this constant comparison and deeper understanding of all – I repeat – of all – our past" (Steiner 2014: 3–21).

Following Riccardo Steiner and Pearl King, and especially the approach of Marjorie Brierley, it is crucial to study the work of our analytic ancestors in order to continually "re-examine what we do", (Winnicott in Abram 2013: 312). An authentic appreciation of how our concepts have evolved and con-tinue to evolve needs to be founded on the analysing situation, that is, the Freudian single case study research (Abram 2022a & b).

Notes

1 This was only nine years after an Act of Parliament allowed women to vote on condition they were house owners and over 30 years old! In 1928 all women over 21 were allowed to vote.

2 As we know from Riccardo Steiner, it was Edward Glover who, along with Ernest
   Jones, held a position of considerable power in the training and organisation of the
   BPAS for almost 30 years. Glover was also the analyst of Melitta Schmideberg
   (Melanie Klein's daughter), and although welcoming Melanie Klein in 1926,
   joined with her daughter in attacking the Kleinian developments during the Controversial Discussions.
3 Cf. Leopoldo Bleger's review of the book, *Une Guerre Pendant La Guerre* (Bleger
   1994).
4 I am grateful to Nellie Thompson who sent me a copy of this letter that is held in
   the New York archives.
5 From Brierley's 'Armistice' letter to Mrs Klein, 21 May 1942: "... It seems to me
   imperative for the Society to secure a temporary armistice in which scientific
   inquiry can proceed ... If the Society splits now, it will fragment from emotional
   tension. If it splits after investigation (and, as you know, I do not regard this as
   inevitable) it would then divide on honest grounds of proved incompatibility ... I
   should like to suggest that the Society pass a self-denying ordinance in respect of
   all current charges and counter-charges, personal attacks, vendettas, party politics
   and so forth. It should require ALL members to refrain from over-stepping the
   bounds of legitimate criticism in discussion ... It does seem to me a simple fact
   that, up to now, your own attitude and that of your friends, towards your work,
   has been felt by many members to be a difficulty in the way of getting to grips with
   the work itself ... Various labels have been attached to this subtle something in
   attitude from time to time. They might be summed up in the phrase 'inadequately
   scientific'... conditions seem to have made her [Susan Issacs] rather too anxious to
   support your work, rather than to explain it ..." King & Steiner (1991): 164–165.
6 From Brierley's 'Memorandum on Technique', 25 October 1943: "... I was alarmed by
   the wave of enthusiasm which swept the Society some years ago, a wave which sent
   Members rushing to Mrs Klein to consult her about their cases. I felt it to be so far
   from healthy that I remain one of the few Members who never has consulted Mrs
   Klein in this way ... Science, like anything else, can be idealized but science in itself is
   only systematized knowledge ... The papers we have heard so far ... have done nothing
   to reassure me that her [Mrs Klein] colleagues' estimate and exposition of her work is
   sound ... They tend to treat Mrs Klein's work as an idealized object ... The essential
   doubt is, do they or do they not promote a realistic solution of infantile problems of
   ambivalence, especially ambivalence regarding the mother? ... The relevance to training is twofold ... we cannot afford to train Candidates to promote unrealistic solutions
   of their own or their patient's ambivalent conflicts ... If Klein trainees did finish
   training identifying their analysts as 'idealized objects', they would inevitably tend to
   identify themselves totally with their trainers and would have to become follow-my-
   leader copyists. They would remain under the psychic necessity of swallowing their
   training whole and never using their teeth upon what they are taught. In such circumstances there could be no hope of steady progress ... But while the trainee
   remained the echo of the trainer the result in both theory and practice could only be
   sterile repetition ... I am grimly determined not to pre-judge this issue ... I propose to
   insist upon my right to make up my mind on the evidence that I hope Mrs Klein will
   be good enough to provide, both in this enquiry and in her forthcoming papers. I
   should also like to emphasize that we cannot crystallize psychoanalysis; we cannot
   keep it fixed in any shape or form, however desirable these may appear at any given
   time. Analysis cannot live unless it grows, and it cannot grow without undergoing
   modification. The essence of analysis, as of any science, is realism. We can safely
   release analysis to the care of oncoming generations if we train them as realists, but
   only if we train them as realists" King & Steiner (1991): 624–628.

7 Writing in 2022 it is difficult for any analyst trained at the BPAS to be truly independent from any grouping. Lineage is as important now as it always was and, for
example, a newly qualified analyst is regarded to be in the same group as their
analyst. The majority of analysts recognise that there are clear convergences and
divergences of theoretical orientation between Kleinians, Freudians and Independents, and this is how one is usually identified. There are analysts who are not
members of any group and may describe themselves as 'non-aligned' i.e. non-
aligned with the main three groupings. There are very few analysts who are truly
independent – nevertheless, if they write or speak it is clear what basic analytical
theoretical assumptions underlie their approach.
8 The original Group of Independent Psychoanalysts changed its name in 2007 to
the Association of Independent Psychoanalysts.
9 This original review on the evolution of the concept of countertransference fails to
include Brierley's work.
10 'Personology' was a term she borrowed from J.C. Smuts who published his book
Holism and Evolution in 1926.

References

Abram, J. (2022a). *The Surviving Object: Psychoanalytic Essays on Psychic Survival-
of-the-Object*, London & New York: New Library of Psychoanalysis, Routledge.
Abram, J. (2022b). Response to Letter to the Editor IJP. April 2022.
Abram, J. & Hinshelwood, R. D. (2018). *The Clinical Paradigms of Melanie Klein and
Donald Winnicott: Comparisons and Dialogues*, London & New York: Routledge.
Abram, J. (2012). 'D.W.W.'s Notes for the Vienna Congress 1971: A Consideration of
Winnicott's Theory of Aggression and an Interpretation of the Clinical Implica-
tions'. In: *Donald Winnicott Today, Chapter 14*, London & New York: New Library
of Psychoanalysis, Routledge, 2013.
Abram, J. (ed.) (2013). *Donald Winnicott Today*, London & New York: New Library
of Psychoanalysis, Routledge.
Abram, J. (2013a). 'On Winnicott's Area of Formlessness', *EPF Bulletin*, 67.
Antonis, B. (2014). 'Controversial Discussions: Independent Women Analysts and
thoughts About Listening to Experience', *British Journal of Psychotherapy*, 2015.
Antonis, B. & Wolf, E. (2008). 'Affect and Body. The Contributions of Independent
Women Psychoanalysts'. In: J. Raphael-Leff & R. Jozef Perelberg (eds), *Female
Experience: Four Generations of British Women Psychoanalysts on Work with
Women*, London: The Anna Freud Centre, 316–329
Bion, W. (1962). 'A Theory of Thinking', *International Journal of Psychoanalysis*, 43: 4–5.
Birksted-Breen, D. (2021). *Translation/Transformation: 100 years of the International
Journal of Psychoanalysis*, London & New York: New Library of Psychoanalysis,
Routledge.
Bleger, L. (1994). 'Une Guerre Pendant La Guerre', *L'Inactuel*, No. 1, Printemps,
1994.
Brierley, M. (1932). 'Some Problems of Integration in Women', *International Journal
of Psychoanalysis*, 13: 433–448.
Brierley, M. (1936). 'Specific Determinants in Feminine Development', *International
Journal of Psychoanalysis*, 17: 163–180.
Brierley, M. (1937). 'Affects in Theory and Practice'. *International Journal of Psycho-
analysis*, 18: 256–268.

Brierley, M. (1939). 'A Prefatory Note on "Internalized Objects" and Depression', *International Journal of Psychoanalysis*, 20: 241–245.

Brierley, M. (1942). '"Internal Objects" and Theory', *International Journal of Psychoanalysis*, 23: 107–112.

Brierley, M. (1943). 'Theory, Practice and Public Relations', *International Journal of Psychoanalysis*, 24: 119–125.

Brierley, M. (1944). 'Notes on Metapsychology as Process Theory', *International Journal of Psychoanalysis*, 25: 97–106.

Brierley, M. (1945). 'Further Notes on the Implications of Psychoanalysis: Metapsychology and Personology', *International Journal of Psychoanalysis*, 26: 89–114.

Brierley, M. (1947). 'Notes on Psychoanalysis and Integrative Living'. *International Journal of Psychoanalysis*, 28: 57–105.

Brierley, M. (1951). *Trends in Psychoanalysis*. London: International Library of Psychoanalysis, Hogarth Press.

Brierley, M. (1969). '"Hardy Perennials" and Psychoanalysis', *International Journal of Psychoanalysis*, 50: 447–452.

Faimberg, H. (2005). *The Telescoping of Generations: Listening to the Narcissistic Links Between Generations*, London & New York: New Library of Psychoanalysis, Routledge.

Green, A. (1977). 'Conceptions of Affect', *International Journal of Psychoanalysis*, 58: 129–156.

Green, A. (1991). 'On Thirdness'. In: *André Green at the Squiggle Foundation*, Abram, J. (ed.) (2000), London: Routledge.

Green, A. ([1973] 1999). *The Fabric of Affect in Psychoanalytic Discourse*. London: The New Library of Psychoanalysis, Routledge.

Hayman, A. (1986). 'On Marjorie Brierley ', *International Review of Psychoanalysis*, 13: 383–392.

Heimann, P. (1950). 'On Countertransference', *International Journal of Psychoanalysis*, 31: 81–84.

Holmes, J. (2014). 'Countertransference Before Heimann: An Historical Exploration', *Journal for American Psychoanalytic Association*, 62(4): 603–629.

Hughes, J.M. (1989). *Reshaping the Psychoanalytic Domain: The Work of Melanie Klein, W. R. D. Fairbairn, and D. W. Winnicott*, Berkeley, Los Angeles & London: University of California Press.

Huppke, A. (2014). 'Ein Blick in die Frühzeit der Londoner Middle Group (A look into the early days of the London Middle Group)', *Luzifer-Amor*, 53, 2014: 52–70.

Isaacs, S. (1948). 'The Nature and Function of Phantasy', *International Journal of Psychoanalysis*, 29: 73–97.

King, P. & Steiner, R. (1991). *The Freud-Klein Controversies 1942–1945*, London & New York: New Library of Psychoanalysis, Routledge.

Kohon, G. (ed.) (1986). *The British School of Psychoanalysis: The Independent Tradition*, London: Free Association Books.

Kuhn, T. (1962) (1970 2nd edition). *The Structure of Scientific Revolutions*, Chicago: University of Chicago Press.

Parsons, M. (2014). 'An Independent theory of Clinical Technique'. In: *Living Psychoanalysis*, London and New York: New Library of Psychoanalysis, Routledge.

Rapaport, D. (1953). 'On the Psychoanalytic Theory of Affects', *International Journal of Psychoanalysis*, 34: 177–198.

Raphael Leff, J. & Jozef Perelberg, R. (eds) (1997). *Female Experience: Three Generations of British Women Psychoanalysts on Work with Women*, London: Routledge.

Steiner, R. (2014). 'Controversies Terminable or Interminable?', *British Psychoanalytical Society Bulletin*.

Thompson, N. (2021). 'Marjorie Brierley's Contribution to the International Journal of Psychoanalysis'. In: Birksted-Breen, D. (ed.) (2021). *Translation/Transformation: 100 Years of the International Journal of Psychoanalysis*, London: Routledge.

Winnicott, D.W. (1949). 'Hate in the Countertransference', *International Journal of Psychoanalysis*, 30: 69–74.

Winnicott, D.W. (1960). 'A Theory of the Parent-Infant Relationship', *International Journal of Psychoanalysis*, 41: 585–595.

Chapter 5

Paula Heimann

Becoming Independent

Emily Alster

Shortly before she died, Paula Heimann was preparing the introduction to a book of her collected papers; she was 83 and had been working as an analyst for over 50 years. Her introduction was never finished but in the notes she left behind, made as she looked back at over 30 publications, she wrote of her 'changed philosophy' (Tonnesmann 1989, 14). It was a restrained choice of words to describe a career spent profoundly rethinking her understanding of the origins of mental illness and the work of psychoanalysis.[1]

Her papers show that she constantly re-examined her ideas. Frequent references to 'alterations', 'revisions' and 'postscripts' to her earlier work speak of her ability to change her mind and integrate new ideas from others – a capacity that was possibly made easier by her growing belief that psychoanalytic work does not rest on the theories, and particularly not on the theoretical certainties, of the analyst.

The paper that made her name, 'On Countertransference' published in 1950, was the first of her publications that she was to describe as truly her own writing. And it is here that for the first time she points to where she believes the work of psychoanalysis rests, 'my impression is that it has not been sufficiently stressed that it is a relationship between two persons' (Heimann 1950). It was a simple description that was to transform what was required of the analyst. In this 'relationship', any claims to certainty or to a neutrality that attempted to hide the analyst's naturalness and humanity would bring the work to a halt. Instead, the analyst's most important tool was her freely roused emotional sensitivity, that was 'extensive rather than intensive, differentiating and mobile' (1950). Paula Heimann was not going soft or getting in a muddle; she was demanding constant self-examination. It was an analytic attitude that required more rigour not less.

'Crown Princess'

As Heimann selected the papers for her book, she also wrote to her editor apologising that her writing was 'unconventional' and 'not welcomed in all quarters' (Tonnesmann 1989, 14). This was also a restrained choice of words.

DOI: 10.4324/9781003296690-8

The publication of her famous paper 'On Countertransference' was just the beginning of growing theoretical differences with her analyst and mentor Melanie Klein, differences that eventually led to an open split between them that sent a jolt through the British Society.

Paula Heimann was not the only analyst to leave Klein's group but she was the most significant (Keene 2012, 6). She had been a principal figure there since 1943 when she was one of only two analysts chosen by Klein to help defend her theories at the Controversial Discussions of 1941–1945. In two highly regarded papers, one presented individually and one with Susan Isaacs, she emphatically expounded the tenets of Kleinian thinking, including the central role of the death instinct and intrapsychic conflict from the beginning of life.

> One conceives of the human mind by its very nature compelled to manipulate constantly between two basically opposed forces, from which all emotions, sensations, desires and activities derive. It can never escape conflict and can never be static, but must always go on, one way or another, must always employ devices to mediate for an equilibrium, between its antithetical drives. And since the instincts are inborn, we have to conclude that some form of conflict exists from the beginning of life.
>
> (Heimann 1943, 501–531)

Over the following years Paula Heimann grew to become, in Pearl King's memorable phrase, Melanie Klein's 'crown princess' (King 1989, 6). She was a staunch supporter of Klein and trusted as a supervisor to many of the next generation of Kleinian analysts, including Wilfred Bion and Hanna Segal. She frequently stood in for Melanie Klein at Society meetings and it was reported that she could be relied upon to lay out the Kleinian position with, 'a blessing or a rebuke or a lecture' (Ibid.).

From around the time of the publication of 'On Countertransference', Paula Heimann's and Melanie Klein's theoretical ideas were diverging. Initially these differences were in private but in 1955 they broke out into the open when Paula Heimann said that she could not agree with Melanie Klein's description of envy as part of the death instinct. She was asked to resign from the Klein Trust and she gave a statement to a meeting of the British Society to say that she no longer wished to be considered a member of the Klein Group. Training candidates who chose to stay in analysis with her would now also be unacceptable as members and Melanie Klein requested that Paula Heimann's teaching seminars were handed over to other analysts. When Paula Heimann was asked by the analyst Sylvia Payne to write a paper summarising her theoretical differences with Klein she declined, saying later that she had felt 'too traumatised to do so' (Ibid., 8).

Sylvia Payne invited Paula Heimann to join the Middle Group, where there were already many other analysts who wanted to be free of a requirement to agree with either Melanie Klein or Anna Freud. Her arrival must have felt quite a coup. If the Middle Group already suffered from the charge that they were not 'middle' but 'muddled' (Kohon 1986), it was not a charge you could lay at Paula Heimann. She had a formidable reputation as a theoretician and as an exacting analyst, and she continued to write firmly on the dangers of everything from the analyst making seductive jokes to ever sharing their feelings with a patient: 'As the real person the analyst is as useful to the patient as any Tom, Dick or Harry' (Heimann, 1960). Her arrival coincided with the Middle Group deciding that they needed a new name, and the one they chose was suggested by Paula Heimann (King 1989, 8). It was a name that made it clear that its members were not part of a 'school'. From now on they would be known as the Group of Independent Psychoanalysts.

'Why is it that I see everything so differently?'

Very few psychoanalysts can claim to have written a paper that is acknowledged as a turning point in the history of psychoanalytic theory and technique, but Paula Heimann's 1950 paper 'On Countertransference' is acknowledged to be one of them (Rayner 1991, Kohon 1986). Her argument, that the analyst's feelings are an essential instrument of her work, toppled Freud's pressing instruction:

> I cannot advise my colleagues too urgently to model themselves during psychoanalytic treatment on the surgeon, who puts aside all his own feelings, even his human sympathy, and concentrates his mental forces on the single aim of performing the operation as skilfully as possible.
>
> (Freud 1912)

Pearl King wrote that, at first, Paula Heimann's advice was received as 'heresy' (King 1989, 6).

> My thesis is that the analyst's emotional response to his patient within the analytic situation represents one of the most important tools for his work. The analyst's counter-transference is an instrument of research into the patient's unconscious.
>
> (Heimann 1950)

Challenging Freud and earning a place in psychoanalytic history might have seemed unlikely when Paula Heimann came to England in July 1933. She was fleeing Berlin after briefly being arrested, while seeing a patient, when Hitler came to power. Her husband had already fled to Switzerland, and for a short while she had to leave behind her eight-year-old daughter, Mirza, in the care of a Catholic family. She was 34 years old, had only just qualified as an analyst and, as she later recorded, 'I arrived in England with £10' (Rayner 1991).

It was less than a year later that she heard of the death of Melanie Klein's son Hans, and she wrote to her. She was already interested in Klein's emphasis on aggression and the death instinct, something she felt had been understated by her own teachers in Berlin. In London Melanie Klein asked Paula Heimann to visit regularly, telling her how much she appreciated being able to talk about her loss in German and how she found the English 'too alien' (King 1989, 3). When Melanie Klein began work on a new paper on mourning, Paula Heimann became her secretary, 'I offered to write while she talked' (Rayner 1991). But when Melanie Klein told her that she thought she also wanted an analysis with her, offering a low fee to make it possible, she was surprised. As she was later to record, 'it would just not have been done in Berlin' (Ibid.). But Paula Heimann was lonely and worried about her future (Robinson, 2019) and, after thinking it over, she accepted.

Paula Heimann said that she was grateful for the help she received in her analysis, especially in the years before the war. However, she also thought that she had attempted to look after Melanie Klein, taking on the role of a replacement child for her after the loss of her son and estrangement from her daughter Melitta. It was an interesting repetition. Paula Heimann, born in Danzig in 1899, was the youngest of four children and the third child, a girl, had died, leaving her to feel that she had been conceived to care for and to comfort her depressed mother (King 1989, 8). Later Paula Heimann was to say, 'history repeated itself, my childhood history repeated itself which was never analysed. And then I became very attentive to this – in myself and my patients' (Rayner 1991).

According to Paula Heimann it was her paper 'On Countertransference' that was the beginning of her break with Melanie Klein. When she read her paper at the International Psychoanalytical Congress in Zurich in 1949, it was the first time she had presented a paper without showing it to Klein first. While Ernest Jones congratulated her, Paula Heimann said that Melanie Klein was angry and tried to persuade her to withdraw it (King 1989, 6). It was published in the International Journal of Psychoanalysis the following year.

Pearl King described the publication of 'On Countertransference' as Paula Heimann's 'first gesture of freedom and assertion of her own creativity' (Ibid., 8). But perhaps the roots of her interest in the analyst's emotional responses also lay in her work with her first analyst Theodor Reik in Berlin. Reik had his own differences with colleagues who he felt relied on an overly 'scientific' technique. He warned his students not to put logic before emotional experience and wanted to teach them the art of courting 'surprise' and using their intuition, ideas he later presented in his book *Listening With The Third Ear* (Reik, 1948).

We know from a warm letter that Paula Heimann wrote to Reik just after she qualified that she felt at ease with her analyst and here, at the very beginning of her career, she also seems to know of her struggles to come.

Why is it that I see everything so differently from everyone else? ... [I]t seems to me that I have to decide: shall I—as decency of character would demand—remain isolated and swim against the current? This is a very hard thing to do: it gives me no joy, and that matters a great deal. Or shall I forget about it (and you), disowning my better and different judgement, for the sake of fitting in? Am I capable of doing that?

(Rolnik 2008)

Towards the end of her career she recalled her first analyst. Writing about the analyst's need to listen to their patient on many different levels, she joked, 'Reik spoke of the analyst's third ear, I think he needs more than three' (1977).

'Lay the ghost'

Many other analysts had already been interested in the analyst's emotional responses to their patients including Ferenczi (1933), Ella Freeman Sharpe (1930) and Donald Winnicott (1949). But Paula Heimann's paper 'On Countertransference' (1950) was to become a turning point, perhaps because it was the first time that such a direct 'invitation' (Symington 1986, 276) had been issued to all analysts to make use of their feelings.

Paula Heimann said that she wrote her paper to, 'lay the ghost of the "unfeeling", inhuman, analyst' (1960, 153). Her concern was that her students were so anxious to follow Freud's injunctions to be like a 'surgeon' or a 'mirror' that they had become afraid of their feelings, and so guilty that they saw them as 'nothing but a source of trouble'. For her the implications were serious, with detached analysts making poor and 'inhuman' interpretations. In her paper she is unequivocal, the emotions aroused in the analyst 'are much nearer to the heart of the matter than his reasoning' (1950).

Although Melanie Klein was unhappy with this paper and wanted it withdrawn, it is hard to read it and not see its strong roots in Klein's thinking and in particular her concept of projective identification (Groarke 2018). Paula Heimann is clear, countertransference feelings are the patient's creation, 'The analyst's countertransference is not only part and parcel of the analytic relationship but it is the patient's creation, it is a part of the patient's personality' (Heimann 1950). Countertransference as projective identification was enthusiastically taken up by a new generation of Kleinian analysts, including her supervisee, Wilfred Bion.

But in the same paper Paula Heimann also describes analysis as a 'relationship between two persons' and this is a much more complex idea than just one person having feelings and putting them into the other. In 1960, she wrote a second paper on the subject, 'Countertransference', where she stated that she wanted to clear up a misunderstanding.

I have had occasion to see that my paper also caused some mis-understanding in that some candidates, who referring to my paper for justification, uncritically, based their interpretations on their feelings. They said in reply to any query 'my countertransference', and seemed disinclined to check their interpretations against the actual data in the analytic situation.

(1960)

Here in 1960, she regrets that her 1950 paper had contributed to a confu-sion about what belongs to the patient and what belongs to the analyst, and she reminded people of the crucial line in her 1950 paper that analysis is a relationship between two people. As she was to tell the analyst Gregorio Kohon, she always maintained that the psychoanalytic situation implied two transferences, two resistances, two unconsciouses (Kohon 1992).

According to the analyst Margret Tonnesmann, who edited the *Collected Papers* and had access to all the unpublished notes and transcripts, Paula Heimann only referred to so-called projective identification and objected strongly to interpretations which assumed the patient to have split off unwanted aspects of themselves and successfully projected them 'into' the analyst (Tonnesmann 1989, 20). In her 1960 paper on countertransference, Paula Heimann gives what she says is the correct description of what is hap-pening between analyst and patient, and it is a less mechanical picture. The analyst's emotional responses are the analyst's *own* human responses to com-plex unconscious process in the patient.

The analytic situation is a relationship between two persons. What dis-tinguishes this relationship from others is not the presence of feelings in one partner, the patient, and their absence in the other, the analyst, but the degree of feeling the analyst experiences and the use he makes of his feelings, these factors being interdependent. The aim of the analyst's own analysis is not to turn him into a mechanical brain which can produce interpretations on the basis of a purely intellectual procedure, but to enable him to sustain his feelings as opposed to discharging them like the patient.

(Heimann 1960)

She was arguing that Freud's metaphors were the problem. The analyst was not a 'mirror' or a 'surgeon' but a human being trained to listen to and sus-tain her feelings and put them to use. Paula Heimann's work on counter-transference is much closer to another metaphor used by Freud when he described how the analyst 'must turn his own unconscious like a receptive organ towards the transmitting unconscious of the patient. He must adjust himself to the patient as a telephone receiver is adjusted to the transmitting microphone' (Freud 1912).

For Paula Heimann what was essential was not so much Freud's 'evenly suspended attention' but the analyst's 'freely roused emotional sensitivity', which was 'extensive rather than intensive'. This was the tool that would allow her to explore the transference in the service of the patient, as a supplementary and supportive ego. When she heard an analyst reporting that 'the patient projected into me', she felt this was a sign that the analyst was acting as super-ego and 'blaming' her patient (Tonnesmann 1989, 21).

Her evolving description of psychoanalysis was not one of active intrusions by the patient but instead the failure by the analyst to, as yet, consciously discern the aspect of the transference object that the patient brings. The unsettling disturbance in the analyst's feelings is her unconscious picking up on the unconscious communication, and her delay in understanding is inevitable. Conscious understanding is always, in one of Paula Heimann's many memorable phrases, 'lagging behind' the unconscious.

In her writing she frequently uses the technical term 'countertransference', but she also uses her own phrase, the analyst's 'emotional response'. This gets closer to describing the unconscious communication of affects in all relationships between two people, including patient and analyst and infant and mother. This 'emotional response' is not an automatic or intellectual route to the patient's unconscious. Instead, she writes, it is a starting point for an exploration. The analyst must sit with her unsettling feelings; she must wait, explore, and only interpret when it makes sense with everything else she knows of her patient.

> As he waits – which he must do in order not to interfere with an ongoing process in his patient, and in order not to obscure the already puzzling situation still more by irrelevant and distracting interpretations – the moment comes when he understands what has been happening. The moment he understands his patient he can understand his own feelings, the emotional disturbance disappears and he can verbalise the patient's crucial process meaningfully.
>
> (Heimann 1960)

In Paula Heimann's work we see a restrained use of the analyst's 'emotional response' – a technique that was to take root in the work of many Independent analysts who followed her: Pearl King, Enid Balint, Nina Coltart, Harold Stewart, Adam Limentani, Michael Parsons, Christopher Bollas, Neville Symington, Patrick Casement and many others.

'The Origins of Cruelty'

As she listened to her patients, Paula Heimann was also revising her understanding of the origins of mental illness. And in three key papers, all written in the 1960s, she made what she describes as 'important alterations' to her previously held views. Here she reverses her view that adult pathology rests on instinctual conflict from the beginning of life and argues for the foundational role played by the infant's first real relationships. Arguing in her own language, she was becoming increasingly in-step with a growing number of colleagues including Michael Balint, John Bowlby, Ronald Fairbairn, Masud Khan, Marion Milner and Donald Winnicott, who were already arguing for the place of early trauma in adult pathology.

The title of the first of these papers makes Paula Heimann's break with Klein's concern with the death instinct clear. In 'Evolutionary Leaps and the Origins of Cruelty' (1964) she begins by gently reminding analysts of what she calls a familiar fact, that the analysis of patients with severe pathological states, whose inner worlds are dominated by cruelty and sadism, uncovers material pointing to evidence of severe disturbances in the relationship between mother and infant.

> The analysis of such patients uncovers material pointing to severe disturbances in early maternal care; that is, to a substantial psychopathology on the part of the mother and/or of the mother-father relationship, or to physical illness of the mother or child. This material points, in other words, to an early disturbance of the relationship between infant and mother that was not corrected in the further course of the patient's development.
>
> (1964)

In this paper she was joining many others in arguing that Freud's model of early life had overestimated the capacity of maternal care to fully satisfy an infant's needs (Keene 2012, 3) and that bad objects were created when the infant's ego is helpless against the intrusion of an aggressive object. She writes that while cruelty is normal in humans it is also dependent on the objective care of the infant.

> The child experiences the primary power of life or death through its mother (or her representative) depending on the care, or lack of care, attention or neglect, love or hate she shows it.
>
> (1964)

In thinking close to Winnicott's, she goes on to describe how if the child is frustrated beyond the ability of its defensive hallucinations it experiences sensations approaching those of death. For Paula Heimann this experience is left as a trace that can be activated later in life. She argues that it is the activation of this anxiety that awakens cruel impulses, with the desire for others to suffer cruelly going hand-in-hand with a magical belief that after this everything will be fine.

A few years later, in her paper 'Postscript to Dynamics of Transference Interpretations' (1969), she returned to revise her 1955 paper of the same

name to make what she describes as 'important alterations'. In an unequivocal reversal of her earlier view, she now writes that she no longer has any
clinical use for the concept of a death instinct. For her, human aggression was
in the service of life.

> Personally what I no longer find convincing is the relation between the
> hypothetical death instinct and the primary destructive drive.
>
> (1969)

She freely admits that up to now she has spent her professional life as an
enthusiastic supporter of the idea of a death instinct, but now Freud's theory,
and the 'cosmic speculation' it involves, does not fit with what she observes in
her clinical work. It was a remarkable turnaround, in a paper that is written
with new spontaneity and confidence.

> What we can observe as psychoanalysts is that our patient's want to live
> and to live well … but before deducing from this a life instinct that
> evolved at the same time as a death instinct, it is safer to assume that the
> person wishes to survive … in other words, one sees that a living person
> (and living creatures in general) want to go on living.
> What then is the death instinct? There are many situations in which
> our patients tell us they want to be dead. I believe it is more correct to
> say they want to be dead than say they want to die; indeed analysis
> reveals that the wish in question concerns a state that is painless, while the
> fact of dying is usually strongly invested with phantasies of pain. Behind the
> wish to be dead what one really finds is the wish to be free of pain, whether
> physical or psychical, such as shame, guilt, intolerable fears, anxiety,
> depression, confusion, despair, and so on or we find phantasy wishes to be
> revenged upon or to kill an object with which the patient has unconsciously
> identified.
>
> (1969)

She writes that of course patients can present with negativism, indifference,
contempt for pain, apathy, lack of reaction to stimuli and psychotic states of
melancholy depression. However, she writes that these clinical phenomena
cannot be explained away so simply by an 'instinct'. Instead they are 'problems of great complexity involving childhood experiences and imposed
identification (intrusions on the part of bad parents in early infancy) or
desired, but ill-judged identifications, cumulative trauma' (1969).

With her new understanding of the fateful role of the early environment,
she also returned to the topic of countertransference. In her paper 'Comment
on Dr Kernberg's paper on "Structural derivatives of object relationships"'
(1966), she writes that many instances of 'so-called' projective identification
'should be defined as the reactivation in the patient of his infantile

experiences with his rejecting and intruding mother'. Paula Heimann, following Ferenczi, was now linking countertransference to trauma.

> I have become attentive to the existence of 'bad internal objects' which could be traced to serious deviations from the average in maternal care, beginning in the earliest phase and extending throughout childhood.
>
> (1966)

She writes that it would be wrong to diagnose a patient as full of destructive impulses, as in many instances this is not correct.

> In the analysis at crucial points transference and countertransference revolve on this quality, rejection and intrusion, and many instances of 'so called' projective identification should be defined as the reactivation in the patient of his infantile experiences with his rejecting and intruding mother.
>
> (1966)

This was a profound development in the understanding of countertransference. As Margret Tonnesmann, who completed the task of publishing Paula Heimann's *Collected Papers*, put so clearly in her introduction.

> There is certainly a substantial difference between on the one hand an interpretation based on the assumption that there is a conflict from the beginning, the anxieties aroused by it setting into motion the defence mechanisms of splitting and projection and on the other hand an interpretation which conceives of it as a transference manifestation in a reversal of roles. In the latter the patient's identification with an aspect of a bad internal object results in the analyst being exposed to feelings similar to those which the patient had when the early mother failed him.
>
> (Tonnesmann 1989, 21)

Paula Heimann's evolving understanding of the emotional responses in the analyst was developed in the influential work of her pupil Pearl King, writing on the impact of parental pathology and the use of the analyst's affective response in the reverse transference (King, 1978).

'A Partner in the Work'

Paula Heimann's 'changing philosophy' was inevitably influencing her understanding of the working of psychoanalysis. Her emphasis always remained on the central role of work in the transference, after all she is the author of the famous line passed on to all aspiring analysts: 'why is the patient now doing what to whom?' written in 1955, the year she left Klein's group. But in the same paper she also makes a small aside to describe the realistic level of the analytic relationship, operating alongside the patient's projections.

> Although the patient re-enacts his past object relations in the transference, the analyst has to consider the reciprocal fact that his own personality, no matter how much he controls its expression, is perceived and reacted to by the patient … The analyst's personality is one part of the analytic situation and of the patient's problems on a realistic as well as on a phantasy level.
>
> (Heimann 1955)

It was a significant step towards a more Independent way of thinking and working (Groarke 2018), and one which allowed for the idea of a therapeutic alliance between patient and analyst.

Later in this paper she also goes on to describe times in an analysis when she believes patients are not engaged in transference communications but are instead recounting deeply emotional memories and painfully recovering the value of their lost objects. She says these are times when the analyst should just listen, remaining vigilant, but remaining 'a listener and bystander' who is accepted as being there and sharing the patient's experiences with him. Paula Heimann's technique was changing and was increasingly in tune with seminal papers on technique written in the 1940s by the Middle Group analysts Marjorie Brierley, Ella Freeman Sharpe and Sylvia Payne (King & Steiner 1991).

Two years later, in her paper 'Some Notes on Sublimation' (1957), she describes other clinical material that should not be interpreted in the transference. She refers to the work of Marion Milner, and discusses a patient who had momentarily withdrawn from her and who had started to recite a poem in a self-absorbed way. She stresses the importance of letting the patient withdraw into their own primary creative activity, and says it is vital that this is not interpreted in the transference as a hostile turning away from the analyst. 'Her withdrawal was not motivated by hostility or fear, but by her urge to engage in creative ego activity, she withdrew towards her own depth' (Heimann 1957).

She spelt out her evolving understanding, again in a postscript to earlier writing, in her paper 'Postscript to Dynamics of Transference Interpretations' (1969). Here she describes how beside the work of verbal interpretations there is another crucial aspect to the analytic situation – a 'milieu', operating quietly in the background. For her, analysis was now more than the work of the transference, it also rested upon the environmental facilitation provided by the analyst. The 'milieu' was the analyst's arrangements – her room and couch, the session times and the fee – but it was also her stable, uninterrupted presence and continuous attention, her symbolic unspoken care, which she said was something that belonged to the patient without having to be questioned.

The 'milieu', a word she said she chose as it represented both an environment and a centre, repeats the original undifferentiation between the infant and maternal care. It could allow the patient to relive illusions with loving parents, as well as the loss of these illusions, and could allow for the development of basic trust. She writes that this unspoken 'milieu', and the verbal 'working team', are complementary, and neither can be taken separately, but at times the 'milieu' is the focus of the work. In states of distress and regression it is the 'milieu' that allows pre-verbal states and trauma to be re-experienced.

Paula Heimann's emphasis was also now increasingly on making space for the patient's own explorations and creativity. Central to her thinking, and in agreement with Winnicott (1969) and Marion Milner (1987), was her belief in fostering what she saw as the ego's own innate creativity and its own potential to work towards growth and development.

> To work with the transference does not mean that the analyst refers to himself whenever he communicates something to his patient. Although he must be constantly alert to grasp the meaning of the transference (wish, drive, fear, and so on) he must also be attentive to the importance of events outside the psychoanalytic situation; for example, to emerging memories after a dream, and also to the need to do just what he pleases, which is sometimes inherent in the patient's behaviour. Similarly when the patient is engaged in the process of creative work, or in the work of mourning, the task of the analyst is that of a person who is simply there and remains vigilant. This is part of his role as partner in the work.
>
> (Heimann 1969)

This belief in supporting and fostering the ego's innate potential led her to give specific advice to analysts. Interpretations, she writes, can usefully be 'a mere "hm?" or a "hm!"', but they must contain a questioning, an urging on, a request to the patient's ego so he will go on searching. The analyst must keep an optimal distance between her and her patient's understanding; if she fails to see how much her patient can take in at that moment, if she tries to be too clever, or if the timing is wrong, she will fail. In this her writing again appears close to Freud:

> When you have found the right interpretation, another task lies ahead, you must wait for the right moment at which you can communicate your inter- pretation to the patient with some hope of success ... you will make a bad mistake, in an effort perhaps of shortening the analysis, if you throw your interpretations at the patient's head as soon as you have found them.
>
> (Freud 1926)

Paula Heimann writes that when the interpretation is ready, it must be vivid, warm and personal and not gloomy, didactic or schematic. She describes the analyst as following the principle embodied by the maternal function, and wrote that this was decisively important when offering the child, and the adult patient, new concepts he does not have. To prevent false or distorted development interpretations must be appropriate to the patient's development in that moment and never have the quality of an attack or of something alien. Ultimately the analyst was there to support the patient's own exploration and development and, in agreement with Winnicott, it was the patient's own discoveries, and not the analyst's need to interpret, that mattered. 'It is only through a process of work carried out by oneself, though within one's relationship with one's analyst, that one can arrive at a solution' (Heimann 1969).

'Tamed Naturalness'

Towards the end of her career Paula Heimann wrote her most liberated and personal paper, 'On the necessity for the analyst to be natural with his patient' (1978). Here her writing finds its own naturalness as she fights for the vital importance of naturalness in the analyst. And it is here that she offers her unforgettable warning to any analyst tempted to pretend that they are 'neutral' or to suppress their own feelings, 'In my opinion there is only a short distance from the neutral analyst to the neuter'.

In this enjoyable paper she takes a swipe at clinical 'taboos' and 'nonsense'. On the 'rule' that analysts should not ask the patient a question she writes, 'Why can't I simply and honestly ask my patient for the information I need to understand his associations if he can easily provide it? Of course we all have our peculiarities but dogmas are at a different order of magnitude'. And on the requirement that analysis requires five sessions a week she writes, 'another bit of nonsense … that five hours a week equals analysis and that fewer than five are sins'.

Perhaps most significant is when she describes taking herself by surprise and breaking her own rule that the analyst should never share her emotional responses with her patient. In a clinical vignette she describes how she unintentionally made a spontaneous comment to one of her patients, telling her that something she had said 'made me shiver'. Her comment shocked her, and her patient was indignant, but this natural response then led to a moving development in the work. She writes that the communication of her feelings, in violation of her own rules, had also appeared to her as something natural. Later she saw how this offering of her feelings to her patient, an unwanted child and unnoticed by her mother, was a response to a person who had needed this intuitive emotional perception from her analyst. She argues that this function in the analyst is based in her natural humanity and her own personal experiences of early privations and illness and that it is this quality in the analyst that keeps the therapeutic process alive. Here her clinical work foreshadows the classic work of both Nina Coltart (1986), Neville Symington (1983) and the writing of her supervisee Christopher Bollas (1987) on expressive uses of the countertransference.

Of course, Paula Heimann knew that such an approach was full of traps and dangers but she writes that these dangers simply have to be faced, and points out that anyone wanting an easy job should get out of being an analyst as quickly as possible, in her own interest and that of her patients. For her the goal of analysis had now long since ceased to be the relief of symptoms but 'a liberation to naturalness and honesty', and this could only be achieved by the patient if it was also achieved by the analyst.

> Violation of the natural way of acting; that is, violation of the funda-mental principle and goal of analysis. Each participant in the analytic process seeks and struggles for both, internal and external truth. The acknowledgement of reality, to which all psychic progress and opportu-nities for happiness are tied, require that each exhibit a natural honesty.
>
> (1978)

She wrote that the work took courage, that courage was a prerequisite for a human way of acting, and without it the goal of analysis could not be achieved. For her the analyst must break free of a 'Procrustean bed of ana-lytic rules' (1978) in order to find the analytic attitude that will allow her to listen to, understand and help to free her patients. Here, once again, she was in step with the pioneering Independent women, Marjorie Brierley and Ella Freeman Sharpe writing more than 30 years earlier. 'I am more inclined to alter my preconceived notions to fit the patient's new pattern than to cut the pattern to fit my notions' (Brierley, 1943). 'Nobody can hand over a ready made technique except as an artefact' (Sharpe, 1943).

Paula Heimann knew that people might see her suggestions as an invitation to do wild analysis, but she wrote that it was the opposite, as it rested on a deep trust in the unconscious and the analytic process combined with a demand for critical self-observation, continued self-analysis and self-supervision. She termed the resulting balance 'tamed naturalness', 'As so often both in analysis and in the human condition, there is a paradox: only tamed naturalness is creative' (1978). Tamed naturalness made the need for analytic listening more rigorous, as the analyst Patrick Casement discovered when he asked to see Paula Heimann for an urgent consultation after agreeing to hold a patient's hand in the following session. After listening to the case, Paula Heimann was clear that it was of profound importance that he did not hold this patient's hand. When Patrick Casement replied that he could not now withdraw his offer, she told him that he must not do this to follow a rule, or just because she said so. The problem was that he needed to follow what his patient was really showing him, which was that he, like the others in her life, was unable to bear the impact of her feelings (Casement, 2000).

Swimming against the current

As a young analyst Paula Heimann feared that to 'swim against the current' would lead to isolation and perhaps to some degree this came true. Her work after 1950 is not so well known. But her influence is profound and while some might think it a contradiction to even attempt to define an 'Independent' it seems that Paula Heimann came close to personifying what it might mean to be one. Central to this is that she found a freedom to develop her own way of understanding psychoanalysis based on her clinical observations. At the heart of this was her understanding of unconscious communication and her argument that for the analyst to really listen to her patient she must find the freedom to listen to herself. Her clinical work led her to be increasingly in step, and find a home with many others who saw the foundational role of early relationships in emotional development and a growing understanding that many patients come to analysis to communicate and find help with the affective experiences of their early life.

For her the analyst's most important tool in her work is not her theories but her natural, tamed, humanity. In a paper she wrote on the qualities needed to make a good analyst, 'The evaluation of applicants for psychoanalytic training' (1968), she recalled a casual remark made by a colleague as they waited for a lift home from a conference: 'No matter how sophisticated our concepts have become what we really expect in a psychoanalytic candidate is that he should have a good heart and that he should have gone through some suffering without denying it'. For her this was not, 'wishy washy sentimental goodiness' but a simple truth. Analysts were ordinary people who had been through the difficult process of reflecting honestly on themselves.

> Driven by his suffering the patient turns to the analyst in the hope of finding help. The analyst can provide help if he originally came to analysis as someone who was ill – and in some regards still is ill – but had the courage to do without falsehoods and tricks, in this way making something creative out of his illness.
>
> (1978)

Note

1 For a detailed description of all the developments in Paula Heimann's work see Margret Tonnesmann's introduction to the 'Collected Papers' (Tonnesmann 1989, 10–25).

References

Bollas, C. (1987). 'Expressive Uses of the Countertransference: Notes to the Patient from Oneself'. In: *The Shadow of the Object: Psychoanalysis of the Unthought Known*, London: Free Association Books, 200–235.

Brierley, M. (1943). 'Memorandum on her Technique'. In: King, P. & Steiner, R. (1991). *The Freud Klein Controversies 1941–45*. London & New York: The New Library of Psychoanalysis, Routledge.

Casement, P. (2000). 'The Issue of Touch: A Retrospective Overview', *Psychoanalytic Inquiry*, 20: 160–184.

Coltart, N. (1986). 'Slouching Towards Bethlehem ... Or Thinking the Unthinkable in Psychoanalysis'. In: *The British School of Psychoanalysis: The Independent Tradition*, Kohon, G. (ed.), London: Free Association Books.

Fairbairn, W.R. (1952). *Psychoanalytic Studies of the Personality*, London: Tavistock Publications.

Ferenczi, S. 1949 (1933). 'Confusion of the Tongues Between the Adults and the Child (The Language of Tenderness and of Passion)'. *International Journal of Psychoanalysis*, 30: 225–230.

Freud, S. (1912). '*Recommendations to Physicians Practising Psycho-Analysis*'. In: *The Standard Edition of the Complete Psychological Works of Sigmund Freud*, Volume XII, London: Hogarth Press, 109–120.

Freud, S. (1926). 'The Question of Lay Analysis'. In: *The Standard Edition of the Complete Psychological Works of Sigmund Freud*, Volume XX, London: Hogarth Press, 177–258.

Groarke, S. (2018). 'Making Sense Together'. In: *British Psychoanalysis: New Perspectives in the Independent Tradition*, Kohon, G. (ed.), London: Routledge, 133–147.

Heimann, P. (1943). 'Some Aspects of the Role of Introjection and Projection in Early Development'. In: *The Freud Klein Controversies 1941–45*, King, P. & Steiner, R. (eds), (1991). London & New York: The New Library of Psychoanalysis, Routledge, 501–531.

Heimann, P. (1950). 'On Counter-Transference', *International Journal of Psychoanalysis*, 31: 81–84.

Heimann, P. (1955). 'Dynamics of Transference Interpretations', *International Journal of Psychoanalysis*, 37: 303–310.

Heimann, P. (1957). 'Some Notes on Sublimation'. In: *About Children and Children-No-Longer: Collected Papers 1942–80*, Tonnesmann, M. (ed.), London & New York: The New Library of Psychoanalysis, Routledge, 122–137.

Heimann, P. (1960). 'Counter-transference'. In: *About Children and Children-No-Longer: Collected Papers 1942–80*, Tonnesmann, M. (ed.), London & New York: The New Library of Psychoanalysis, Routledge, 151–160.

Heimann, P. (1964). 'Evolutionary Leaps and the Origins of Cruelty'. In: *About Children and Children-No-Longer: Collected Papers 1942–80*, Tonnesmann, M. (ed.), London & New York: The New Library of Psychoanalysis, Routledge, 206–217.

Heimann, P. (1966). 'Comment on Dr Kernberg's Paper', *International Journal of Psychoanalysis*, 47: 254–260.

Heimann, P. (1968). 'The Evaluation of Applicants for Psychoanalytic Training—The Goals of Psychoanalytic Education and the Criteria for the Evaluation of Applicants', *International Journal of Psychoanalysis*, 49: 527–539.

Heimann, P. (1969). 'Postscript to Dynamics of Transference Interpretations'. In: Tonnesmann, M. (ed.), London & New York: The New Library of Psychoanalysis, Routledge, 253–261.

Heimann, P. (1978). 'On the necessity for the analyst to be natural with his patient'. In: *About Children and Children-No-Longer Collected Papers 1942–80*,

Tonnesmann, M. (ed.), London & New York: The New Library of Psycho-analysis, Routledge, 311–323.

Keene J. (2012). 'Reflections on the Evolution of Independent Psychoanalytic Thought'. In: *Independent Psychoanalysis Today*, Williams, P., Keene, J. & Dermen, S. (eds), London: Karnac Books, 3–62.

King, P. (1978). 'Affective Response of the Analyst to the Patient's Communications', *International Journal of Psychoanalysis*, 59: 329–334.

King P. (1989). 'Introductory Memoir'. In: *About Children and Children-No-Longer Collected Papers 1942–80*, Tonnesmann, M. (ed.), London & New York: The New Library of Psychoanalysis, Routledge, 1–9.

King, P. & Steiner, R. (1991). *The Freud Klein Controversies 1941–45*, London & New York: The New Library of Psychoanalysis, Routledge.

Klein, M, (1946). '*Notes on Some Schizoid Mechanisms*'. In: *Envy and Gratitude and Other Works: 1921–1945*, London: Hogarth Press, 1–24.

Kohon, G. (1986). 'Countertransference: An Independent View'. In: *The British School of Psychoanalysis: The Independent Tradition*, Kohon, G. (ed.), London: Free Association Books, 51–73.

Kohon, G. (1992). 'Book Review. About Children and Children-No-Longer', *International Journal of Psychoanalysis*, 73: 164–165.

Milner, M. (1987). *The Suppressed Madness of Sane Men: Forty-four Years of Exploring Psychoanalysis*, London & New York: The New Library of Psycho-analysis, Routledge.

Payne, S. (1943). 'Memorandum on Her Technique by Sylvia M. Payne'. In: King, P. & Steiner, R. (eds) (1991). *The Freud Klein Controversies 1941–45*, London & New York: The New Library of Psychoanalysis, Routledge.

Rayner, E. (1991). *The Independent Mind in British Psychoanalysis*, Maryland: Aronson.

Rayner, E. Date unknown. Unpublished transcript of recorded interview in private papers.

Reik, T. (1948). *Listening With the Third Ear: The Inner Experience of a Psycho-analyst*, New York: Farrar, Straus & Co., 1983.

Robinson. K. (2019). '*A Brief History of the British Psychoanalytical Society*', https://psychoanalysis.org.uk.

Rolnik, E.J. (2008). '"Why is it that I See Everything Differently?" Reading a 1933 Letter from Paula Heimann to Theodor Reik', *Journal of the American Psycho-analytic Association*, 56: 409–430.

Sharpe, E.F. (1930). 'The Technique of Psycho-analysis', *International Journal of Psychoanalysis*, 11: 361–386.

Sharpe E.F. (1943). 'Memorandum on Her Technique by Ella Freeman Sharpe'. In: King, P. & Steiner, R. (eds) (1991). *The Freud Klein Controversies 1941–45*, London & New York: The New Library of Psychoanalysis, Routledge.

Symington, N. (1983). 'The Analyst's Act of Freedom as Agent of Therapeutic Change', *International Review of Psychoanalysis*, 10: 283–291.

Symington, N. (1986). 'Melanie Klein: Part 2'. In: *The Analytic Experience, Lectures from the Tavistock*, London: Free Association Books, 263–276.

Tonnesmann, M. (1989). 'Editor's Introduction'. In: *About Children and Children-No-Longer Collected Papers 1942–80*, Tonnesmann, M. (ed.), London & New York: The New Library of Psychoanalysis, Routledge, 10–25.

Winnicott, D.W. (1949). 'Hate in the Countertransference'. In: *Collected Papers: Through Paediatrics to Psycho-analysis*, Khan, M. (ed.), London: Hogarth Press, 194–203.

Winnicott, D.W. (1969). 'The Use of an Object', *International Journal of Psychoanalysis*, 50: 711–716.

Chapter 6

Marion Milner
The pliable self

Maia Kirchkheli

Art Creates Nature.

(Milner, 1952b, p. 99)

'I am one of those people who think in images', reiterated Marion Milner throughout her life. The image that comes to my mind is her painting 'A Thought Too Big For Its Concept', the only one hanging in The Institute of Psychoanalysis. There are splashes of yellow and orange in the centre of the canvas, each framed by lines of blue, red and purple opening on one end or the other to give birth to an ever-expanding self into a bigger frame … It describes the *process* of continuous re-birth in colour. I came to think of it as a metaphor for her idea of psychic development rooted in the basic human paradox that one is bigger than oneself.

If I single out a psychoanalytic paper from her oeuvre that goes with it, it is 'The Role of Illusion in Symbol-formation', previously entitled 'Aspects of Symbolism in Comprehension of the Not-self'. The original title captures the essence but lacks the dynamism of the later one, where emphasis is on the *process*. This paper has the particular feeling of a collage – different fabrics are juxtaposed, and various textures are tangible; the attempt at uniformity is resisted. Milner opens her paper with an outline of existing views on symbolism having a defensive function which frames the clinical material that is dense and compelling and out of which something new emerges.

Another reason for likening this paper to a collage is the creative cutting I feel Milner performed in this work. Milner was for some years in supervision with Melanie Klein, who emphasized the role of sadism, loss and anxiety in the process of symbol-formation. The clinical case that she discusses was supervised by Klein as part of her training in child analysis. The first cut was done at this juncture of fellowship and the next at the theoretical level: Milner focuses on the significance of fusion (rather than its defensive function) to give meaning to separation.

Central to this cut, I think, was the meeting of Milner's two sides: that of analyst and of artist, which marks the conceptual birth of her analytic identity. In her collected papers – the fruit of 44 years of exploring psychoanalysis – two papers, 'The Framed Gap' and 'The Role of Illusion in Symbol-formation', both

DOI: 10.4324/9781003296690-9

appear in 1952 in this suggestive sequence. I see the former as a prelude to the latter. Milner used psychoanalysis to comprehend the creative process and her artistic sensibility to contribute to the study of psychic development.[1] Out of this cross-fertilization, the main thesis of this paper is constituted: psychic growth is fundamentally a creative process carried out through the expanding capacity of the individual for symbol-formation that is in the service of meaningful adaptation to external reality. A symbol is an affective conception of the encounter with the Not-self.

Fundamental to creative process is the experience of illusion. Both papers selected here examine necessary conditions for illusory encounters. The primary environment is expected to provide a framed space and a pliable medium to foster the emerging self's capacity for creative surrender.

Milner focuses on the role of paints and toys as examples of pliable medium. Out of my reverie on Milner's way of thinking and writing, I realized that she used and offered herself as a pliable medium. Hence, I have arrived at the concept of a *'Pliable Mind'* – a human mind that lends itself to being used as a medium while not losing its framework to think. It is the analyst's state of mind intrinsically linked to qualities such as receptivity, elasticity and pliability. These psychic features define the analyst's willingness to be affected and reshaped by the experience. Words and thoughts are offered like playdough, the material to play with, the substance for illusory experiences.

Each medium has a consistency and a life of its own. Here lies the subjectivity of the analyst whose psychic make-up determines the limitation of its pliability. The encounter with the firm, unmodifiable aspect of the medium represents the externality – the otherness which must be accepted if it is to be used creatively.

The framed gap

Consider a quote from an artist's studio:

> [T]here comes a moment, when painting some object from the outer world, when the *excitement about whatever it was made you want to paint* and immediately complicated practical problems of how to represent that feeling in colour, shape, texture, and so on, all disappear as conscious problems. One becomes lost in a moment of intense activity in which awareness of self and awareness of the object are somehow fused, and one emerges to separateness again to find that there is some new entity on the paper.
>
> (Milner, 1952a, my emphasis)

The creative quest is *how* to represent the feeling state about the object. The symbol is meaningful if it holds and evokes this affective state.

Milner compared two ways of drawing that are essentially two ways of engaging with an object. First, she described the painstaking process of drawing when her eyes were moving from object to pencil. The intention to produce an exact copy generated a growing despair in her. Milner discovered that she achieved a far better result if she held the excitement, and kept her eyes on the object while her hand drew quickly. This absorption with the object requires the mental surrender to the affective state. Integral to it is the corporal surrender to the artist's tools, the medium. It is a conscious choice of giving up the controlling and directional function of the will. Instead, the will is applied to hold the inner space, to frame the inner gap. Milner noticed that in this instance

> an inner organising pattern-making force other than willed planning seemed to be freed, an inner urge to pattern and wholeness which had then become externally embodied in the product there for all to see.
>
> (Ibid., p. 80)

Elsewhere she calls them 'the free drawings'. It is evocative of the free associations – the fundamental rule of psychoanalysis, another kind of medium to get hold of the primary process. At this point we can see that the shift took place in the meaning of the framed gap from the blank canvas framed by its edges to the state of mind described in visual terms as the inner blank space framed by the will. The reciprocity is established between a canvas, (the background to a new symbol), and an inner blank space which is the site of emotional experience.

I would like to illustrate this kind of reciprocity between the elements of the creative process delineated in the artist's studio and those in Milner's clinical paper, as they constitute the structure for her theory of psychic growth.

1   A *pliable medium* – paint, which would be similar to the way toys and words are used in an analytic situation. This is facilitated by the analyst's pliable mind with an emphasis on the analyst's willingness to be transformed by the mutuality of the experience with the patient.
2   A piece of canvas that is a limited surface, *framed* by its edges. A psychoanalytic session is *framed* both in time and space. The frame marks inside from outside; 'what is inside [the frame] has to be perceived, interpreted in a different way from what is outside; they mark off an area within which what we perceive has to be taken as a symbol, as metaphor, not literally' (Ibid., p. 81).

As noted above, the inner space also needs to be framed by the will to create a receptive state of mind.

3   *Surrender*, both physical and affective to painting, playing, free associating
to the process driven by something other than his will to encounter the
Not-self.

Therefore, I am describing two kinds of shift: from the physicality of the
painting to the state of mind of the artist, and from the artist's studio to the
psycho-analytic room. The artist's studio is a metaphor for the consulting
room and an analyst's inner room. It allows us to have a glimpse of Milner's
state of mind, through which she perceived the clinical picture in the psychoanalytic room.

Pliable Medium – Pliable Mind

Now, consider the following quotation from the analytic playroom:

> [H]e seemed to me to be trying to express the idea of integration, in a
> variety of different ways. Thus the fire seemed to be here not only a
> destructive fire but also the fire of Eros; and not only the figurative
> expression of his own passionate body feelings, not only the phantasy
> representative of the wish for passionate union with the external object,
> but also a way of representing the inner fire of concentration. The process
> in which interest is withdrawn temporarily from the external world so
> that the inner work of integration can be carried out was, I think, shown
> by the boiling or melting down of the various ingredients in what he
> called 'the fire cup', to make a new whole.
>
> (Milner, 1952b, p. 96)

In place of a painter, we have 11-year-old Simon playing with toys: melting,
fusing, adding. His inner fire of concentration must be his surrender to the
affective process of making a new object. Here, we have an alchemic description of symbol formation and Milner's young patient is indeed a budding
scientist. It is reminiscent of the process of psychic metabolism: destruction,
digestion, assimilation, using the Not-self as a medium to expand, to form a
new whole.

Simon suffered from an inhibition of learning. The school became 'too
much identified' with the mother's body, at once desired and hated. I think
Milner describes the case of *symbolic equation*, when the symbol and the
object it symbolises are not distinguished (Segal, 1950). Simon could not hold
the gap between the two elements of the symbol: internal and external to the
self, subjective and objective.

> He nearly always began the session with the bullying tone and insistence
> that I was not ready for him at the right time, whatever the actual time of
> starting; but as soon as he had settled down to using the toys as a *pliable*

medium, external to himself, but not insisting on their own separate objective existence, then apparently he could treat me with friendliness and consideration, and even accept real frustration from me.

(Ibid.; p. 92, my emphasis)

In this brief excerpt we see the transformation of the patient's pattern of relatedness across the session: from the inability to bear the analyst's otherness, the loss of the self while playing with toys, and emerging out of it with a 'newly created object' into an apparent ability to tolerate his analyst's separateness. Milner's understanding of Simon's use of the toys is captured in the following reflection:

As soon as he moved a toy in response to some wish or phantasy then the play-village was different, and the new sight set off a new set of possibilities; just as in free imaginative drawing, the sight of a mark made on the paper provokes new associations, the line as it were answers back and functions as a very primitive type of external object.

(Ibid., p. 92)

After some time, the receptive quality of toys was replicated with the school. Simon ran an after-school photography club with friends. At this point, the school accepted his request to hold meetings in the building during the time assigned for special activities. Thus, the school was receptive to his need and provided the spatial and temporal frame for 'his playing'. It had a profound impact on Simon. He was overjoyed and his bullying tone disappeared in the sessions.

What he had felt to be the mechanized, soulless world of school had now seemed to him to have become humanized, by the *taking into its empty trucks of a bit of himself, something that he had created.*

(Ibid., p. 93, my emphasis)

Milner comments that the school tried to help him many times, but it seemed to become meaningful only when Simon was ready to turn to the school with his own gesture. By this point, from his experiences with his analyst, Simon must have acquired a confidence in the receptivity of the Not-self, the school.

Milner's reflections on this clinical material mark the divergence from the Kleinian school of thought, according to which primitive object relationships operated from birth and primary narcissism, the fusion of the object and self, are the defence against the awareness of separateness. Segal, (1983), summarizing Klein's thoughts on the theme, puts it succinctly: if one believes in primary narcissism, envy would be secondary to disillusionment; if one believes in primary envy, narcissism is seen as a defence against envy. Milner did not share the basic assumption in primary envy and this theoretical difference has an implication for technique. The Postscript of Milner's paper (1952b, p. 106) illuminates some of these points.[2] Klein's comments on Simon's predicament are about his sadism, which she insists to be consistently interpreted in the transference. Milner argues that she initially took up Simon's projection mechanisms, sadism, and persecutory defences but this only exacerbated Simon's anxiety. Aggression, while omnipresent in the clinical material, could not yet be meaningfully owned by Simon.

Progressively, Milner wondered whether Simon's play suggested his fundamental struggle with the earliest phase of establishing object relationships and relating to external reality. How does a developing self move from the primary object that is a fusion of mouth and breast, self and object? This question presupposes a starting point of psychic non-differentiation – primary narcissism.

Thinking in terms of projection and introjection failed to account for Milner's patient's constant preoccupation with burning, boiling down, and melting – the various forms of dissolving the shape of the objects into a substance, a medium. To interpret this as the defensive effacement of the perceived boundaries between the self and the Not-self would leave out the transformative aim of his actions. This aspect of Simon's play suggested a sense of *destruction of the objects' boundaries* on the one hand and an *integration* into a new whole on the other. It is different from the destruction of the object. The aggression is used to transform the object to the extent of *creating* a new one. At the same time, there is an emphasis on the importance of the externality of the toys – objects whose qualities are modifiable. The need for an object's existence is not denied, but it is too alien to be used in its original form. It is treated ruthlessly, turned into a medium. Milner quotes the *Concise Oxford Dictionary* that defines medium as:

> 'an intervening substance through which impressions are conveyed to the senses;' and this pliable stuff that can be made to take the shape of one's phantasies, can include the 'stuff' of sound and breath which becomes our speech.
>
> (Ibid., p. 99)

This definition emphasises the communicative aspect of medium that is being used to convey psychic reality called transference. Milner notes:

> He so often treated me as totally his own to do what he liked with, as though I were dirt, his dirt, or as a tool, an extension of his own hand … In fact it certainly did seem that for a very long time he did need to have the illusion that I was part of himself.
>
> (Ibid., p. 94)

Relentlessly subjected to being 'a dirt' evoked negative countertransference in Milner who was unaware of it for some time. She did register exhaustion and intermittent despair, but Milner is sparse in sharing it with us. For the contemporary reader what might be surprising was another point of controversy: the use of countertransference.[3] Yet, Milner is explicit that when she grasped the negative aspect of her countertransference and dealt with it, her mind became open to transformations. The boundaries between existing psychoanalytic ideas and her personal creative experiences melted into a new whole. A pliable analyst was born.

> When I began to see and to interpret, as far as I could, that this use of me might be not only a defensive regression, but an essential recurrent phase in the development of a creative relation to the world, then the whole character of the analysis changed; the boy then gradually became able to allow the external object, represented by me, to exist in its own right.
>
> (Ibid., p. 104)

In my view, implicit in this understanding is that a pliable medium is a particular property of the analyst's mind which lends itself to be moulded by her analysand.[4] It is the openness to be affected by the Not-self. Milner's mind became refashioned 'in response to the vividness of his [Simon's] belief in the validity of his own experience' (Ibid., p. 105).

For a patient, the analyst's mind becomes a modifiable aspect of the external environment. Eventually, what gets internalized is a belief about the psychic growth being an ongoing movement from medium to symbol. Toys were pliable enough and brought a temporary relief to Simon. But the use of toys *only* could not undo the developmental arrest. What must have made a structural difference to Simon's psychic state was Milner's pliable mind. Milner was not only tolerating being treated as her patient's extension and 'dirt' but when appropriate she would put this developmental necessity into words to him. Albeit becoming a medium, Milner never gave up her symbolic functioning. Thus, she acted as a symbol to Simon: Milner became his creation but separate enough to speak about their experience to him without directly challenging the fusion.

Illusion and symbol

> It seemed as if it was only by being able, *again and again, to experience the illusion that I was part of himself,* fused with the goodness that he could conceive of internally, that he became able to tolerate a goodness that was not his own creation and to allow me goodness independently.
>
> (Ibid., p. 103, my emphasis)

The psychoanalytic frame fosters the development of the illusion conceptualized as transference, the idiom embraced by analysts of the Independent Group.

Analytic work is founded on the development of transference neurosis: a patient transfers his/her unconscious beliefs onto the analyst who is experienced as an archaic parental figure (Klauber, 1987) and it becomes the therapeutic factor in an analytic situation when the internal reality emotionally comes alive through illusory dramatization (Kleimberg, 2012, 2018). The gradual dissolution of transference is driven by the process of disillusionment through which the patient discovers the otherness of the analyst.

The concept of illusion is central to Milner's thinking as it gathers all the constituent elements of the creative process – pliable medium, act of surrender and frame – like a thread that links up beads in a whole. It describes the psychic state when the primary object and the symbol, *while perceived as different, are felt as one and the same.* The feeling state about the union with the lost object is retained and expressed through a new form. Then, the new object has an affective colour of the old one – it feels alive. This capacity for creatively finding a new form for feelings makes the experience of separateness from the object bearable and meaningful.

The OED defines illusion as an instance of a wrong or *misinterpreted perception* of a sensory experience. In ordinary usage, illusion has a negative connotation of being deceived, something contrary to the true state of affairs. I am often struck by the pride taken in the statement: I have no illusions. This attitude amongst many things is a residue of infantile amnesia (Kleimberg, personal communication), the repression of the folie à deux of babyhood. Yet, the price of not having illusions turns out to be emotional impoverishment, '… and we are poor indeed if we are only sane' (Winnicott, 1945, ft., p. 150).

But what does *misinterpreted perception* mean?

Milner (1950, p. 32) quotes Santayana: 'In imagination, not in perception, lies the substance of experience …', and she concludes that the *substance of experience* is what we bring to what we see. Milner's contemporary, Enid Balint (1963), coined the term *imaginative perception* to denote the subjective quality of perception. However, the vivid description of the concept (without using the word illusion but naming it as a fiction) can be found in Freud's paper, 'Two Principles of Mental Functioning', where he examines the dialectic of pleasure and the reality principle for a developing mind.

> It will rightly be objected that an organisation which was a slave to the pleasure principle and neglected the reality of the external world could not maintain itself alive for the shortest time, so that it could not have come into existence at all. *The employment of a fiction like this is, however, justified when one considers that the infant – provided one includes with it the care it receives from its mother –* does almost realise a psychical system of this kind. It probably hallucinates the fulfilment of its internal needs; it betrays its unpleasure, when there is an increase of stimulus and an absence of satisfaction, by the motor discharge of

screaming and beating about with its arms and legs, and it then experiences the satisfaction it has hallucinated.

(Freud, 1911, p. 220, my emphasis)

I quote it here for two reasons. Firstly, it illustrates a dual perspective: an infant thinks that s/he satisfied his/her needs through hallucination while for an adult it is obvious that the real milk secured the satisfaction. If we take both perspectives into account – the real breast met the hallucinated one[5] – we arrive at a transitional space where the two realities overlap (Winnicott, 1971). This is the essence of illusion.

Secondly, Freud is explicit about the *substance of experience*: it is a belief in the hallucinated breast. In order to hallucinate the satisfaction, the baby has to have had sufficient experience of it, so-called mnemic traces, that could be remembered and revived.

An analysand brings his *own substance of experience* with which he imbues the analyst. Although fusion between internal and external versions of the person can only take place in phantasy, it is linked affectively to and corroborated by the external object's pliable presence. Simon 'bullied' his analyst into becoming toy-like for him, and her main role in the transference was to embody his lost rabbit. In terms of technique, at this point of emotional development, participation in the patient's script matters more than interpretation of it. Milner's clinical thinking was also informed by her own introspective findings on the 'problems to do with how one ever comes to believe in the full reality of the "other" at all' (Milner, 1950, p. 37).

Milner devotes a chapter to the necessity of illusion in her book, *On Not Being Able to Paint*, where she examines the relationship between perception and imagination, thing and thought. Through careful analysis of her own experiments on the creative process, she concludes that in the primary experience, dream and perceptions are not distinguished. At the beginning there should be sustained illusion of oneness with the world. Her understanding is shared by Winnicott who comments on her paper:

> For an infant, at the start, there is no good or bad, only a not yet defused object. One could think of separation as the cause of the first *idea* of union; before this there's union but no *idea* of union, and here the terms good and bad have no function. For union of this kind, so important for the founding of the mental health of the individual, the mother's active adaptation to the infant's needs which can only come about through the mother's devotion to the infant.
>
> (Winnicott, 1952b, p. 112)

Milner understood her young patient's predicament as being disillusioned and defused too early, which resulted in premature ego-development. Simon's history of frequently interrupted feeds alluded to the misfit between his need and the primary environment. This primary deprivation meant that for the sake of self-preservation when still an infant *he* had to *react*, and fit in with his environment. Consequently, the separateness and the demands of the reality were accepted at the cost of giving up his primary creativity. Fusion in the analytic situation was the primary way of linking with the external object: regressive in its mode, progressive in its aim. Milner writes in *Not Being Able to Paint*, where an object of scrutiny is her own selfhood: '... a going back to look for something, something which could have real value for adult life if only it could be recovered'.

Capacity in the self: the creative surrender

The capacity of the self to surrender to the Not-self, I think, constitutes the inner condition for illusory experiences. The process of symbol-formation requires letting go of old forms, familiar ways of being, for new ones to emerge. The self needs to feel safe to die in between. Milner links the development of this capacity with the experience of taming the fear of psychic death. She studied this question in her book, *An Experiment in Leisure*.

> I had guessed that if you accept the thought of death with any after-thoughts of immortality it is not a full acceptance. There must be at least one moment of complete blank extinction, a plunge into nothingness.
>
> (Milner, 1937, pp. 107–8)

In my understanding, there could be no unconscious belief in the reversibility of the loss of sense of self otherwise. Consequently, there is no sense of safety to let go. This capacity is foundational for the development of a pliable quality of the mind. It is evocative of the ability for primary maternal preoccupation likened by Winnicott (1956) to illness when the mother lends herself to her baby to provide the maximum adaptation to her newborn's needs. We can draw a parallel to the specificity of the analyst's listening. Parsons articulates Milner's analytic activity consisting of,

> a particular kind of attentiveness to her own state of mind. She needed to keep herself in a state which facilitated his [Simon's] experience of her as a pliable medium of that sort. The detail of the material shows how she enabled him to experience her as partly as aspect of himself, created and controlled by him, and partly something other than himself that had its own responses. She functioned for him, in fact, as an answering activity ... she was able to do this through being in contact with her own Answering Activity.
>
> (Parsons, 2000, pp. 152–3)

Parsons picks up another term coined by Milner to capture her receptivity to her own otherness. Characteristically to Milner, the Answering Activity is not defined but explored and lived through various visual images and scenes in her autobiographical books, *An Experiment in Leisure* and *Eternity's Sunrise*.[6] She describes the Answering Activity being both 'I' and 'not I' (Milner, 1987, p. 57) and alludes to its being rooted in one's inner body awareness. At one point she is talking about a state of being when one feels 'breathed' just like we once were in the mother's body. It is certainly a dialectical experience in which 'I' actively takes passive position in relation to 'not I'. I understand the Answering Activity as the emotional surrender, the psychic movement of self-effacement against the backcloth of one's own body as its frame to reach 'not I', the inner Not-self. Meta-psychologically-speaking, it involves the shift of the cathexis from secondary to primary mode of thinking to being shaped by the inner pattern of organising as opposed to the one that is imposed from without. It is a quality of engagement peculiar to a pliable mind that could treat its unknowable depth as the medium, the source of endless knowledge about oneself and the other. Milner warns us that answers from the inner Not-self usually come as a surprise and those 'surprising', if not disturbing responses, like dream images, need to be further thought about, understood, and integrated in the self.

Khan (1953), in his review of Milner's book, *On Not Being Able to Paint*, advises us to read the book with what I think involves exercising our Answering Activity. As he aptly summarizes: 'Only a passionate attitude of surrendered attention will yield rapport with it' (p. 333). This brings me to the role of regression in analytic situation which supposes the same sort of rapport between patient and analyst.

Dea was in her early thirties and suffered from major inhibitions when she embarked on five-times weekly analysis with me. During the first two years, every time I expressed a thought, her response had a distinct psycho-somatic sequence. Dea would sigh deeply as if trying to exhale my toxic otherness from her body. This act was accompanied with a tangible sense of deflation. Then, she would go quiet and remain frozen on the couch until the end of the session. I would let her know that I recognised the existential threat my separateness posed to her. It felt like I should not make a claim of existing, yet I had to exist. Perhaps through this paradox I could convey what it means to be a living medium.

Dea *felt* alive only when she was with me in the room. Separations were agonising. 'Readiness is all', Milner quotes from Shakespeare (1952a, p. 82, 1937, p. 171).

'*Now, I can let you go because I can keep you*', Dea told me when gradually emerging out of this phase of regression. She had arrived at a creative paradox: she could keep the experience of our union in the absence of our togetherness; she could tolerate the gap between her version of me and the Me that existed outside her control, because her version of me inside her felt real to her. The virtual link between the inner and the outer was maintained. Milner captured well this reciprocity in her reflection: '… by the temporary fusion of dream and external reality, the dream itself becomes endowed with the real qualities of the peg that momentarily carries it' (Milner, 1950, p. 36).

Following various changes in her inner and outer realities, after five-and-a-half years, it felt pertinent to reduce the frequency of her sessions from five to three. The absence framed by the last session on Friday, and the first session in the week on Wednesday, became longer than the presence itself. This made the loss central to the analytic work. A few months later, she brought a dream.

> I dreamt of being in a large room, there was a dining table, and some people. I was sitting next to you and I leaned towards you, putting my head onto your shoulder. It felt cosy. I felt supported, grounded … safe … simply happy! It felt blissful but I knew that I needed to leave. I thought that 'I would love to stay forever with you but I need to leave.' With this thought I got up. You didn't say a word, but you knew that I had to leave. It was at once painful and joyful: I felt I was taking with me what it felt like being with you. There was more in the second half of the dream, but I only remember a few disjointed bits. My boyfriend was there. I remember some coins … as if he was to pay for something and he removed his watch from his wrist suggesting that he was paying with his watch … it strikes me that the end of the dream is so obscure. I simply do not know what it means while I am so clearheaded about the beginning. I mean what concerns us.

Dea woke up feeling a mixture of profound satisfaction and sadness. In part, she wanted to stay forever with me. It was so alluring to be part of me, and she often feared never being able to leave me. But now, something in her knew that she needed to leave. This inner necessity to differentiate had become stronger and drove her away towards expansion. As I followed the movement in her affective state from ecstatic realisation that she could have this feeling of security in my absence, which was profoundly liberating to the pain of the loss that underpinned this very process, I was experiencing an aesthetic moment. Like Milner felt when she watched Simon closing the shutters of the consulting room and lighting dozens of candles, it was her imagination which caught fire. Milner drew our attention to the lack of conceptualisation of this aspect of the analytic process: '… a word is needed for the emotional experience of finding the substitute, and it is here that the word ecstasy may be useful' (1952b, p. 87).

The dream was rich in its affect, containing layered forms of meaning. It could be thought of as an accomplished symbol that marked the moment of developmental readiness to transfer her dreams from the analytic object to her boyfriend. Her experience of dreaming had acquired a new quality – it became the source of aliveness which in my view demonstrated her capacity to get in touch with her own Answering Activity, the appreciation of the other within.

I pointed out to her that this profound sense of security stemmed from her ability to sustain the link with me in my absence.

The preoccupying question that arose from her associations was: 'Can I surrender to my boyfriend the way I surrender to you? He is my reality. Perhaps, it is time I do that.' There was tangible anxiety about how successful it would be. One must make a leap of faith in the receptiveness of the other person. For illusory experiences the external people's willing participation is crucial. The dream shows the move from the maternal object to the paternal one. From an eternal, timeless bliss, to time that is governed by the paternal clock; from primary to secondary femininity.

This psychic shift also suggested her anxious question: what was the cost for the loss of the known, the familiar analytic object and space, while the future with her boyfriend was something unknown? In part, the answer was in her dream: only time can show.

Rhythm of psychic growth

There is a fundamental sequence in establishing contact with reality. The conception of the self starts with the experience of illusion of oneness with the maternal object. One needs to become aware of this stage of fusion before one can reach the relief of de-fusion. De-fusion is the vicissitude of disillusion-ment which reveals the *gap* between the self and the Not-self.

> It was only when he [Simon] could become conscious of the relief of de-fusion that we were then able to reach his depression about injuries that he had felt he was responsible for, both internally and externally, in his family situation and in relation to me.
>
> (Milner, 1952b, p. 104)

The depression becomes meaningful *if* an affective bond with the de-fused object could be retained and a new form for this feeling state is created. Then, an individual is equipped to mourn the lost union. Creating a symbol feels like re-finding the lost object.

The question of different kinds of depression is essential to understanding the process of symbol-formation. Another child patient of Milner, when painting the roof of the house black, remarked: 'There are two kinds of black, horrid black and lovely shiny black' (Milner, 1987, p. 183). This child is talking about two different experiences of loss. When the maternal object is gone and 'nothing is there', the nothingness that gets filled up with infantile traumatic experiences is a horrid black. This would be the case of melancholic depression.

'Lovely shiny black' would stand for the experience when the lovely feelings about the 'gone object' can be reached despite the pain and anxiety. It is the *belief* that one can retrieve a feeling of goodness and with it the associated safety that underpins the capacity to surrender to its frightening nothingness. Then, the black can shine. This is the depression, full of the potential for transformation of the gap into the symbol.

A sufficient encounter with a pliable mind at the beginning of one's life facilitates the development of a belief in illusory experiences. The mother who is pliable enough to adapt, to tolerate being the medium, being intermittently created and re-created as well as allowing temporary regressions throughout the child's development supplies her child with creative confidence in the framed spaces and the pliable medium. Whilst emotional growth is about losing childhood illusions, the capacity for creating new illusions needs to be retained as a vehicle of symbolisation and creative living. This capacity is an internalized sequence of establishing the contact with the Not-self – both within and without. The rhythm of pliability, that of merging and emerging, is established as the ongoing process of re-shaping one's perceptions and affective states into symbols. One acquires a pliable mind; becomes a living symbol. Creative engagement with external reality could be described as a journey from a pliable medium to a symbol.

The essence of the concept of the pliable mind is well captured in Milner's response to Ricardo Steiner[7] who pointed to her paintings on the wall and asked whether she gave titles to them. 'They give *me* titles!' Marion Milner was 93 at the time. One recognizes her openness to be defined by the Not-self so characteristic of her. In the last of the autobiographical trilogy, *Eternity's Sunrise*, she describes this receptive position as the capacity to give up the investment in one's self-image. There is certainly the shift of investment from the known to the unknown aspects of the self. The latter could only become known when symbolized. Within the illusory framework of a belief in reciprocity – in the world's pliability to accept our own bit of the dream and in our pliability to lose the shape – we go on creating new forms and new meanings. These enriched patterns of experiencing are the foundation of feeling alive. In the Milnerian paradigm of psychic growth, we surrender to something that is bigger than we are, with a view to emerging bigger than we were.

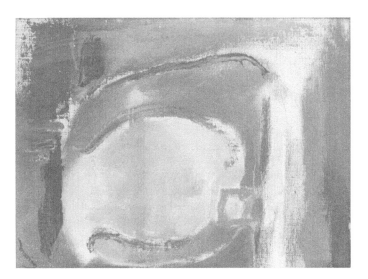

Figure 6.1 'A thought too big for its concept' by Marion Milner

Notes

1 Later in her life when she retired from practicing psychoanalysis, she turned her consulting room into studio (Letley, 2014).
2 Melanie Klein supervised the case of Simon.
3 In 1949–1950, the rift happened between Klein and her disciple, Paula Heimann, following Heimann's paper on countertransference where she argued for the value of the analyst's emotional response.
4 My friend and colleague Nina Chichester-Clark shared with me a thought that perhaps a prerequisite to the pliable mind is that the analyst's *state* of mind must be one of reverie.
5 Winnicott conceptualized this as the illusion of omnipotence (Abram, 1996). Milner and Winnicott were friends and close colleagues. Their minds were two overlapping circles, as Milner (1972) put it pictorially, and the discussion about their conceptual similarities and differences merits a separate paper.
6 These books are fascinating accounts of self-analysis. With *A Life of One's Own* (1934) they form a trilogy.
7 It is a poignant interview conducted by P. King and R. Steiner in 1993. The recording is available in the archive of IOPA.

References

Abram, J. (1996). *The Language of Winnicott*, London: Karnac Books.
Balint, E. (1963). 'On being empty of oneself'. In: *Before I Was I: Psychoanalysis and the Imagination*, Mitchell, J. & Parsons, M. (eds), London: Free Association Books.
Freud, S. (1911). 'Formulations on the Two Principles of Mental Functioning'. In: *The Standard Edition of the Complete Psychological Works of Sigmund Freud*, Volume XII, London: Hogarth Press, 177–258.
Heimann, P. (1949/1950). 'On Countertransference'. In: *About Children and Children-No-Longer: Collected Papers 1942–80*, Tonnesmann, M. (ed.), (1989). London & New York: The New Library of Psychoanalysis, Routledge, 122–137.
Khan, M. (1953). 'On not Being Able to Paint: By Joanna Field. (London: Heinemann, 1950, p. 174)', *International Journal of Psycho-Analysis*, 34: 333–336.
Klauber, J. (1987). '*The Role of Illusion in the Psychoanalytic Cure*'. In: *Illusion and Spontaneity in Psychoanalysis*. London: Free Association Books.
Kleimberg, L. (2012). 'The Illusion of Belief: A Not So Uncommon Misbelief'. In: *Independent Psychoanalysis Today*. Williams, P., Keen, J. & Dermen, S. (eds) (2012). London: Karnac Books, 297–311.
Kleimberg, L. (2018). 'Illusory Dramatization – The Fiction Between Material Truth and Historical Truth', *The Bulletin of the British Psychoanalytical Society*, Vol.54. No.7, September.
Letley, E. (2014). *Marion Milner: The Life*, London: Routledge.
Milner, M. (1934). *A Life of One's Own*, Letley, E. (ed.), London: Routledge.
Milner, M. (1937). *An Experiment in Leisure*, Letley, E. (ed.), London: Routledge.
Milner, M. (1950). *On Not Being Able to Paint*, Letley, E. (ed.). London: reprinted 2010 by Routledge.
Milner, M. (1952a). 'Framed Gap'. In: *The Suppressed Madness of Sane Men*, London & New York: The New Library of Psychoanalysis, Routledge.

Milner, M. (1952b). 'The Role of Illusion in Symbol Formation'. In: *The Suppressed Madness of Sane Men*, London & New York: The New Library of Psychoanalysis, Routledge.

Milner, M. (1972). 'Winnicott: Overlapping Circles and the Two-Way Journey'. In: *Donald Winnicott Today*, Abram, J. (ed.), London & New York: Routledge.

Milner, M. (1987). *Eternity's Sunrise*. Letley, E. (ed.), London: reprinted 2011 by Routledge.

Parsons, M. (2000). 'Creativity, Psychoanalytic and Artistic'. In: *The Dove that Returns, the Dove that Vanishes*, London: Routledge.

Winnicott, D. (1945). 'Primitive Emotional Development'. In: *Through Paediatrics to Psychoanalysis – Collected Papers*, (1958). London: Karnac Books.

Winnicott, D. (1952). 'The role of illusion in symbol formation: References'. In: *The Suppressed Madness of Sane Men*, The New Library of Psychoanalysis, London & New York: Routledge.

Winnicott D.W. (1956). 'Primary Maternal Preoccupation'. In: *The Collected Works of D.W. Winnicott*, Vol.5, Part 2. New York: Oxford University Press, 183–188.

Winnicott D.W. (1971). *Playing and Reality*. London: Tavistock Publications, Ltd.

Santayana, G. (1934). *Little Essays*, Smith, L.P. (ed.), London: Constable.

Segal, H. (1950). 'Some Aspects of the Analysis of a Schizophrenic', *The International Journal of Psychoanalysis*, 31, 268–278.

Segal, H. (1983). 'Some Clinical Implications of Melanie Klein's Work: Emergence from Narcissism', *International Journal of Psycho-Analysis*, 64: 269–276.

Chapter 7

Doing things differently

Pearl King's independence

Ken Robinson

Years ago, when I had recently qualified, I felt stuck with a patient and mentioned him to Pearl. She listened and said: "do something different, dear". She was suggesting, I think, not so much that I *act* differently but that I *be* different, that I give myself the freedom to create a space internally where I could be alongside the patient, both inside and outside the patient's world. Over time it worked. As Pearl puts it in her paper 'On a patient's need to have "bad parents"', "the motto of such patients is, 'If you don't at first succeed, try, try, try again' not 'try another way'" (2005, p. 81).[1] For the analyst to try another way is, at least potentially, to break the mould.

"*Do something different*" may stand as a motto for Pearl's life, personally and professionally. Whether she was helping to found a masonic movement in which men and women worked equally together, or being one of the first to take advantage of civil partnership, or helping Winnicott to foster psychoanalysis in Finland, or creating the 1952 Club with Masud Khan, or establishing and structuring the Archives of the Institute of Psychoanalysis, or with Riccardo Steiner making the Controversial Discussions available after decades of suppression – the list is longer – Pearl did things differently and made a difference.[2]

Such activities show the common concerns of her work in institutions, the consulting room, in supervision and teaching, right across her own life cycle as a psychoanalyst. I shall concentrate on Pearl's clinical and theoretical work, but I'd like, by way of introduction, to recount an incident in her pre-analytic work within an institution, in her own words. It is a telling story about how she used her role in her first job as a Labour Officer in a Royal Ordinance factory in Yorkshire before she had even considered training as a psychoanalyst. She told me how she worked in a section of a munitions factory responsible for making 12,000lb bombs, employing both men and women:

> There was a male officer in charge of the men and there was me in charge of the women. When people came to see me I asked them to sit down. After all I was also a woman and a communist and they were working class: we had a lot in common. But my male companion who was not

DOI: 10.4324/9781003296690-10

secure in himself made them stand up. One morning the women came along to me and complained: "we're short of money again, they've docked our money for being late and it wasn't our fault. The buses were late again. I said: "That's terrible". But I didn't know how to read a wage card, so I said that I would consult the male shop steward and ask him to come round with me so that I could take down all that they were short of and that I would stay over and take the details up to headquarters and get them to do something about it.

When he heard about this the male Labour officer said: "You can't do that sort of thing". I thought he meant go to headquarters, so I said: "Why can't I? It'll save us having a strike here". But that wasn't what was worrying him. He said: "But look how you let these girls behave, letting them sit down, and all that. They should stand up in front of you, like the men do with me". You see what I mean?! This idea of dignity. I threw all that out of course. Later I had a row with the manager of the section, because when he got news of what I was proposing to do he forbade me to enlist the help of the male shop steward. He said he couldn't afford the male worker coming around as the shop steward and helping me. So I said: "Well okay then you'll bring about the possibility of a strike". Then he quickly thought it over and said: "All right, you go ahead".[3]

Pearl never stopped drawing on her "operational research", indeed as one of those who tried to encourage research in the British Society from 1962 through to 1999, she worked on the basis that "there were in fact many parallels between Psycho-Analytic Research and research into the dynamics at work in groups and in institutions" (King 1999, p. 3).

Pearl's account of her role in the Royal Ordinance factory encapsulates so many of the qualities and concerns that she carried over into psychoanalysis and which are evident in her analytic papers. In trying to put herself in the place of the other, so as to understand from the inside another way of seeing and doing things, in her commitment to democracy (which has driven so much of her work within the institutions of psychoanalysis), and in challenging assumptions operating behind the received way of doing things within the factory, she was concerned to free those in the system from the unthinking dead hand of the past. In the consulting room she sought to help her patients to free themselves from the compulsive repetition of patterns of thinking, feeling, behaving and relating, which had been established unconsciously in the past, and were still active in the present of the transference neurosis. For her a good ego structure in the individual was as necessary as a good social structure in an organisation, as she argued at the Stockholm Congress in 1963 when she proposed revised statutes for the IPA.

In a wonderful letter that Pearl wrote to Masud Khan in 1963, she describes the impasse of being trapped in a closed system. As she put it, "there is a period when analysis [with some patients] has to be, and is experienced as a closed system, but to be successful it must eventually be turned into an open one". As she saw it, the analyst's provision of free-floating attention is key to that development. It "is terribly important," she wrote, "as it does protect us from being seduced to a one-pointed vision or [from] collud[ing] in a narrow consideration of a small area of the patient's life to the exclusion of much wider problems". Without it "we lose touch ... with a number of terribly important signposts about what is happening in the patient and which non-verbal (subliminal) problems he is reliving in the analysis situation" (King 1963).

Pearl's paper, 'A patient's unconscious need to have "bad parents"' (1963/ 1974), published for the first time in her *Selected Papers* (2005), is a good example of such a situation and the qualities that she brought to it. It also highlights another quality: her capacity to bring her patients (and her work with them) alive in her reports. It shows how she could respond to the challenge that all patients bring of how to accommodate creatively to questions asked of her understanding and technique.

In this paper Pearl writes of an almost intractable analysis. She came to realise that her patient needed "*to keep intact his myth of unsatisfactory parents*" (p. 73), leaving her with the

> real clinical headache ... of how to discriminate between [on the one hand] the 'return of the traumatic experiences' in the transference in the analytic setting, where the main therapeutic task is the re-assimilation by the stronger adult ego of experiences that were overwhelming to the infantile ego, and [on the other] the exploitation of these traumatic experiences for the maintenance of unconscious and infantile omnipotence. In this latter case, they are not re-assimilated, but perpetuated.
>
> (pp. 68–69)

Pearl offers an important reminder of the many and complex ways in which transference can be used as a resistance.

She describes a man who lived in what felt to him to be a "life-and-death struggle to establish *magical omnipotent control* over [his] objects and [his] environment, as [he] really *believe[d]* that this was the only way to survive and to maintain the safety and coherence of [his] ego" (p. 80, original emphasis). Internally, and unconsciously, he encapsulated "an *idealized 'good' object/parent* (with whom no ordinary human being [could] successfully compete)" (original emphasis), attributing all bad experience to figures in the external world, whether actual parents, friends, work colleagues or his analyst. I shall focus on the analyst. Pearl felt that he sought to control her like a puppet by turning her into a "bad parent". At the same time, he needed her and brought to bear on her a placatory false self to woo her into looking after him. Pearl records how she felt "cut off from access to [her] real spontaneous self" just as the patient denied his own severely impoverished real self (p. 82). *"A placating or false self of the patient confront[ed] this puppet-parent or parent-surrogate and the result [was] a stalemate"* (p. 81, original emphasis). Pearl's paper portrays the ups and downs of this process and the way that she freed herself, through increasing analytic understanding and her use of her affective responses to the patient, to re-find her creativity.

The analysis lasted for ten years in three phases. The patient saw Pearl for three years, broke off the analysis, resumed after a few months for a further four years, broke off again and then after 18 months returned for another 18 months. When he stopped after the second phase Pearl "was far from satisfied with the results". One way in which she did something different was in agreeing to see the patient first once a fortnight and then weekly in the chair as a sort of postscript. This postscript began as a "'supervision' of his analytic work with himself". He told her that when he lay on the couch it did not feel like his real self lying there so he had "escaped taking part in his analysis". It seemed to Pearl that "he used his new position in space and the change in his relation to [her] as symbolic of a *different him* making a relationship to a *different me*". The patient "re-lived crucial phases of his analysis, from a different viewpoint" (p.74). Pearl found that, with the benefit of this different viewpoint, he could in time relinquish his omnipotent "myth of unsatisfactory parents" which had kept them unreal and protected him both from his fears of harming them in phantasy and reality, and from his own vulnerability. He acknowledged that Pearl had survived, had not written him off and had perceived "the screaming child" in him and now he could recognise, humbly and sadly, that his mother too had seen it (pp. 77–78).

As a footnote, it is interesting to note that Pearl had presented her paper to a Scientific Meeting of the British Psycho-Analytical Society in March 1963 and again, in the same year, at the pre-Congress in London before the IPA Congress itself in Stockholm. In the London audience was Jacques Lacan, who asked her for a copy of her paper. Lacan's interest was kindled by her analysis of the transference as an illusion. In fact, he was so struck by it that he devoted a whole session of Seminar XII to her paper on 3 February 1965. (Perhaps he was also struck by Pearl with whom he danced: she was, he said, "fort active et fort aigue, fort intelligente … et après tout, non sans quelque audace" (Lacan 1965).) His admiration is even more striking because there are such fundamental differences between his and her thinking, as his seminar shows.

Pearl revised the paper in 1974 as a tribute to Paula Heimann for her 75th birthday. In her summary of the case, she is at pains to stress the importance of being able to use her own affective responses, following the example of Heimann who was for Pearl a figure who herself did something different. Pearl started her paper by remembering an experience with Heimann to which she was fond of referring. It had happened when she was in training in the late 1940s:

She was taking a seminar on Freud's Papers on Technique, and she ... asked me to summarize the main points in his paper 'Recommendations to Physicians practising Psycho-analysis'. When I came to the recommendation that analysts should take as a model, "the surgeon, who puts aside all his own feelings, including that of human sympathy, and concentrates his mind on one single purpose, that of performing the operation as skilfully as possible" (Freud, 1912), Paula Heimann to my surprise, strongly disagreed with Freud's emphatic recommendation. She formulated her point of view later in her paper entitled 'On Counter-transference', which she read in 1949 ... In this paper she stated, "My thesis is that the analyst's emotional response to his patient within the analytical situation represents one of the most important tools for his work. The analyst's counter-transference is an instrument of research into the patient's unconscious".

(p. 67)

Notwithstanding that we know more now about the status of Freud's so-called "recommendations" and the centrality of empathy in his theory and practice, to Pearl and her fellow students, Heimann had, in Pearl's words,

given sanction to make use of a whole range of our affective capacities, which we had previously considered should be taboo. It was now possible to draw on these sources of data not only to help discover how our patients were using us, but also to explore the subtle distortions that take place in the interplay between phantasy and reality, delusion, and despair, as patients attempt to come to terms with both their good and bad experiences with their actual parents and the psychic elaborations of these experiences.

(p. 68)

Later Pearl came across Otto Fenichel's *Problems of Psychoanalytic Technique* and underlined passages that deal with how "fear of the countertransference may lead an analyst to the suppression of all human freedom in his own reactions to patients", and how "the patient should always be able to rely upon the 'humanness' of the analyst" (Fenichel 1941, p. 74), a point that Heimann revisited in her wonderful 1978 paper 'On the necessity for the analyst to be natural with his patient'.

Pearl returned to the theme of countertransference in 1978 in her acclaimed and perhaps most important paper, 'The affective response of the analyst to the patient's communications', which is a model of clarity in the often-confusing literature on countertransference. Such clarity of definition, often informed by the history of a given term, is characteristic of Pearl's work. (She admired Joseph Sandler's work with the 'Hampstead Index' project [King, 1999, p. 5].) Her paper contains much about her distinctive clinical technique.

There was a danger (and still is) that the term "countertransference" would cover indiscriminately all the analyst's feelings in the transference-counter-transference field. Pearl distinguishes three types of reaction to the patient in the analyst. First, she turns to the original meaning of the term "counter-transference" as, technically, a pathological phenomenon. Second, she defines the affective response of the analyst as

> the perception by the analyst of feelings and moods, unrelated to his personal life, and which may even feel alien to his normal way of react-ing, but which when placed in the context of the patient's material and the psychoanalytic setting, illumine and render meaning to those trans-ference phenomena that are in the process of being experienced, con-sciously or unconsciously, by the patient.
>
> (p. 91)

Finally, in a characteristically straightforward way, she stresses that not all the analyst's affective responses should be understood in relation to transference or countertransference. Some will be the ordinary human reactions of the analyst as one human being to another human being who is in mental pain and asking for help. She confines "countertransference" to its original mean-ing. Affective self-awareness in the analyst needs, she believes (building on Heimann), to be combined with a capacity for taking up a position of neu-trality or "non-attachment" – she borrows the concept from Eastern philoso-phy – which allows the analyst to "*monitor*" her affective responses without discharging them (p. 96, original emphasis). She had already argued in her contribution to a panel discussion on 'Curative factors in psychoanalysis' (1962) that this attitude "is a crucial factor in the curative process, and one of our main therapeutic tools" (p. 58). It makes it possible for the analyst to play those roles required unconsciously of her by the patient in the playground of the transference, on the "psychological stage" of the analytic relationship, so as to "become aware of what or whom [she is] being made into or treated as, and why" (p. 56). And it involves *waiting* "without preconceptions for what-ever our patients communicate to us, whether through words, gestures, tones of voice, images, silences or facial expressions", as well as "*monitoring* our own affective responses to what is going on both between ourselves and our patients, and intrapsychically *within* our patients" (pp. 96–97). Anyone familiar with Ella Sharpe's work, especially her lectures on technique (1930–31) and her 'Memorandum on technique' in the Controversial Discussions (King & Steiner 1991, pp. 639–647), will hear Pearl's indebtedness to Sharpe's line of independent thinking, especially on transference and the analyst's adaptation to each patient as unique, as well as to Heimann's. Pearl took from both, and what she inherited she made distinctively her own.

Pearl recognised that whilst the analyst's response to the patient's unac-knowledged affects is important in all analyses, it is particularly important in the realm of the pre-verbal, with patients "whose pre-verbal experiences were traumatic and in whom the consequent damage was in part the result of the affective responses of the patient's psychologically disturbed mother" (p. 90). She emphasised the importance of analysts using their affective responses with these patients, who had suffered problems in their primary affective development, paying tribute to the contributions of Middlemore, Winnicott and Bowlby, whose work with infants emphasised the importance of the mother's affective response to the child and the child's vulnerability to the mother's psychopathology.

> If the patient's mother was psychologically very disturbed during the early infancy of her child … using the infant for the gratification of her own neurotic needs and as a receptacle for her unwanted impulses and affects, the infant's affective development would be seriously distorted, his basic trust precarious, and his capacity to relate to objects inhibited by fear of 'invasion' by the other person. Thus, instead of contributing progressively to the maintenance of the infant's protective shield (Freud, 1920), her psychopathology would have resulted in the protective shield being cumulatively damaged (Khan, 1963) and consequently her infant's sense of himself as a person with a viable ego boundary would also have been damaged.
>
> (p. 89)

Pearl was alive to the difficulty that analysts face working with their affective responses to such patients, including the obstacles within the analyst, particularly the analyst in training, to being able to use them. Where the feelings evoked in the analyst are ego-syntonic it might be difficult to appreciate their transference significance, and if they are ego-alien it might be difficult to accept them.

The developmental point of view (which, she saw as also under threat from the slippage away from basic Freudian concepts) is central to Pearl's achievement. It is evident from her earliest papers to her last; from her work with a four-year-old boy to her thinking about older age. In 'Change: the psychoanalysis of a four-year-old boy and its follow-up', which she refined over more than 50 years (1951, 1953, 2003), Pearl wrote a paper which is unique in the psychoanalytic literature, for it records the history of her work with a patient, Philip, referred to her by Winnicott, with whom she stayed in touch for over 50 years, from four-year-old boy through his troubled adolescence to her final years. The patient himself provided a postscript to her paper in his middle age when it was published in her *Selected Papers*. Although Philip was in formal treatment with her only as a child and then briefly as an adolescent, her paper describes the way that beyond this work she sent him presents and cards at Christmas to create a framework within which each had the other in mind and within which he could continue to grow. Throughout her papers there is a sense of patients being impelled by a developmental imperative towards finding relief from their mental pain through psycho-analysis. It is a view that she shared particularly with Anna Freud and Win-nicott. In Pearl's terms "psychoanalytical theory and technique is based on the hypothesis that man has within himself ... a life-promoting force that operates not only biologically but intrapsychically in each individual, which, given reasonably stable and good maturational and environmental conditions, will be stronger than any disintegrative forces at work". Whatever her parti-cular technical emphasis with different patients, the common factor is always her ability to allow the patient to use her not simply in the transference but as a developmental object, in the sense that she provided for the patient an environment in which transference could be explored and understood as part of a technique which is directed towards – she quotes her analyst Rickman – the "removal of the major obstacles to the action of the integrative processes which operate within every living organism, so that these integrative processes will in the end get the upper hand without further analytical aid" (p. 54). This was Pearl in 1962 setting out her own version of how the analyst served the patient's development. She was quoting Rickman from 1950, but the '60s was a period in which there was fresh emphasis on the topic, with, for example, Winnicott and Anna Freud in England and Loewald in the United States (Winnicott 1962; Anna Freud 1965; and Loewald 1960). As so often, there is here a sense of Pearl being engaged in emerging international concerns.

Pearl was a pioneer, along with Hanna Segal, in the discussion of the psy-choanalysis of patients in their later years, writing several ground-breaking papers. I say 'pioneer in the discussion of' because some analysts were treat-ing older-age patients but not admitting to it. There was a tendency, following Freud, to regard patients beyond 40 as unsuitable for analysis, at least offi-cially, but Pearl was not one to stay quiet. Here again she was doing some-thing different. She had been in a post-qualification clinical seminar with Hanna Segal from around 1950 (along with, amongst others, Harold Bridger and Elliot Jaques) and she felt encouraged by the seminar to take on a 63 year-old woman for analysis. Segal had read a short paper on the analysis of an old man at the Paris Congress in 1957 and Pearl felt that she had learnt a lot from her way of working and thinking about a patient. Older-age patients became an important theme in her own work. She gave her first paper touching on middle and older age in 1972 at the English Speaking Conference and her first paper devoted to old age the following year to the Society for Analytical Psychology. And then in 1979 she delivered the first ever full-length paper on middle-aged or older patients to an IPA Congress. She con-tinued to write about old age until 2003. Because in general Pearl had taken an interest in patients who suffered early, pre-genital, developmental failure or arrest, she had become especially concerned with narcissistic problems and techniques appropriate to their treatment. This is why she found the ideas of Winnicott, Milner and Kohut so germane. She extended this interest in narcissism into her work on later years. Her first discussion of old age in 1972 was significantly part of a paper on 'Sexuality and the narcissistic character' (1972). The vicissitudes of narcissism in old age became one of her central concerns. I shall focus on her 1979 Congress paper: 'The life cycle as indicated by the nature of the transference in the psychoanalysis of the middle-aged and elderly' (1980), which describes some of the narcissistic vulnerabilities that might prompt patients to seek help: the fear of the loss of or diminution in sexual potency; the threat of retirement; redundancy or displacement by younger colleagues; anxieties in marital relationships when children have left home; ageing, illness and dependency; the inevitability of death.

Pearl lays out some fundamental guidelines.

> Middle-aged and elderly patients may be functioning within a number of different time-scales. These may include a chronological time-scale, a psychological one, and a biological one, alongside the time-scale of unconscious processes, which are paradoxically, timeless. An understanding of the time-scale within which an elderly patient is currently functioning in the analytic session gives the analyst an important key to the understanding of transference phenomena in such patients. The analyst can be experienced in the transference as any significant figure from the elderly patient's past, sometimes covering a span of five generations, and for any of these transference figures the roles may be reversed.
>
> (1980, p. 138)

In her experience the developmental phases that most often need to be worked through in the transference of middle-aged and older patients are those of puberty and adolescence, the analyst being experienced (whatever his actual age) as significant adults from those phases of the patient's life cycle. One of her clinical examples is the 63-year-old patient whom she had taken to the seminar with Segal – a woman who had so narcissistically invested her professional role as the head of a children's home that it had become the main source of her self-esteem and identity. She did not enjoy an adequate image of herself apart from her role, and she had no appropriate sense of ontological security; retirement, therefore, threatened her with collapse.

Pearl's interest in old age was not confined to thinking about patients. In 'On being a psychoanalyst – integrity and vulnerability in psychoanalytic organisations' (1989) and again in 2002 in 'On becoming an ageing psychoanalyst' she charts the developmental tasks of the analyst as she establishes and re-establishes her identity in the progression from candidate to Associate Member, Member, Training Analyst, and retirement. She recognises that the analyst, no less than her 63-year-old patient, may suffer if she uses her role, her patients and her professional activities as the main source of her worth and identity, making it difficult to retire without suffering considerable instability.

For all that Pearl was a pioneer and did things differently, she was also rooted in a tradition that she defended fiercely, a Freudian and Independent tradition. She dedicated her *Selected Papers* (2005) to her "teachers and colleagues … who passed on to [her] their knowledge and understanding of how to practise psychoanalysis" including John Rickman, Sylvia Payne, Marion Milner, Michael Balint, Paula Heimann and Donald Winnicott (p. viii). She came to believe that there was a danger that British psychoanalysis was losing its way by making the affective relationship between analyst and analysand the focus of analysis, reducing analysis to a sort of relational therapy which substituted for transference as Freud understood it. In this relational therapy, therapist and patient concentrated on their "here and now" relationship shorn of its historical antecedents, whereas transference proper is living history, the past alive in the present through repetition in the here and now of the transference neurosis. She had first voiced this in 1992 at the English Speaking Conference in London. In 1996 she addressed her concerns more fully in a fine polemic paper, 'What has happened to psychoanalysis in the British Society?', presented to the 1952 Club. With the loss of the historical dimension to transference, she argued, other interlocking clinical concepts (free association, free floating attention, the repetition compulsion, and so on) were also endangered. Analysts of different persuasions had voiced similar worries for some time. Melanie Klein was already complaining of "here and now" analysis in her unpublished notes on technique (Bott Spillius 2004), Limentani (1986) addressed it in his Presidential address to the IPA in 1985, and later André Green would warn of it in his contribution to the celebrations for Pearl's 80th birthday (Steiner & Johns 2001). But within current British psychoanalysis it fell to Pearl to raise it, much as she voiced the complaints of munitions workers all those years ago or later argued, for example, for the rights of Associate Members. It took strength and courage to do so.

Pearl began 'What has happened to psychoanalysis in the British Society?' with a quotation from Marjorie Brierley and ended with one from Sylvia Payne, both from the Controversial Discussions. These two figures would, of course, become leading members of the Middle Group, later the Independent Group, and Pearl was their heir, as she was also Paula Heimann's and Ella Sharpe's. Brierley had set out the fundamental question to be debated in the Controversial Discussions: "Is a theory of mental development in terms of infantile object relationships compatible with a theory in terms of instinct vicissitudes?" and she answered in the affirmative citing Freud's most recent definition of instinct in support of her opinion: "An instinct may be described as having a source, an object and an aim" (King 2004, p. 123). Pearl worked out, independently, her own affirmative answer, just as her analyst John Rickman had done. (He had been analysed by Freud, Ferenczi and Klein and left the Kleinian group during her analysis with him.) But she was worried about a tendency that had crept in "to work in terms of the analysis of the vicissitudes of the current Object relationships of the patient and the analyst … with little reference to the vicissitudes of instincts, indicating that perhaps the two theories have not proved compatible, but that one theory has replaced the other" (King 2004, p. 124). She reminded her colleagues that, as Payne had put it:

> The basic conceptions of Psychoanalysis are: 1) The concept of a dynamic psychology 2) The existence of the Unconscious 3) The theory of instincts and of repression 4) Infantile sexuality 5) The dynamic of the transference.

And she continued:

> This is our heritage. If we want to continue to call ourselves Psycho-analysts, those of us who value this heritage and what we have learnt from Freud, have an obligation to understand and to explain his con-tributions to our colleagues, and especially to those who come after us.
>
> (King 2004, p. 124)

Her quotations from Brierley and Payne lead us to Pearl the historian and archivist, to her many papers on the history of British psychoanalysis, in which she increasingly enjoyed that she herself was a piece of living history. In parti-cular, they lead to her magnificent edition, with Riccardo Steiner, of the Discus-sions. Nowhere had she been more determined to do things differently. We all know the scholarship of the edition: I'd like to emphasise what an achievement it was to get the Discussions into print given the trauma of the Discussions. The publication history of the Discussions is witness to how difficult it has been to lift the silence around them. The possibility of publication was first and briefly mooted within the British Society in 1954 and came to nothing. It was another 12 years before Joseph Sandler, as editor of the Bulletin, was granted permission to include papers in the Bulletin. When she heard about his plans, Sylvia Payne contacted the then President, Donald Winnicott, to argue strenuously against Sandler's plan. Sandler went ahead but, after two Bulletins, in 1967 further pub-lication was suspended after Paula Heimann objected. Publication was discussed again in 1970 and 1971, once more to no avail. It was not until 1985 that a limited typescript edition was completed on Pearl's initiative. In 1991 this became pub-licly available in revised form in Pearl's and Riccardo's magnificent edition. They broke a silence of virtually four decades – a silence that, I think, speaks of a fear of opening old wounds and retraumatising the Society (Robinson 2015). The book's epigraph speaks loudly of Pearl: "If we do not learn from history we are doomed to repeat it."

Finally, how did Pearl face the challenges of old age and retirement? There is a clue in the title of a paper revised in 2003 when she was 85: "in age I bud again"! She turned to research and writing, and at last collecting some of her papers together for publication, after the efforts of colleagues in the past to help had come to nothing, though Pearl remained grateful to them: Jennifer

Johns, Bernard Barnett and Susan Budd. It is a shame that we did not manage to pull together a planned collection of her papers on the history of British psychoanalysis. Before her final illness she phoned me rather excitedly: she had decided to take up cello, what did I think?!

When we gathered Pearl's papers and decided which to include in her selected papers, *Time Present and Time Past*, Pearl became anxious about whether they had stood the test of time. Over a period of two years or so we read and talked through each one with an eye to the light that it might shed on past and current cases – she was still engaged in a little supervision – and Pearl became sure that they were still valuable and worth revising where necessary, or even added to.

By way of summary it is fitting, in this book about Independent women analysts, to end with a more general insight into what it meant for Pearl to practise as an Independent. In one of her many unpublished notes she listed "Points that strike me re the Technique of the British School (Independents)" (2003):

1   Great concern with the influence of the repressed UCS.
2   Importance of patient as a 'person'.
3   While keeping firmly to a base line in technique, they are flexible enough to see the subtle individual differences and complexities of each patient.
4   They do not feel forced to take up either all positive or all negative aspects of a patient's material, but being centrally aware of conflicts and ambivalence.
5   They stress the importance of reconstruction (re-living) in analysis of childhood/adolescent, as well as infantile experiences, without imposing preconceived ideas or theoretical constructions on the order or timing of them.
6   The concept of transference as the 'transfer' or projection of various people in various roles, experienced in the past, onto the Analyst, alongside the gradual perception of the discrepancy, and the diminution of paranoid mechanisms.
7   Analytic work consists in discovering what/who these roles refer to, to what developmental stages they are relevant, what conflicts are involved, what affects are attached to them, what defences are being used and what part of the structural apparatus (id, ego, or super ego) is predominantly involved.
8   A three-pronged approach to understanding the material of patients before analysts can consider that they have adequately worked through the influence of 'Transference'. This means covering

   i   the infantile/childhood material
   ii   current life material and
   iii the relationship with the analyst.

9   The order may differ with different patients.

In her 1963 letter to Khan, Pearl also commented not only on free-floating attention but on the underlying "perception of a clinical process in the analyst ... [a] perception [that] is held and understood and then returned plus understanding to the patient ... Communication has to take place from the analyst to the patient of the skill of making sense of chaotic and threatening experiences". She was describing analytic listening. For the cover of her *Selected Papers*, she selected her self-portrait as an owl, who was, as she put it at the launch of the book's publication in 2005, "a very serious Owl, ... respectful of Freud and Psychoanalysis". After publication she was delighted when a colleague directed her to the rhyme, "A wise old owl" (Opie & Opie 1997, p. 403), which she quoted at the launch of her *Selected Papers*, and which encapsulates the wisdom that comes with years of experience as an analyst. As a wise old analyst, she saw more and spoke less, and the quieter she became the more she heard.

Notes

1 All references to and quotations from Pearl King's work are from this edition of her *Selected Papers*, unless otherwise stated.
2 Although this is a paper about Pearl King's clinical and theoretical contributions, I would like to indicate briefly something of her service to the institutions of psychoanalysis. She held many offices, among them Secretary of the British Psychoanalytical Society (BPAS) (1956–58), Honorary Secretary of the International Psychoanalytical Association (1957–61), Secretary of the EPF (1953–1967) and Deputy President of the BPAS (1964–66). In 1982 she became the first president of the BPAS not to have been trained as a doctor, retiring in 1984 to become its Honorary Archivist until 1994.
3 Personal communication. Little (1993) gives a slightly different version of this story.

References

Bott Spillius, E. (2004). 'Melanie Klein Revisited: Her Unpublished Thoughts on Technique'. *Bulletin of the British Psychoanalytical Society.* 40(iv): 13–28.
Fenichel, O. (1941). *Problems of Psychoanalytic Technique.* New York: The Psychoanalytic Quarterly. King's copy is dated September 1951.
Freud, A. (1965). 'Normality and Pathology in Childhood: Assessments of Development'. In: *The Writings of Anna Freud*, VI. New York: International Universities Press.
Green, A. (2001). 'The Passion of History Confronted with the Failure of Psychoanalytic Historical Thinking'. In: *Within Time and Beyond Time: A Festschrift for Pearl King*, Steiner, R. & Johns, J. (eds), London: Karnac Books.
Heimann, P. (1950). 'On Counter-transference', *International Journal of Psycho-Analysis*, 31: 81–84.
Heimann, P. (1978). 'On the Necessity for the Analyst to be Natural With His Patient'. In: Tonnesmann, M. (ed.) (1989). *About Children and Children-No-Longer. Collected Papers 1942–1980*, London: Routledge.
King, P.H.M. (1947–48). 'Task Perception and Inter-personal Relations in Industrial Training, Parts I and II'. *Human Relations.* 1: 121–142 and 373–412.

King, P.H.M. (1963). *Letter to Masud Khan*, 11 July 1963, from a copy in the author's possession.

King, P.H.M. & Steiner, R. (eds) (1991). *The Freud-Klein Controversies 1941–1945*. The New Library of Psychoanalysis. London: The Institute of Psychoanalysis and Routledge.

King, P.H.M. ([1996] 2004). 'What Has Happened to Psychoanalysis in the British Society?' In: *Who Owns Psychoanalysis?* Casement, A. (ed.), London: Karnac Books.

King, P.H.M. (1999). *Can We Learn From Our History.* Unpublished.

King, P.H.M. (2005). *Time Present and Time Past: Selected Papers of Pearl King.* London: Karnac Books.

Lacan, J. (1965). *Seminaire XII: Problèmes cruciaux pur la psychanalyse*, 3 February 1965. Unpublished stenotype, École Lacanienne de Psychanalyse.

Limentani, A. (1986). 'Presidential Address Variations on Some Themes', *International Journal of Psychoanalysis* 67: 235–243.

Little, G. (1993). *The English Analyst.* Unpublished.

Loewald, H.W. (1960). 'On the Therapeutic Action of Psycho-Analysis'. *International Journal of Psycho-Analysis*, 41: 16–33.

Opie, I. & Opie, P. (1997). *The Oxford Dictionary of Nursery Rhymes.* 2nd edn. Oxford: Oxford University Press.

Robinson, K. (2015). 'Remembering, Repeating and Working Through: The Impact of the Controversial Discussions', *British Journal of Psychotherapy*, 31(1): 1–151.

Rickman, J. (1950). 'On the Criteria for the Termination of an Analysis'. *International Journal of Psycho-Analysis*, 31: 200–201. Reprinted in *Selected Contributions to Psycho-Analysis.* London: International Psycho-Analytical Library and Hogarth Press, 1957.

Steiner, R. & Johns, J. (eds) (2001). *Within Time and Beyond Time: A Festschrift for Pearl King.* London: Karnac Books.

Winnicott, D.W. (1962). 'The Development of the Capacity for Concern'. In: *Collected Works of D.W. Winnicott*, Vol. 6, (2016), Oxford: Oxford University Press, 351–356.

Chapter 8

Nina Coltart's colourful ways of listening

Paola Somaini

In her interview with Antony Molino, Nina Coltart describes herself with humour as "the most independent representative of the Independent Group" (Molino 1997, 177).

In this paper I would like to reflect on my experience of reading and encountering Coltart. I intend to sketch my own portrait of this analyst whom I think truly stands out for her originality and the sense of adventure and passion with which she embraced both her work and life.

Reading Coltart is a unique experience. It feels like going on a journey with her. She thought of herself as an "armchair traveller" and, as a reader, one feels taken on by her on her analytic journeys[1], invited into her world and into a friendly and personal relationship with her. Her humorous and no-nonsense conversational style is immediately intimate. The impression is of meeting a real person, emotionally present and almost alive on the page in flesh and blood. Many have remarked on her gift for friendship and her capacity to facilitate an almost immediate, vital and enthusiastic rapport with another human being.[2] Like Winnicott, she is one of those writers who work out their thoughts in the process of writing, so one ends up inside her own process of thinking while her ideas are taking shape. As Coltart herself says,

> I have to say that my sense of writing as something central and confirming is one I get when I am actually writing, or when I become aware that I am writing … [it] makes me aware of a deeper level, perhaps an unconscious level, of thinking – so it's been very valuable to me. It's helped shape up quite a lot of my ideas.
>
> (Molino 1997, 183)

Coltart comes across as a brave, bold, original, at times irreverent analyst, with an almost revolutionary and challenging voice. It is her humanity[3] and openness that I think is particularly poignant and moving for the reader. She puts her own personality centre stage in a way that I find unique and at times challenging. Unusually for an analyst, she talks about her own life and history – her own suffering and "unhealed wounds" – so her pain and vulnerability are very palpable (Molino 1997,

DOI: 10.4324/9781003296690-11

195). I believe that it is this authenticity – this uncompromising freedom to be her own person – that is at the core of her analytic identity.

Coltart is certainly not interested in hiding or holding back,

> When one writes in the way I do, which, when it is not a case history, is mainly free-associative thoughts on the experiences, and style of a working therapist, one cannot help but give quite a detailed picture of oneself. In fact, it is important not to be afraid of doing so. The work of therapy is so intensely personal and, I believe, so influenced both in process and in outcome by who one is that to try to shrink into a corner or pretend that one is not intimately involved in every step on the way is a sort of false humility and adds nothing to enhance the readability of what one is trying to express.
>
> (Coltart 1996, 166)

Figure 8.1 Portrait of Nina Coltart by Paola Somaini

In this paper I would like to focus on some aspects of Coltart's analytic presence and listening that I find most original and challenging. I will start with a drawing of my own.

Firstly, a portrait through a blind drawing: the value of enjoyment

I had the impulse to draw Coltart. I made the sketch above from a portrait picture which I found in her last book, *The Baby and the Bathwater* (1996).

I see Nina Coltart's writing as her authentic and agile gesturing towards the other; a way of offering herself to be used, absorbed, read and above all enjoyed. This sketch is my own personal response to this gesturing with something that I enjoy – drawing and painting. Coltart indeed gives great importance to the need to enjoy our work, to find a place for humour and enjoyment in our daily analytic practices.

I have used a sketching technique called 'blind drawing' by which I only look at the subject of my drawing and never look at what my hand holding the pencil is doing on the piece of paper. So I did this drawing by looking and focusing only on the picture of Coltart whilst allowing my hand and pencil to move freely on paper. I have recently discovered this technique in a book entitled, *You Will Be Able to Draw by the End of This Book* by Jake Spicer (2017). Well, I have not got to the end of the book and in fact not even gone beyond page four! The point is that I am thoroughly enjoying myself, and am intrigued by this technique that leads to a process of discovery that is free and creative.

I believe that this drawing technique captures something of the quality of the analytic encounter, where we embark on a process where we are on some level blind yet our focus (Coltart would say our 'Bare Attention') through all our senses – our eyes, our heart, our body (Coltart would also include our spirit) – is both a deep internal focus on our own selves and an intense focus towards the other who is at the centre of our receptive curiosity.

I am drawing in the dark and yet at the same time my eyes are intensely focused on the other. I postulate that by introducing a disconnection between my eyes and my hand I am bypassing my rational and conscious self – perhaps I am sedating my critical Super Ego? – and instead creating the possibility for a deeper and more spontaneous connection with the subject of my drawing. It is this that facilitates a more creative drawing. We could say that this technique and the 'squiggle game'[4] have similar origins in that they both find a way of emerging more directly and immediately from our true self and are thus closer to the unconscious. The drawings sort of pop up! I am struck by the certainty with which my hand moves on the piece of paper, as if the hand *knows* what she is doing. I wonder if the true self has found a way of expressing itself and that is why the drawings to me feel beautiful, truthful and always meaningful. Is this spontaneity that brings enjoyment? The joy of the true self who has found a way of expressing itself, like a child who is engrossed in playing and is enjoying playing itself?[5] Sometimes the drawings that emerge are obscure. They always stimulate a state of reverie in me; sometimes stories come to mind as if emerging directly from the drawings themselves.[6]

The artist Paul Klee described this kind of line that is free to go where it will, for movement's sake and in its own time, as the most active and authentic. As he memorably put it, "The principal and active line [that] develops freely ... goes out for a walk so to speak, aimlessly for the sake of the walk" (Klee 1921/1961, 105).[7]

The Coltart that emerges from this 'blind drawing' is not obscure. She is firmly grounded, with an imposing body, eyes of different size – one seems to be closer than the other, the lenses of the glasses are also different in size; perhaps they put different things into focus – and a mouth that is reaching down towards the heart. Her gaze conveys to me something warm and caring and a great deal of stillness. Overall, I see a face that has its own harmony yet whose single features stand out in their unique and different ways.

Coltart stresses that in order to Survive-with-Enjoyment[8] as a psychoanalyst, one does not just need a good analyst or good supervisors, or to attend the right conferences, one also needs a garden to tend: "in an ideal world, all psychotherapists would have a garden" (1993b, 98). That is, one must seek that "primitive sort of satisfaction" the body feels when "it uses all one's muscles" with the aim of reaching "alertness in one's very perception as well as one's muscles". And then she adds, "But perhaps even more than the body, the spirit, in a job as absorbing and demanding as ours, needs stimulation, change, refreshment, expansion". As analysts we need to feed our spirit – and so attain psychic nourishment – from activities beyond the consulting room and find ways to expand our psychoanalytic selves.

By the end of this paper, I will add colour to this sketch as I hope that my thoughts about Coltart will add substance to her analytic persona and her ideas.

A special atmosphere: bare and loving attention

Coltart's clinical work takes place in a special atmosphere. In the words of her analysand, Muriel Mitcheson Brown,

> From the start, analysis with Nina was a totally different experience: she made it seem natural, desirable, and above all, full of potential for change ... a fascinating mix of a very correct, classical approach to technique and an intensely real personal relationship ... a rare mix of rigour and spontaneity.
>
> (Mitcheson Brown 2011, 11–26)

Coltart sums up her analytic presence under the concept of Bare Attention, which is the "scaffolding of everything else we do" (Coltart 1993a, 181). It is the activity of continuously observing, watching, listening and feeling in silence. It is this kind of Attention that is the source of creativity in analysis. Amedei and Boffito point out that in choosing "evenly hovering attention" over "evenly suspended attention", Coltart is putting emphasis on the work and investment required by the analyst:

> [T]he difference lies precisely in the application of the will and in a certain sense, of creativity. Any object that is light enough can remain suspended, but hovering requires an effort, a degree of intentionality, and even a certain amount of playfulness.
>
> (Amedei and Boffito 2011, 155)

> Bare attention has a sort of purity about it. It's not a cluttered concept. It's that you simply become better, as any good analyst knows, at concentrating more and more directly, more purely, on what's going on in a session. You come to concentrate more and more fully on this person who is with you, here and now, and on what it is they experience with you: to the point that many sessions become similar to meditations.
>
> (Molino 1997, 205)

It is a form of concentration that is grounded within ourselves, in our hearts and our bodies: it is "ultimately a kind of love", a muscle that needs to be continuously worked on. Love in the sense of *agape* – not falling in love – is a capacity that can be learnt; its qualities are "patience, endurance, humour, kindness and courage" (Coltart 1993a, 119).[9]

A seminar by Michael Parsons during my training entitled 'Listening to Ourselves Listening to Others' comes to mind. Thinking about it now, I believe that this seminar could be seen as a series of tasks aimed at helping us with exercising and keeping toned our 'attention muscle' and thus entering into a deeper focus on ourselves and our surroundings.

In the seminar, we read poems aloud and reflected on our experience of letting the poems get inside ourselves. We had to pay careful attention to what they evoked in us, to how the words and their sounds made us feel from inside. We did a 'Show and Tell' in which we all brought to the seminar three objects that had a special value to us. We sat around in a circle and put the objects on the ground at the centre of the circle. We all immediately felt that these objects were very precious; our shared attention and focus put them under a special light. We treated them with care, we asked the owner permission to touch and hold them in our hands. The atmosphere in the seminar became intense, charged, almost sacred. Parsons invited us to think about our patients as bringing things to us, to think about every session as an offering. How are we going to respond to these offerings? Would we treat them with care, attention, wonder?

The third and final task was an exercise in listening to the night. We had to sit in the dark, ideally in the countryside and as much as possible in an open space, far away from light and simply sit there for at least one hour (or maybe it was only half an hour?). I remember how hard it was for me to sit in this silent and dark night. I struggled to quieten my mind, I felt vulnerable, scared and assaulted by paranoid thoughts. When I gradually calmed down, I noticed how I brought the attention onto myself. I felt the air touching my skin, a slightly warm yet also fresh sensation. Things seemed very still, the silence felt deeper and I could hear and feel the air around me and inside me. My focus shifted onto my breathing. I remember thinking of being in labour; when the pain and the contractions intensified it felt reassuring to focus deeply on my own breathing and just think about breathing in and breathing out. I noticed that my eyes were gradually able to 'see' more; the dark was not all black. I started looking at the grass and I remember thinking that I could see it very clearly. In fact, I had never looked at it so carefully in my entire life.[10] I imagined little bugs – or maybe I could see/feel them? – there was so much life and activity going on in the grass. My sense of smell also became heightened. I remember thinking that I was smelling the humidity in the air and what an intense and distinct smell it was. Time didn't seem to matter, until towards the end when I felt cold and wanted to go back inside. I have never meditated but simply writing this down makes me think that this exercise brought me close to the practice of meditation.

Coltart was an analyst and also a Buddhist and practised meditation for over 30 years. She was thus exercising this 'attention muscle' on a daily basis in her consulting room, and in her meditation practice. I believe that her capacity to sustain this type of intensely focused attention allows her to create the deepest atmosphere in which analysis can take place (Coltart 1996, 176). It is this atmosphere that facilitates what she calls a shift into "fifth gear ... when our listening ear seems to be directly connected with our tongue and speech" and our mind reaches a state of creative reverie through a "specially sensitive deployment of (a) blend of identification, imagination and intuition" (Coltart 1993a, 150). This, I believe, is the true self of the analyst, who is speaking in a deeply felt way that is creative and spontaneous. Such moments or passages of time elicit a deep sense of fulfilment and enjoyment in the analyst.

Coltart's listening is both receptive and alert, respectful of the patient's needs and defences including, perhaps especially, the need for silence. Silent patients, she says, "need, above all, that we ourselves should be silent partners" (Coltart 1993a, 79–94). In a silent analysis both participants are listening and studying each other; it is a two-way-process, "the patient is studying the analyst's silence with just as much keenness as the analyst is studying his".[11]

Coltart seems to have had, like Bion, a special capacity for silence.[12] Coltart's seminars with Bion during her training had a profound impact on her,

Dr Bion was a distinguished and in some ways an awe-inspiring analyst. He was one of the first analysts to teach the use and value of silence, and he could be very intimidating in his way of doing it. He would come into a student seminar and sit down and stare at us in silence ... He tended to provoke anxiety and the seminar frequently turned into something rather more like a therapeutic group. And he would then interpret how we were handling the experience.

(Coltart 1993a, 192–193)

She found Bion's unorthodox style unnerving and intimidating, even traumatic, though she also felt that it was "brilliant teaching" which left a mark on her that she has never forgotten. It is curious that similar comments have been made about Coltart, who was also said to inspire awe and have a powerful and commanding presence, alongside a private and silent side of her personality.[13]

As we shall see later, this quietness of mind does not mean emotional dullness. On the contrary, this Bare Attention is akin to internal stillness, a "sort of observatory in our own minds" that provides a firm ground especially at times of heated emotional storms (Coltart 1993a, 186). This loving attention is indeed "the trustworthy container in which we may have to *feel* hatred, rage or contempt for varying periods of time" (Coltart 1993a, 121).

The act of faith: the unconsciousness of the unconscious and its rough beasts

Coltart seems to be able to thrive in the area of Negative Capability, to tolerate darkness – and enjoy it! – and uncertainty, and to be prepared to sit it out with a patient for as long as it takes. Her most famous paper, 'Slouching Towards Bethlehem ... or Thinking the Unthinkable in Psychoanalysis' (1993a, 1–14) is a sort of testament of her analytic identity, and I think that it is here we discover how her strength as an analyst resides in the strength of her analytic foundations. The two pillars on which her foundations rest operate like two points on a compass[14] that orientate both her mind and heart: they are the faith[15] in the analytic process and in the power of the unconscious. Faith, with a small f, is the faith in "this strange process that daily we create with our patients", in the unknown and unthinkable things in our patients, "the sheer unconsciousness of the unconscious" and ultimately "that between the analytic couple things happen" (1993a, 3). Knowing that the analytic process is working and unfolding all the time, quietly or noisily – depending on what is going on! – is a source of great support for the analyst who is in a sense never alone.

Sustained by this faith the analyst aims to reach towards a "deeper nexus of feeling, fantasy and wordless experience" and is able to wait for the "true pattern" to emerge (Coltart 1993a, 3). The analyst is reaching towards a mysterious "rough beast" that inhabits the deep unconscious and who is waiting to be born within the analysis.

This immersion of ourselves into the depths of the unconscious and reaching towards the non-verbal realm of experience is accompanied – and perhaps in the 'young' analyst with even more intensity – by a sense of dread: "The act of faith may feel like a spontaneous regression to complete unknowing, and may well be accompanied by dread; it can be disturbing to the analyst and seem like a serious self-induced attack on his ego, which in a way it is" (Ibid., 7). This sense of dread is paradoxically exhilarating for Coltart who says that it is when darkness closes in that the fun can begin. She warns us against the danger of being tempted to interpret too soon in order to catch something prematurely and thus create a distorted beast – a "deformed monster" – out of our own anxiety. This will possibly push even further back the unconscious beast that truly belongs to the patient: "the true creature who is not yet ready for the light of day retreats backwards into the darkness again" (Ibid., 6).

We need to ask ourselves, whose unconscious are we talking about? Coltart simply reminds us that the analyst is also a "rough beast" so we then need to keep in mind that in the room there are two "rough beasts". The analyst's emergent self and identity, like the patient's, are both born out of the process of doing analysis. All along we need to be mindful of the fact that we as analyst have our own resistance to the discovery of the unconscious. Kleimberg talks about our own "enemy within", "the everlasting resistance to the unconscious knowledge of ourselves … the resistance to the 'frightening unknown'" (Kleimberg 2012, 57–58).[16] Our continuous efforts to try to capture the unconscious run thus against our own resistance to the analytic process itself (so the support I was talking about earlier is complex and far from straight-forward).

Fear, dread and an awful feeling of ignorance[17] are thus the familiar companions in an analytic journey, and if they are not we should ask ourselves why. Patient and analyst are both vulnerable participants in the process: confusion, suffering and emotional turmoil are the main ingredients of this mysterious journey.

I would like to add here a reflection on Coltart's own life. Coltart suffered the sudden and tragic loss of both her parents in a train crash when she was eleven years old.[18] At the time she had been evacuated because of the war to Cornwall with her sister and her beloved nanny – "a salt of the earth person" (Molino 1997, 191). Her sister became very sick. The local doctor was worried and sent for the parents who got on the night train straightaway. This train crashed and the parents never arrived, while Coltart waited for hours at the local train station. At the end of the following day, the news came that the parents had died. In her interview with Antony Molino, she poignantly remarks that, "A tragedy like that fractures your life completely, and from then on you're a different person … It's from such events that one knows about handling death, about handling grief and trauma … or rather, about not always handling them successfully" (Molino 1997, 191).

Coltart identifies this fracture as the seat of a psychotic core in her own personality and the experience of waiting as the source of "unbearable psychotic anxiety" (Molino 1997, 196). Of her own analysis with Eva Rosenfeld[19] Coltart says that it "never got near the core of this psychotic anxiety" (Molino, 1997, 195). It helped her very much with her depression though did not go far enough.[20] I find it poignant and remarkable that Coltart makes the very experience of waiting and not knowing the central tenet of her analytic presence and listening, *knowing* that this would take *her* to the edge of what is bearable for her and ultimately take her close to her own psychotic core. The agony of waiting becomes the pillar of her analytic identity.

The role of spontaneous and authentic affect

Coltart firmly states that our work as analyst must come from within our most authentic self:

> I believe with some authority that we can do no harm to a patient by showing authentic affect, within the limits of scrupulous self-observation. I am talking about being not doing ... I am not arguing for emotionally directed action – such as touching, caressing, hitting, walking out – but for truth in our emotional being with a patient.
>
> (Coltart 1993a, 161)

What stands out mostly for me in Nina Coltart's riveting clinical accounts is her bravery in experiencing and working from a position of distress. She is brave enough to go to the edge of an emotional experience, to almost stretch herself to the limit of what she can bear: she literally soaks up her patient's "primary hatred of a genuinely powerful mother" (Ibid., 10) and when she cannot stand it anymore she shouts; she stays in silence with her "profoundly silent patients" for months (one patient slept on her couch without speaking for seven months – this was the least orthodox of her treatments and yet probably the most successful she tells us) (Ibid., 92–93); and she bursts into laughter and sees great value in humorous exchanges with her patients (Ibid., 11–12). I believe that it is her trust in the analytic process, her act of faith, that allows her to surrender to these emotional states, that are formless and disorganized, and from these depths she is able to come out and up towards new understanding and discoveries.

I will try to map out how Coltart uses her affective responses as a transformative factor in the analysis. Coltart allows firstly the feelings to emerge within herself, then to become *real* feelings experienced *between* her and the patient, and finally it is her capacity to use these emotional experiences for further understanding and working through that allows her to reach to transformative constructions of the patient's history. Coltart indeed places great importance in knowing the patient's history, in gathering information during initial consultations and starting "treatment armed with a good, detailed history" (Coltart 1996, 164) in order to build up a picture of the patient's main object-relationships of not only early life, but up to late adolescence.[21]

Once patient and analyst survive the "emotional storm", to borrow a term from Bion, the work of the analyst is then a "gathering together ... (of) hitherto meaningless fragments of the patient's mental and verbal elements into a thinking process, and communicate this back to the patient" (Coltart 1993a, 5). In her clinical accounts we can see that this gathering together is done in collaboration with the patient. The constructions[22] are thus co-constructions. This work of co-construction is very complex and can lead to a "functioning insight" only if its conviction is equally shared and strong in both analyst and patient.[23] Therefore, this movement from not knowing and Negative Capability towards discovering and knowing takes place through a detailed work of co-construction and a thorough analysis of the transference-countertransference in which both patient and analyst are engaged.

Coltart's freedom in using her spontaneous and authentic affective responses points towards a more open use of the countertransference. What is centre stage in her method of enquiry is the analytic situation and its emotional reality. The task of the analyst is to be open to experience the full emotional intensity of the feelings that emerge in the here-and-now of the analytic encounter and to be free to struggle[24] with her feelings in an open and authentic way. Her words read like a poem: we need to be prepared, she says, to go down "the emotional darkness of the underground river of (our patients') affective life" (Coltart 1993a, 160).

While Coltart is struggling with the eruption of silent black waves of hatred and despair, Harold Searles[25] is alarmed by the emergence in himself of strong loving and erotic feelings towards his patients. Searles describes how during a session with a schizophrenic patient, "while we were sitting in silence and a radio not far away was playing a tenderly romantic song ... I suddenly felt that this man was dearer to me than anyone else in the world, including my wife" (Searles 1959, 185). I read this sentence a while ago and it stayed with me as I think it so powerfully coveys how strange – at times even mad – an analytic experience can be, how far one can be from reality and yet at the same time how emotionally real the experience can feel.

Searles's view is that if the analyst is able to move beyond his anxiety, embarrassment and guilt in experiencing romantic and erotic feelings towards his patients, patients can greatly benefit from knowing that their feelings are reciprocated by the analyst and that they are engaged in a mutual experience, "a deeply-felt, but minimally-acted-out relationship" (Searles 1959, 189). In order for a successful analysis of the Oedipus Complex the analyst must fall in love[26] with the patient while recognizing that his wishes will never be realized:

The patient's self-esteem benefits greatly from his sensing that he (or she) is capable of arousing such responses in his analyst ... I have come to believe that there is a direct correlation between, on the one hand, the *affective intensity* with which the analyst experiences an awareness of such feelings – and of the unrealizability of such feelings – in himself towards the patient, and, on the other hand, the depth of maturation which the patient achieves in the analysis.

(Searles 1959, 183)

Christopher Bollas, a close friend[27] of Coltart's, is another analyst who is advocating for a less private use of the countertransference which he calls the 'Expressive Uses of Countertransference' (Bollas, 1983). His belief is that it may be very helpful for the analyst to find a way of expressing to the patient his own subjective states, "even when he does not know what it means" (Bollas 1983, 2). The analyst's own associations, affective responses, fantasies can thus become an object of enquiry between the analytic couple. By surrendering to the process and getting lost into the environment created by the patient, to the point of losing his own identity, the analyst becomes *situationally ill*. Soaked up in experiencing, with at times very little understanding and knowing, the analyst should be prepared to share something of his illness with the patient – usually something that remains private and within his own mind – with a view of making this very subjective state the object of analytic enquiry (for Bollas the countertransference itself is the *Other patient*[28] in the room). This subjective state – experienced by both patient and analyst, though the former may be completely unaware of it – through this communication is now situated *between* the patient and the analyst and can thus become something that the analytic couple can work and play with.

Because of her bravery in surrendering to the analytic process, to regress inside the analytic situation and become situationally ill, Coltart reaches towards a level of disturbance that is too strenuous for her to bear any longer. This is why she ends up shouting; the cry for freedom is as much for her own sanity as for that of her patient:

I had given up trying to understand this patient, given up theorizing and just sat there day after day without memory and desire in a state of suspension, attending only with an empty mind to him and the unknowable truth of himself, which had shaped his life, until such a moment as I was so at one with it that I knew it for the murderous hatred it was, and had to make a jump for freedom – his as well as mine though I did not think that out at the time – by shouting. These acts of faith can feel dangerous.

(Coltart 1993a, 10)

Her screaming is both an act of freedom and her way of surviving creatively. The strain that she feels comes from the trauma that the patient had himself endured in infancy. In Winnicott's language we could say that she reaches to the *failure situation* that had remained frozen inside the patient and that needs to be relived in the present of the analysis in order to then belong to the past and be forgotten (Winnicott, 1974).

Coltart is challenging the idea of the neutrality of the analyst, without obviously advocating thoughtless discharge of affect or gross acting out. She is leaving us with many questions, I think. How free we are as analysts to be truly spontaneous with our patients? Are we frightened of our most spontaneous self? Spontaneous emotional responses – like a laugh and a shout – erupt from inside ourselves and we do not have much control over them. Can we think with Coltart that "laughter and enjoyment can be therapeutic factors in psychoanalysis" (1993a, 11)? How prepared are we to reach towards depths of disturbance that could derange us and make us feel mad with fury and rage or with love and passion? If we are suffocating something in ourselves, are we suffocating something in the process and in the patient too? After all, if the analyst is concealed behind a façade, how can the patient develop his own personhood and truly know himself as a feeling person?[29]

The overarching difficult and central question that remains to be clarified – and it may well be that it cannot be clarified – seems to be, what is the difference between suffocating an affective response and containment; between hiding from our spontaneous self and holding something inside ourselves in a state of Bare Attention, allowing for both suspension and suspense?[30]

Coltart's sincerity in writing her paper 'Slouching Towards Bethlehem...' and bringing into the open her shouting during an analytic session is another act of bravery on her part. Another analyst could have chosen not to share this experience, could have maybe decided after a while that the patient was not analysable and possibly even found a reason to terminate the treatment. Coltart instead takes us with her to the core of her struggle to survive this "black silence" and tells us that, after a long while, all she could do was to shout. Did she not survive? Or is she confronting us with the emotional truth of the effort and strain – at times immense – that is at the core of psychic survival? A mother, like an analyst, knows how hard it is to survive and how one can only survive in the way that is humanly and personally possible to the individual at the time. There are not many choices in surviving. So could we say that Coltart survived in the way that was available to her, and by being truthful to her own emotional being with her patient she was able to reach the patient where he needed to be reached and understood. Her authenticity, her internal compass, guided her there.

Authentic love and hate on the part of the analyst are necessary factors in an analysis for our patients to develop fully their own capacity truly to love and hate.[31] What do we think of these acts of freedom, these emotional upheavals in which *both* patient and analyst are involved? Could we see them, along with Coltart, as important therapeutic factors necessary to bring about therapeutic shifts in an analysis (and to work though deep transference neurosis)? If there is a deeply felt relationship between patient and analyst where there is spontaneity and freedom, then the ground is fertile for a passionate involvement between the two parties. Love and hate can come to the fore and the analyst's survival, in whatever shape it may come, opens up the possibility for growth, and maybe even for Growth-with-Enjoyment. Winnicott gets hold of this joy in surviving and finds words for it in the imaginary conversation where subject meets object and says, "'Hullo object!' 'I destroyed you.' 'I love you.'" (Winnicott 1969, 713).

I find myself one more time returning to Coltart's life, to show again how deeply grounded her analytic self is in her own personal history. Coltart tells us that in her analysis with Eva Rosenfeld the interpretations about her anger and guilt towards her parents "never clicked with (her). They did not become real" (Molino 1997, 196). It is outside her analysis that Coltart finds an experience that allows her to reach to this maddening rage and terror. It is in her humorous and profound essay, 'Two's company, three's a crowd', that Coltart, in her typically light and funny way, tells us about her "adventure" of enrolling in an introductory course at the Institute of Group Analysis when she was already a senior analyst and Director of the London Clinic (Coltart 1996, 41–56). In the experiential group she has a traumatic experience that has a profound effect on her. When some members of the group are late and Coltart is confronted with their empty seats, she has a panic attack and relieves the intense anxiety and childhood trauma of waiting for her parents who never turned up. It is in this moment that she is in touch with her own murderous rage towards the group leader who, like her mother, Coltart says, "failed" to rescue her from the terror and anxiety of abandonment. She is able to use this experience by letting herself be cared for by the group who "looked after her" and then let her be and gave her time to recover from her panic and gather herself together.

Once again, this violent rage that she found so hard to get in touch with and tolerate within herself becomes the core of her brave authentic listening, where she is open to soak up her patients' rage and murderousness. Therefore her acts of creative survival become both her patients' and her own healing experiences. Ultimately I am saying that she is finding creativity in her own deepest suffering and disturbed self. Did Coltart shout because she had a reservoir of murderous hatred towards her own mother that came into contact with the patient's own hatred towards his own mother, and this resulted in an explosive climax that had to come alive in the consulting room in the shape of a shout – inchoate words – and could not be translated into an interpretation? I think that Coltart is here reaching deep into that scary and mysterious river – "the emotional darkness of the underground river of affective life" (1993a, 160) – both her own river and her patients'. It is very possible that disorder and chaos cannot be avoided at these depths of experience; the waters are very deep and dark indeed.

The search for life experiences that can foster growth and further development is in all of us. I am reminded of Neville Symington who decided to challenge himself by learning to fly a plane as a way of getting in touch with deep fears in himself: "In learning to fly I directed myself at the place where my fear was the greatest …" reaching to "a panic fuelled by a mass of disconnected fragments inside" myself, an "inner terror" (Symington 2018, 334–335).

By reaching towards our own "frightening place", as Symington calls it – in his case the pilot seat on a flying plane, in Coltart's case the sight of some empty seats – we get in touch with our infantile self and we feel most vulnerable, at times terrified. The question for me is do we need sometimes to find these terrifying places which can be great catalysts for self-analysis in order to expand our own capacity for experiencing life and growth, both in our own lives and in our analytic lives?

Figure 8.2 Multicolour Coltart by Paola Somaini

Multicolour Coltart

I would like to end by adding colour to my sketch (unfortunately the image printed here is in black and white so you will need to imagine the colours I am describing). Continuing in the spirit of the 'blind drawing' technique, I simply picked up the colours that I spontaneously found. Again, I followed an impulse without thinking too much.[32] They feel like the 'right' colours because they emerge from this free-spirited attitude that I see as Coltart's stance in life and psychoanalysis. Moreover, colours make me think of affects, sensations and feelings and the intensity of her creative aliveness. The yellow on her face makes me think of light and vision, the deep red of her hair – fiery hair? – of her heated emotional outbursts and the blue of her blouse of the infinity that opens up in encountering Coltart. A deep blue sea with its rough-beasts-sea-monsters and also its endless potentiality for discovery.

I have done this Coltart and immediately I would like to do another one! A part of me is not satisfied and would have liked to have used even more colours and reached to a sort of kaleidoscopic effect with the hope of giving better justice to Coltart's analytic aliveness and depth of creative receptivity. I have recently read in *The Economist* that apparently Wittgenstein, when teaching at Cambridge in the 1930s, used to sit among students, rattling off questions along the lines of "Why might we think that blue is closer to green than red?" (Wittgenstein 1930/2021, 75–77). How to answer this question? It feels impossible, maybe like answering the question: are these the 'right' colours for Coltart? I believe that Coltart can only remain a multicolour creature, deeply alive to her own emotional self, the infinite combinations of the colours in a kaleidoscope, though her contour – the strength of her personality, intellect and analytic foundations – is in the black line that is the sketch itself. The frame contains the storm – her aliveness that is like a storm. I imagine Coltart's consulting room to be bare and minimal, profoundly silent and with a splash of vivid colours, the explosion of intense emotions, her laughs and shouts: a space where there is potential for both Bare and Bold Attention.

I do not think it is possible and I would not want to assume that I have captured the essence of this analyst. She remains mysterious and complicated and perhaps the only thing one could say with certainty about her is that she was a one-off. In her own words, "In all of us there are some things which will never be within reach; there is always a mystery at the heart of every person, and therefore in our job as analyst" (Coltart 1993a, 14).

Ultimately you will need to use your own imagination – your own playground and garden – and find your own 'right' colours for Coltart, and so create your own. As Gustave Moreau, teacher of many fauvist painters including Henri Matisse, put it, "If you have no imagination, you will never produce beautiful colours … colours must be thought, dreamed, imagined" (Moreau 1893/1967, 36).

Reaching the end of the line

Coltart's life journey ended in suicide.

When she retired and resigned from the British Psychoanalytic Society in 1994 at the age of 67, Coltart moved from London to Leighton Buzzard in Bedfordshire. She felt that her life had come "full circle" and was eager to experience these later years as a non-practising analyst (Molino 1997, 195). Sadly her health was deteriorating due to an autoimmune illness that within a short period of time would have confined her to a wheelchair. In 1996 she published her last book, *The Baby and the Bathwater*, and in the same year she gave her long interview to Antony Molino who had the uncanny intuition that Coltart was saying her final goodbye. Coltart indeed took her on own life on 24 June 1997.

What to think about this final gesture? Maybe she could not bear this additional agony of waiting for her own, certainly painful and possibly pro-longed, ending? Or perhaps this was her ultimate act of freedom and bravery? In her writings,[33] she talks about the need to have death as a concern[34] of ours in life so that we can be more likely "to die with some grace" (Molino 1997, 207). She advocates for

> a regular contemplation of the very fact of death, so that we familiarise ourselves with it. A discipline of simple meditation as part of one's life makes this sort of approach unalarming, partly because it increases calmness and detachment from the importance of the self.
>
> (Coltart 1996, 147)

Coltart was not interested in endless journeys[35] and, like Winnicott, spoke of her great curiosity about death and of her wish to experience death itself.

So one can imagine that she was ready. In a final empathic gesturing she wrote letters to her loved ones preparing them for her death. She made sure, as much as possible, that they were also ready. As Boffito remarks, "she took them by the hand" with the hope that they would not end up, like her, with an horrific and shocking pain of loss lodged inside themselves (Boffito 2017, XXIII).

In life and in art, Ruskin declares, wisdom lies in "knowing the way things are going":

> Try always, whenever you look at a form, to see the lines in it which have had power over its past fate and will have the power over its futurity. Those are its *awful* lines; see that you seize on those, whatever you miss.
>
> (Ruskin 1904, 91)

Maybe Coltart did get hold of her own "*awful* line", the connection between her "unhealed wounds" of childhood and her approaching death; instead of having an awful ending to her life she decided to "die gracefully", and add a final line and gesturing of her own. She claimed her ending as her own while reaching out once again towards the other, her letters, her graceful signs reaching the loved ones whom she was leaving behind.

She and her line went out on a final walk together.

Notes

1 Nina Coltart indeed loved traveling and liked to keep journals of her trips. Sometimes she wrote plays and humorous stories around anecdotes of her travels. The trilogy of her travel diaries – *The Tran-Siberian Railway, A Tuscan Holiday* and *Hotel Drama in New York* – is an entertaining and gripping read (Rudnystsky & Peston, 2011, 223–246).
2 Her character and personality come alive in all her writing and perhaps with an especially touching immediacy in her own essays, diaries, reviews and in the tributes to her life paid by friends, supervisees, colleagues and former patients, all assembled together in the book, *Her Hour Came Round At Last, A Garland For Nina Coltart*, edited by Peter Rudnystsky and Gillian Preston (Nina Coltart's sister), (2011). In her Obituary, Brafman remarks that "Nina had the rare gift of knowing precisely what help each person needed" (Brafman 1997, 15–16).
3 Ella Shape's words come to mind, "To say that the analyst will still have complexes, blind spots, limitations is only to say that he remains a human being. When he ceases to be an ordinary human being he ceases to be a good analyst" (Sharpe 1947, 4).
4 The squiggle game emerged from Winnicott's own interest in drawing as a way of getting in touch with the child and reach a communication at an unconscious level. He described the game like this: "This game that I like playing has no rules. I just take my pencil and go like that ..., and I probably screw up my eyes and do a squiggle blind. I go on with my explanation [to the child] and say: 'You show me if that looks like anything to you or if you can make it into anything, and afterwards you do the same for me and I will see if I can make something of yours'" (Winnicott, 1968/1989, 301). Winnicott believed that through this spontaneous and mutual process, analyst and child can co-create pictures which are representations at the level of dream and both be surprised by their discoveries (see Winnicott, 1971). As Jan Abram puts it, squiggles are "akin to a pencil drawing of a dream" (Abram, 1996, 309).
5 See Henri Matisse's thoughts on creativity and the bravery required to look at things like a child: "The effort needed to see things without distortion takes something very like courage; and this courage is essential to the artist, who has to look at everything as though he saw it for the first time: he has to look at life as he did when he was a child and, if he loses that faculty, he cannot express himself in an original, that is, a personal way ... The first step towards creation is to see everything as it really is, and that demands a constant effort. To create is to express what we have within ourselves. Every creative effort comes from within" (Matisse 1953/1990, 148).
6 Marion Milner writes about her "doodle method" of free drawing and she notices that "beginning with something that could only be called a scribble there had emerged pictures that had definite stories even though I had no conscious awareness of what they were about while doing them" (Milner 1987, 6–7).
7 Tim Ingold in his book *Lines* (2007) offers a fascinating overview of Paul Klee's theories on drawing (Klee, 1921/1961). The artist contrasts this "free line that goes

out for a walk" with another kind of line that wants to get from one location to another in a hurry, who – as Klee puts it – is attending more like a "series of appointments" than (going for) a walk. "Whereas the active line on a walk is dynamic, the line that connects adjacent points in series is, according to Klee, 'the quintessence of static'. If the former takes us on a journey that has no obvious beginning or end, the latter presents us with an array of interconnected destinations that can, as on a route-map, be viewed all at once" (Ingold 2007, 75).

8 *Survival-with-Enjoyment* is the first chapter of Coltart's book, *How to Survive as a Psychotherapist* (1993b, 3–12). See also Chapter 8, *Leisure and Living* (1993b, 97–114).

9 Coltart refers to Michael Balint's idea that a full capacity for love is not archaic but must be learnt. It is a capacity that the child can learn in the primary relationship: "in true love there is sensitivity, choice, generosity, the ability to be open to a certain sort of identification, and tenderness" (Coltart 1993a, 119).

10 Jonathan Sklar, in a recent yet unpublished paper, makes a link between a fascination with ordinary grass and the analytic focus on free association as a way into the unconscious: "Like many painters, Bacon was interested in small parts of life, like grass. Henry Miller describes grass as follows: 'Grass only exists between the great non-cultivated spaces. It fills in the voids. It grows between-among other things'. An idea that we need to become interested in ordinary grass. Ordinary grass as ordinary associations to find the way into the unconscious" (Sklar, 2021).

11 It is important to point out though that her working in silence and with silence remains always firmly grounded in theory and a deep understanding of development and its corresponding pathology (see her detailed study of a "black silence" in *The Analysis of an Elderly Patient* (1993a, 160)).

12 Sara Maitland's book, *The Book of Silence* (2008), about her experience, both dark and euphoric, of immersing herself in and falling in love with silence is a fascinating read.

13 Mike Brearley (personal communication, January 2021) remembers Coltart's strong and still presence and how one would immediately notice her in a room. He recalls that she was capable of being forthright and also careful and quiet in her intense listening.

14 I have taken this image of a compass from Rudnytsky (2011, 167).

15 We can hear Bion here and Coltart is very aware – with delight and horror – of how close her ideas are to Bion's thinking: "I felt a strong urge to read all the works of Bion, and have done so. I was both delighted and horrified by what I found. Delighted because some of it expressed so clearly some of my own ideas; horrified because it began to look as though I have been plagiarising. But I do not think I can have been … I have concluded that … we had simply developed individually along similar lines in *some* ways" (Coltart 1993a, 4).

16 See also Symington who talks about a "shared resistance" to the analytic process where both patient and analyst are fighting "a slow but persistent battle … against the shared resistance and illusion" (or delusion) activated within the transference-countertransference (Symington 1983, 188).

17 If we are able to accept and bear this state of ignorance we may be able to experience a "flash of the obvious" says Bion: "One is usually so busy looking for something out of the ordinary that one ignores the obvious as it were of no importance. Indeed, one of the reasons for thinking it is time to give an interpretation is that nobody has seen something so obvious" (Bion, 1973/2014, 67).

18 This is what Coltart says in her interview with Antony Molino (1997, 194). Rudnytsky (2011, 168), notices that Coltart refers to the accident having taken place when she was 11 years of age whilst she was in reality almost 13. I find this a

poignant moment when we can see that Coltart the child collapsed inside this tragedy, and Coltart the adult and psychoanalyst is in part still collapsed inside this tragedy that fractured her life and that continues to bring confusion and terror to her and to interfere with her capacity to remember.

19 For a fascinating exploration of the parallels between Coltart's tragic family life and the tragic life (also marked by several losses) of her own analyst, Eva Rosenfeld, see Rudnytsky (2011, 174) who talks about Coltart finding herself entangled in an intergenerational trauma in her analytic family too.

20 Symington is another analyst who unusually writes about his own analysis. See John Klauber, 'Independent Clinician' (Symington, 2018, 3–22).

21 "It is essential, I believe for the smooth development and effective handling of the transference, that the therapist has a firm grasp on the patient's view of the main object-relationships of his/her early life – and by that I mean up to late adolescence, not just the first two or three years of life. If one is going to understand the individual transference, rather than impose a theoretical structure on it – which is then inevitably similar to everyone – one needs to know a lot about what it was like to have been the patient as a child, the details of the relationship to his/her mother, father, siblings, or their surrogates – whoever played important influential roles in the development" (Coltart 1993a, 62).

22 Coltart suggests a distinction between reconstructions and constructions: "'reconstruction' suggests the exact reproducing of a lost memory, a piece of the past, whereas 'construction' gives adequate and respectful weight to the way in which every event in life is *new*, even in analysis" (1993a, 159).

23 In her clinical paper, *The Analysis of an Elderly Patient*, she states that "chronically unconscious meaning, had to be revisited by us in the analysis many times over the next few years; *we stitched it slowly together*" (1993a, 157, my emphasis).

24 Denis Carpy also remarks that "it is inevitable that if the projections are fully experienced, then the countertransference will be acted out to some partial degree … The analyst's partial acting out allows the patient to see, consciously or unconsciously, that she is affecting the analyst and inducing strong feelings in him, and it allows her to observe him attempting to deal with these feelings" (Carpy 1989, 289–292).

25 Searles is one of the authors Coltart's mind turns to when she is reflecting on the analyst's capacity to love as a *matrix*, a trustworthy container of her, at times intense and unsettling, feelings (1993a, 121–122). She quotes from his paper, 'The effort to drive the other person crazy': "… it seems to me that the essence of loving relatedness entails a responding to the wholeness of the other person, including responding to a *larger* person in him than he is himself aware of being, to help restore that wholeness" (Searles 1959/1965, 269–270).

26 See also Gerrard, "My hypothesis is that until and unless there can be felt moments of love for the patient by the therapist the patient is not able to develop fully" (Gerrard 1996, 163).

27 Coltart had been an important mentor and teacher for Bollas. One can feel the great warmth and admiration that he has for her in his Foreword to her final book, *The Baby and the Bathwater* (1996), where he crowns her as the queen of the Independent literary tradition, praises her bravery in being an "outspoken critic of dogma, her forthright defence of true independence of mind … her courage and integrity" and most poignantly recognizes the enormous good she did for the great number of patients who came to her for initial consultations and who were by her most carefully and thoughtfully matched with colleagues. It is because of this careful work, he says, that she is a legendary figure: "when she left London in 1994 for her country home – and the next step in her journey – Nina Coltart left behind

a country that was the better for her" (1996, XVII). When Coltart left London, Bollas bought her house and so also inherited her consulting room which became his own working environment.

28 "The Other source of the analysand's free association is the psychoanalyst's countertransference, so much so, that in order to find the patient we must look for him within ourself" (Bollas 1983, 3).

29 Symington reaches this conclusion (2018, 348).

30 An email exchange (June 2021) with Mike Brearley has helped me to articulate these questions with greater clarity.

31 On this point see Winnicott, "If the patient seeks objective or justified hate he must be able to reach it else he cannot feel he can reach objective love" (Winnicott, 1949).

32 Henri Matisse talks about the feeling of freedom in discovering colour, "Colour, above all, and perhaps even more than drawing, is a means of liberation" (Matisse 1945/1990, 100).

33 The themes of ending, suicide and death run through all her books and could be the focus of another paper. See especially 'Endings', in her last book *The Baby and the Bathwater* (1996, 141–154).

34 A *concern* she says, not in the sense of a worry, that can be "delusional or shallow" (Coltart 1996, 142).

35 "If all things, all phenomena, all beings are transient, then there is no abiding me to go on all these endless journeys" (Coltart 1996, 139).

References

Abram, Jan (1998). 'A Tribute to Dr Nina Coltart', *British Journal of Psychotherapy*, 14(4): 522–526.

Batchelor, David (ed.) (2008). *COLOUR, Documents of Contemporary Art*. London & Cambridge (MA): Whitechapel Gallery & MIT Press.

Bion, Wilfred Ruprecht (1973/2014). 'Brazilian Lectures, São Paulo'. In: *The Complete Works of W.R. Bion*, Mawson, C. (ed.), Vol. VII, 67. London: Karnac Books.

Amedei, Gherardo & Sara Boffito (2011). 'Bare Attention: the Love That is Enough?'. In: *Her Hour Came Round At Last, A Garland For Nina Coltart*, Rudnystsky, P. & Peston, G., London: Karnac Books.

Boffito, Sara (2017). 'Nota Bibliografica'. In: *Pensare l'Impensabile e Altre Esplorazioni Psicoanalitiche, Nina Coltart*. Milano: Raffaello Cortina Editore.

Bollas, Christopher (1983). 'Expressive Uses of Countertransference – Notes to the Patient from Oneself', *Contemporary Psychoanalysis*, 19: 1–33.

Bollas, Christopher (1996). 'Foreword'. In: *The Baby and the Bathwater*, Coltart, N., London: Karnac Books.

Brafman, Abrahão Henrique (1997). 'Nina Coltart (1927–1997): An Obituary'. *Bulletin of the British Psychoanalytical Society*. Vol. 33, (10): 15–16.

Carpy, Denis Vernon (1989). 'Tolerating the Countertransference: a Mutative Process', *International Journal of Psychoanalysis*, 70: 287–294.

Coltart, Nina (1993a). *Slouching towards Bethlehem … And Further Psychoanalytic Explorations*, London: Free Association Books.

Coltart, Nina (1993b). *How to Survive as a Psychotherapist*, London: Sheldon Press.

Coltart, Nina (1996). *The Baby and the Bathwater*, London: Karnac Books.

Gerrard, Jackie (1996). 'Love in the Time of Psychotherapy', *British Journal of Psychotherapy*, 13(2): 163–173.

Flam, Jack Donald (1990). *Matisse on Art*, Oxford: Phaidon Press.

Ingold, Tim (2007). *Lines*, Oxford & New York: Routledge (reprinted in Routledge Classics2016).

Klee, Paul (1921/1961). *Notebooks, Vol. 1: The Thinking Eye*, London: Lund Humphries.

Kleimberg, Leon (2012). 'In the First Psychoanalytic Encounter, could "Missing the Wood for the Trees" have any Effect on the Development of the Psychoanalytic Treatment?' *EPF Bulletin*, 66, 52–69.

MacCarthy, Brendan Francis (1997). 'Nina Coltart (1927–1997): An Obituary', *Bulletin of the British Psychoanalytical Society*, Vol. 33, (10): 14.

Maitland, Sara (2008). *A Book of Silence*, London: Granta Books.

Matisse, Henri (1945/1990). 'The Role and Modalities of Colour'. In: *Matisse on Art*, Flam, J.D., Oxford: Phaidon Press.

Matisse, Henri (1953/1990). 'Looking at Life with the Eyes of a Child'. In: *Matisse on Art*, Flam, J.D., Oxford: Phaidon Press.

Milner, Marion (1988). *The Suppressed Madness of Sane Men*, London & New York: Routledge (first published in 1987 by Tavistock Publications).

Mitcheson Brown, Muriel (2011). 'Ways of Knowing'. In: *Her Hour Came Round At Last, A Garland For Nina Coltart*, Rudnystsky, P. & Peston, G. (eds), London: Karnac Books.

Molino, Anthony (ed.) (1997). *Freely Associated*, London: Free Association Books.

Moreau, Gustave (1893/1967). 'Statement'. In: *Matisse*, Guichard Meili, J., New York: Praeger.

Rudnystsky, Peter (2011). 'In Praise of Nina Coltart'. In: *Her Hour Came Round At Last, A Garland For Nina Coltart*, Rudnystsky, P. & Peston, G., London: Karnac Books.

Ruskin, John (1904). 'The Elements of Drawing', In: *The Works of John Ruskin*, Tyas Cook, E. & Wedderburn, A., Vol. 15, London: George Allen.

Searles, Harold Frederic (1959). 'Oedipal Love in the Countertransference', *International Journal of Psychoanalysis*, 40: 180–190.

Searles, Harold Frederic (1959/1965). 'The Effort to Drive the Other Person Crazy'. In: *Collected Papers on Schizophrenia and Related Subjects*, London: Hogarth Press.

Sharpe, Ella Freeman (1947). 'The Psycho-Analyst', *International Journal of Psychoanalysis*, 28: 1–6.

Sklar, Jonathan (2021). 'Francis Bacon and the Radicality of Free Association', Unpublished paper presented to the AIP (Association of Independent Psychoanalysts) online Conference, On Free Association: Independent Perspectives. London, 12 June 2021.

Spicer, Jake (2017). *You Will Be Able to Draw by the End of this Book*, London: Ilex Press.

Symington, Neville (1983). 'The Analyst's Act of Freedom as Agent of Therapeutic Change', *International Review of Psychoanalysis*, 10: 283–291.

Symington, Neville (2018). *Becoming a Person Through Psychoanalysis*, London & New York: Routledge (first published in 2007 by Karnac Books).

Winnicott, Donald Woods (1949). 'Hate in the Countertransference', *International Journal of Psychoanalysis*, 30: 69–74.

Winnicott, Donald Woods (1969). 'The Use of an Object', *International Journal of Psychoanalysis*, 50: 711–716.

Winnicott, Donald Woods (1974). 'Fear of Breakdown', *International Review of Psychoanalysis*, 1: 103–107.

Wittgenstein, Ludwig (1930/2021). 'Statement'. In: "The "Tractatus" at 100, The Rest is Silence, A short book that Ludwig Wittgenstein wrote on the Eastern Front changed philosophy for ever", *The Economist*, May 22–28, 75–77.

Chapter 9

Enid Balint's imaginative perception

The creation of mutuality in the consulting room

Elizabeth Wolf and Barbie Antonis

What would you think if you heard the following ideas?

The capacity for mutuality comes from good enough mothering, the experience from which the infant's self grows and is the basis for creative life. Here is another: the capacity for mutual concern is the first truly feminine quality (Balint 1993a). And another, usually considered the most important contribution from Enid Balint: to feel alive in the world, a person has to be able to imaginatively perceive it (Balint 1989). Imaginative perception is Enid Balint's phrase for that experience with an other which is the engine for feeling alive in the world. As she puts it, "The infant cannot perceive reality unless it is perceived mutually with someone else. The mother, who can give complete attention to her infant is normally the first person to provide this atmosphere …" (Balint 1989, 102).

Enid Balint developed these theoretical ideas within her psychoanalytic practice, where she noticed the significance for her patients of experiences – or lack thereof – of recognition or misrecognition, feedback (echo) or void, mutual concern and imaginative perception; all early interconnected and essentially relational phenomena between baby and caregiver. Her observations herald Enid Balint's original contribution to psychoanalytic theory, an imaginatively elaborated depiction and theory of the earliest *reciprocity* in the mother-infant relationship, and the consequences of this understanding for clinical technique. In addition, Enid Balint augmented Freud's understanding of unconscious communication as the basis for all psychoanalytic work by perceiving it in action across at least three generations. What is remarkable is that she did not observe mothers and infants together, like Donald Winnicott, but developed her ideas from close observation of herself and of her patients, particularly during periods of regression – benign and malignant.

Today let us bring you our understanding of these ideas from Enid Balint's texts.

For the last ten years we have been teaching candidates the work of a number of British women psychoanalysts – Ella Freeman Sharpe, Marjorie Brierley, Marion Milner, Nina Coltart, Pearl King, Paula Heimann and of course, Enid Balint. This is our family tree as British Independent women

DOI: 10.4324/9781003296690-12

psychoanalysts. We consider Enid Balint a central transmitter of Independent theory and technique. She learned from her analysts and others (Winnicott and Ferenczi) as we have learned from her. We did not meet Enid Balint, who died just before we began our training at the Institute of Psychoanalysis, though she already had a place in our minds through her analysands and supervisees.

Reading Enid Balint teaches us to listen with greater awareness to all of our patients and to ourselves with them. Michael Parsons, who was supervised by her during his training, found it hard to describe exactly her "elusive" yet "distinct" quality of supervision, but he saw that, as he puts it, "After many months I realised I was absorbing something about the business of being with an analytic patient … which certainly made a difference to what happened in a session" (Parsons 1993, 2). Years later, when collecting her papers for publication with Juliet Mitchell, he described Enid Balint's clinical presence by quoting her: "It is the nature of the analyst's participation that matters … To be 'neither distant nor close but there'" (Ibid.). Being "there" means being a "participating observer" (Ibid., 4) who makes a new class of observations by employing "in addition to the scientific objective, detached observations, introjection, identification and reflection" (Balint 1968, 62). In this paper we will introduce Enid Balint, the psychoanalytic clinician, by giving you a picture of her in the consulting room with her patients. We believe that Enid Balint illuminates, elucidates and extends psychoanalytic theory.

But first, some history.

Who was this analyst, this woman, and what were some of the influences on her development as a psychoanalyst that came together in her theorizing and its application across diverse areas such as GP practice and marital therapy?

Jonathan Sklar draws out the pivotal position Enid Balint occupied in the circulation of psychoanalytic ideas after the Second World War. He places her as one of the psychoanalysts central to the establishment and growth of the Independent Tradition. From her first analysis with Rickman, who himself was analysed by Freud, Ferenczi and Klein, to her own analysis with Winnicott, and her second marriage to Michael Balint when she was 50, Enid Balint absorbed the developing analytic ideas and contributed to theories.

Patrick Casement reminded us of the following anecdote recounted by Enid Balint, we think, in her last presentation to a Scientific Meeting. She told the analysts present that she was a senior in her Boarding School when a girl climbed onto the roof, threatening to jump off. The Head thought that Enid was just the right person to deal with this crisis. So Enid climbed onto the roof and, for an hour or more, she sat beside the girl listening to what was troubling her. The girl eventually came back down with Enid, and Enid spoke of this as perhaps her first step towards eventually becoming an analyst. To our minds, this captures her readiness to engage actively and to listen deeply with patience until the girl was ready.

Born in 1903, she grew up in Hampstead in comfortable circumstances and attended Cheltenham Ladies College before going on to The London School of Economics to read Economics. Living in Kent before World War Two with her first husband and two small daughters, she heard about atrocities in Germany, wanted to help and, raising money, bought a house for German refugee children – a kind of home and school. One of her concerns during this time was the difficulty people had to obtain information about housing and assistance with financial problems. Through volunteering as a social worker, she helped to set up the Citizens Advice Bureau. It struck Enid that the details that troubled people so deeply during the Blitz were less about major incidents such as losing their home, than the small, seemingly "irrelevant" details about their relations with their neighbours (Balint 1993b, 222). She recognized something similar later, as a psychoanalyst, which guided her technique. Enid Balint said the analyst had to listen, had to wait for the small details that lead to other things from which dreams, memories held in the body and associations arise. She said the analyst had to wait and see what it is about and not come in too soon with a "set piece" interpretation that would seem to understand what is important but risk "neglecting or misunderstanding the patient by understanding too quickly" (Ibid., 223). The tiniest details are what makes the story alive for the patient, and lead to them telling something different and unexpected. "That is transference in the true sense, not just in the 'here and now'" (Ibid.).

During her second marriage to Michael Balint, they collaborated on developing theories on benign and malignant regression. Their work with junior doctors and psychiatrists in training led to the establishment of what became known as 'Balint groups', which continue as a space for reflection on unconscious processes between doctor and patient.

It was her work with the Citizens Advice Bureau that brought Enid Balint into contact with the Tavistock Institute of Human Relations, where she set up the Family Discussion Bureau, later called the Institute of Marital Studies. Her contacts at the Tavistock included John Rickman, who became her Training Analyst, and Wilfred Bion, who became her supervisor and a lifelong inspiration in her practice (Anna Freud was her other influential supervisor). The analysis with Rickman ended after two years with his death in 1951. Subsequently she went into analysis with Donald Winnicott for three years until she qualified as a full member in 1954. Thereafter, she resumed seeing Winnicott once weekly for a year from 1962 while she was preparing for her training analyst panel (which she passed in 1963) and then again once weekly from the time of her husband's last illness from October 1969. Winnicott died in 1971.

We now look at clinical illustrations, many published in the *International Journal of Psychoanalysis* and later collected in a single volume, *Before I was I*, in which we follow the growth of her ideas on creation of self with an other, from the earliest explorations in 'On Being Empty of Oneself' (1963) to her elaboration in the later papers, 'The Analysis of Women by a Woman Analyst, What Does a Woman Want' (1973), 'Creative Life' (1989) and 'Unconscious Communication' (1990). These cases introduce the interrelated concepts: recognition and its corollary, misrecognition, mutuality, primitive concern and imaginative perception. In 'One Analyst's Technique' (1991), written for this volume, she gathers together her thoughts on clinical technique. The hallmark of Enid Balint's practice was to pay finely tuned attention to the nuances of mood, atmosphere, the body, transference and countertransference, out of which she could imaginatively elaborate the patient's early relationships. In the following excerpts, by necessity abbreviated, we aim to show Enid Balint working as a psychoanalyst, and the genesis of her key concepts.

Sarah

In 'Being Empty of Oneself', Enid Balint describes how a mother's recognition of her infant, an essential experience in the development of self, occurs through the active feedback loop between mother and infant. This illustrates what is meant by good mothering.[1] Sarah, who Enid Balint came to understand as being profoundly *unrecognized* by her mother, illustrates the possible psychogenesis of the feeling of being empty of oneself. It should be noted that Sarah's experience of living in a void, of being empty, is quite distinct from the *alive* empty space Enid Balint describes at the beginning of an infant's life where mutuality with the mother can be observed, and "... there is a development of two people together" (Balint 1993a, 129).

Enid Balint relates the course of the six-year analysis in four stages. Sarah came into treatment acutely anxious, unable to continue the training course for which she had come to England, and broke down soon afterwards. We see the ensuing analysis as a case study of Michael and Enid Balint's ideas on benign regression where the aim is recognition of the nascent self.

In the first phase, lasting about one-and-a-half years, Sarah moved with difficulty between the door and the couch, where she covered herself with the rug and turned away, as she experimented with Enid Balint's capacity to tolerate her confusion and withdrawal; would her analyst "force" her back to work, into mother's world, which Sarah experienced as a "complete void", dreaded more than anything else (Balint 1963, 473)?

The second phase was ushered in when Sarah noticed paper and pencil on a table near the analyst's chair, and asked if she could take them. Enid Balint writes, "... When I agreed, she put the paper on a table near the couch ... and ... began to draw ... with intensity and great effort ... as an attempt to communicate with me" (Balint 1963, 474). Henceforth, part of each session was spent drawing in this way. Enid Balint recognized, "It was not important if I did not understand or interpret her drawings; but I had always to recognise them as communications, respect them and respond to them" (Balint 1963, 474). She later suggested that her response to Sarah's drawings was experienced as proper feedback; Sarah felt accepted by her and not forced to meet her analyst's standards or fit into her world. Over time, Sarah brought her paintings, all of which Enid Balint kept in one place in the consulting room, understood as bits of the patient's self and body gradually becoming more integrated. Only in the third and fourth stages of the analysis was Sarah able to speak about her body, first discovering her intense urge to suck, and afterwards, becoming able to experience feelings inside her body for the first time.

During the crucial third phase, Enid Balint writes that characteristically Sarah "… hit the couch, or the cushions, clenched her fists, flung cushions on the floor, tore up her drawings, and crouched away from me sobbing" (Balint 1963, 474), behaviour which, once Enid Balint had responded, enabled Sarah to collapse onto the couch where she began to suck her fingers. In time, associations followed, during which period Sarah would turn around on the couch to look at her analyst, astonished that Enid Balint could see her "day after day". We note these moments, when Sarah could see Enid Balint seeing her, the feedback loop perhaps being established.

Enid Balint realized that those moments when Sarah turned away again were connected to her countertransference feelings of impatience with Sarah's continued illness, or moments when she misunderstood the seriousness of Sarah's behaviour. Sarah then felt deserted, and turning away was preferable to once again living in a void. Enid Balint's revelation came the moment she realized that, as she puts it, *The void in fact was caused by my presence when I did not understand her*" (Balint 1963, 475, original emphasis). "At those moments, the patient felt unseen and unrecognized like a terrible mismatch between maternal perception and infantile experience" (Antonis & Wolf 2008, 322). Enid Balint went on to flesh out feedback as a key mechanism, operating in healthy primary maternal preoccupation and the mother's mirror response. The infant's behaviour, she writes, "stimulates the environment, and foremost his mother to various reactions. Echo and feed-back can be described as what the mother contributes to the stimulus and reactions out of her self" (Balint 1963, 479). This is how an infant gets to know himself through his mother's experience of him, with the addition of her integrative ego capacities. When mother's responses are distorted by her own pre-occupations or ideas, the infant experiences her responses as not fitting with his own, and Enid Balint thought they then do not make sense to the child. She writes,

> There is no possibility of the development of a healthy self when there is no proper feed-back at acceptable intervals. My idea is that these need not be at fixed moments or periods. A few may be enough – and each can be valuable and start a development.
>
> (Ibid., 479)

Further, Enid Balint hypothesized that Sarah did not experience the additional factor of having unhurried time for development and integration, which her analyst considered necessary for development. The patient's experience of having enough of these moments in the analysis were the foundation of Enid Balint's assertions. Enid Balint actually met Sarah's mother, as well as using the clinical material, transference and countertransference, and her imagination, to reconstruct a story of Sarah's early experiences with her mother.

We wonder, has something occurred in the development of these patients that makes them feel they have lost their essence, or had they never reached that stage of development? We learn as if in passing that there was sexual abuse in Sarah's history. It appears as if Enid Balint did not focus on the sexual trauma as centrally as we might consider it today. In her paper, Enid Balint's aim is to theorize about traumas from earlier failures. For Sarah, Enid Balint may have wondered if her memory from age six was a screen memory of infantile non-recognition or a memory of the trauma of the sexual abuse, which had the effect of undoing integration. Sarah had remembered,

> going into her parents' bedroom in great trouble … [I]t must have been the first time that her brother had had intercourse with her. Her parents had noticed nothing and she had said nothing. They had treated her just as usual; this had made her feel utterly alone and empty.
>
> (Ibid., 476)

We note the crucial factor here of the child feeling something terrible in her body and taking it to mother for it to be accepted, but it being neither seen nor noticed by either parent. Enid Balint surmised, "For Sarah, the nucleus of herself was not based on feelings arising out of body-self sensations, reinforced and enriched by responses from her mother to them" (Ibid., 479). Neither Sarah nor her mother found an echo in the other. We note Enid Balint's emphasis on the joint contribution from mother and infant in the creation of mutuality. Enid Balint's reconstruction suggested that her mother saw Sarah as an empty object in which to put herself, not as an "independent person in her own right" (Ibid., 478). She hypothesized that as a baby, Sarah did not stimulate a response from her mother that fit with Sarah's *bodily* experience in that moment. Sarah did not get proper feedback, but instead received an introject from her mother that felt alien, which led to her feeling that she lived in a void, both inside and outside. Outside was a world that felt out of touch with her bodily sensations and feelings, leaving Sarah feeling unrecognized, empty of herself, while inside all that was left was Sarah's aggression and despair.

Filling out Winnicott's concept of a lived experience together, Enid Balint concentrates on the *mutual* activity in a proper feedback or echo process between two contributing participants; it is not a projection-introjection process with the infant as a passive partner. She describes it thus:

> [It] starts in the child and acts as a stimulus on the mother, who must accept it and recognize that something has happened. Her recognition

results in a kind of integration, and this is then reflected, fed back to the child, in much the same way as on the biological stage the baby's sucking acts as a stimulus for the milk production.

(Ibid., 478)

The baby is there as an active partner. For the infant Sarah, misrecognition led to the impoverishment of her life; she existed in a fantastical nightmare, out of touch with the world; her communications got no response, or what came back was not a proper echo to what she felt, until this "lifeless relationship with the environment" (Ibid., 479) broke down with her breakdown.

In the fourth phase, Sarah increasingly adjusted to reality. She began to have the feeling of her hands as "alive and belonging to her" (Ibid., 475) instead of as being lifeless and made of steel. "As soon as she rediscovered herself and, so to speak, filled herself up ... her projective processes began to operate" (Ibid., 475). Enid Balint believed the recognition feedback processes occur at the earliest stage of development; it is only on the basis of feeling full of oneself does a person come to feel they are really living in their bodies, consistently recognisable to others. These processes are built on over time.

We find ourselves imagining the bodies together, baby with mother, mother with baby. This is about bodily communication: touch, feel, smell, sound, rhythm – full senses and a fully sensual experience. Proper feedback is experienced in the body, for the infant and for the mother, the experience of both together. Enid Balint became as interested in this pre-verbal period of life as she was in the verbal, and she tuned in to her patient's body and physical presence from the moment and manner of their entering the consulting room to every movement on the couch. She placed her chair in a position where she could see her patient's face, saying,

> I sit to one side, a bit but not totally behind the couch, and I certainly watch hands, feet and body, and that is part of what I hear when the patient talks. Both make sense together, or sometimes don't.
>
> (Balint 1993b, 224)

Reading her cases, we hear her time-and-again noticing her own feeling or response in relation to a patient, and how that alerted her to think about something she had not yet understood. When Enid Balint, through her clinical work, imagined these bodies together, she introduces the processes she names as 'imaginative perception' and 'primitive mutual concern', and their place in the developing infant's self.

It was her feelings of unjustified satisfaction that put Enid Balint on her guard in two analyses discussed in 'What Does a Woman Want?', where the work was apparently going well though it was also repetitious and unfruitful.

With these two women patients, Enid Balint noticed there was little change in relation to feelings about and attitude towards their mothers, and to herself. "It appeared that both patients wished to satisfy and please me but since their wish was acted out it was difficult to analyse: in one it was eroticized, in the other not" (Balint 1973, 196).

It is of particular interest to us to draw out Enid Balint's contribution in these analyses when we consider the question, what is feminine? Juliet Mitchell, in her introduction, says the paper offers "an important, highly original understanding of the early formation of a woman's desires and her internal object relations" (Mitchell 1993, 72). Not surprisingly, Enid Balint developed her ideas from her clinical experience analysing women, specifically those whose mothers were either depressed or withdrawn. She came to understand these patients as not having identified with their maternal introject and hence had no integrated internal sense of being a woman; they satisfied their mothers from a distance. These women avoid motherly protection and wish instead to give it to other women and perhaps enjoy it vicariously.

Mrs X

Mrs X secretly imagined satisfying her analyst mother each time she entered the consulting room, which Enid Balint understood as symbolically representing sexual intercourse, after which Mrs X felt free to have intercourse with her various lovers. However, Mrs X's anxiety returned on leaving the consulting room, so great was her need to be a need-satisfying object and be wanted all the time. In sexual intercourse with men this was easy, though she was never happy afterwards, having to wait for the next time, but with women, Mrs X felt her vagina was redundant. After some years in analysis, two important developments occurred. Mrs X gave up her analyst as an external sexual object and was able to get in touch with another primitive introjected object, identified as her first caring nanny, who had remained with her until she grew up (after a string of transient care givers). Mrs X felt truly dependent on this nanny who she experienced as caring and dependable. Enid Balint writes, "The patient had identified with the caring nanny and was herself able to look after – that is, to care for – her when she in turn was ill. A relationship of mutual concern had developed between them" (Balint 1973, 197). Crucially, the nanny had responded to the girl's care, unlike her mother. Enid Balint hypothesized that the mother was kept as an external sexual object, and her secret identification with and relation to the nanny compartmentalized; until Mrs X remembered this, and the nanny was *identified with* and felt to be the only "truly feminine introjected object" (Ibid.) could Mrs X attempt to care for and love her mother. After further attempts to reach her mother, which also failed, Mrs X was able to begin a process of mourning, accept her mother's rejection and experience some liberation from her. This was manifested in the transference as well.

Mrs Y

A second patient, Mrs Y, also had few memories of her early relationship to her mother, a woman who had been a lifelong depressive. From her mother's diaries, which Mrs Y only read some years into the analysis, she learned of her mother's failure to hold her close when feeding, that her mother had to read continuously and smoke to tolerate the feed at all. Mrs Y had relationships with the men in her family but felt her mother as unreachable. Mother "was represented in dreams as a frozen, icy box or coffin or an unreachable bare room ... and seemed a foreign body frozen and untouchable inside her" (Balint 1973, 198), an unintegrated maternal imago. When Enid Balint linked Mrs Y's dreams and associations to the early relationship with her mother, she was faced with Mrs Y's confusion and resistance. The patient could not accept the frozen isolated part of her inner world as a representation of her mother, who could not be thawed. Continuing the analysis of her frequent dreams allowed Mrs Y to get in touch, painfully, with other aspects of her mother: her clothes, her books, the contents of her cupboards, which over time she realised stood for her mother's body. The turning point came when one day, Mrs Y brought a very different dream.

> It was about a piece of marvellous velvet, the most beautiful material, texture, colour, she had ever seen; but it was not hers ... the patient wept. She, the patient, could not have the velvet, or touch it or stroke it ... I never imagined such beautiful stuff. She then spoke about her mother and soon realized that the velvet represented her mother's body.
>
> (Balint 1973, 198)

The subsequent working through of Mrs Y's hopeless relationship trying to satisfy her mother, led eventually to her giving up trying to help unhealable people in the external world. From her work with these women *for whom there was no reciprocal early bodily communication and satisfaction*, Enid Balint hypothesised the necessity for this which she termed "the capacity for mutual concern".

We find it helpful to differentiate mutuality from mutual concern. Mutuality is like an arrow that goes both ways, both partners are active. Mutual concern implies an additional capacity of caring for the (m)other. Enid Balint follows Winnicott in thinking about concern as a developmental achievement, reached from about six months, and many of her written papers focus on her work with patients who had not yet reached this stage. Winnicott describes concern as a "highly sophisticated experience" (Winnicott 1962, 353–4) in the baby's life; it is the fusion of the erotic and aggressive drives in relation to one object, the environment mother and the object mother coming together in the baby's mind. In her conversation with Juliet Mitchell, Enid Balint says,

> If you look at a small baby, it seems that it is born with an ability to experience in a particular way. I do not mean verbal thinking, but there is some kind of registering going on. If the mother is in pain, the baby will cry too. So you start off with a communication of mutuality.
>
> (Balint 1993b, 226)

If nothing happens in the couple to disrupt this process, the capacity for mutual concern grows.

We understand Enid Balint as including mutuality when thinking about the feminine, along with other more usually described maternal/feminine capacities such as holding, containing and a transformational function. By mutuality, Enid Balint means active and reciprocal engagement in its most primitive form between mother and infant, and in her view, "the infant cannot perceive reality unless it is perceived mutually with someone else" (Balint 1983, 102). Furthermore, Enid Balint asserts that mutuality and the capacity for mutual concern are at the foundation of mature object relationships. For Enid Balint, this would be true for all relationships, not restricted to mothers and daughters. We choose to quote Enid Balint in full here:

> I suggest that women want, in their relationships both with men and with women, to use that primitive structure in human relations, namely, the capacity for mutual concern … Owing to its primitive nature it can only be satisfactorily expressed by the body itself, or by feelings in the body based on inner representations of the body and by body memories. The vagina is that part of a woman's body which is felt to be the most important area with which to express mutual concern with men (this does not exclude the use of the rest of her body). However, in her relation with women she is at a loss to know how to express it unless she has herself introjected and identified with a woman's body which satisfied her and which she felt she satisfied when she was an infant. I assume that if she was satisfied by her mother's body she rightly felt that her own body satisfied her mother. I do not think it is adequate to think in terms of identification with parts of a woman's body or of the environment created by the mother. Furthermore, I suggest that unless a woman can experience mutual concern with women her relationship with men is likely to be impoverished and men may be undervalued and not experienced as objects for mutual concern.
>
> (Balint 1973, 200)

We are struck that Enid Balint sees the capacity for mutual concern as an essential human quality, while also describing it as the first real feminine capacity. The male infant naturally also develops the capacity for mutual concern in his relations with his mother and we understand this as his feminine endowment. It is interesting to wonder about the vicissitudes of the male infant's developmental journey and how he might lose or disavow his capacity for mutual concern, which is the core of all loving mature human relationships and creative life. Where there is active registering, mutuality and developing mutual concern between two people, Enid Balint posits the term "imaginative perception" to capture the dynamic inter-relational process in the unconscious mind. These concepts form the matrix describing self-other relationships.

The technical challenges in her work with Mrs X and Mrs Y helped Enid Balint generate the concept of imaginative perception, which relies on the capacity for mutual concern that was lacking in both women. Sarah, too, was not recognized by her mother and therefore could not be imaginatively perceived by her. The processes necessary for healthy development were absent. Enid Balint appreciated the significant place of imagination when she wrote, "External reality can, in any case, only exist for the individual if it is introjected, identified with and then *imaginatively perceived*. Identification alone is not enough" (Balint 1987, 481). Another patient, Kay, described in 'Unconscious Communication', received her mother's disturbance, handed on without being in the conscious awareness of either; in other words, it was not imaginatively perceived by either mother or daughter. Mother's disturbance had been introjected but not identified with. Kay unconsciously lived out her mother's actual loss of her own mother, Kay's grandmother, each time Kay lost something of obvious value, such as jewellery, whose worth she could not perceive. Enid Balint's paper is primarily about Kay's mother's and grandmother's unprocessed losses and grief which were then enacted by Kay. Kay's mother was given up for adoption and never knew her birth mother. Her early history (two years in a children's home) was lost as well; mother thought only of the happy childhood she had with her adoptive parents from age two. Kay's life was dominated by the fear of loss. Enid Balint saw the unconscious introject in Kay "as a foreign body inside the grandchild, which remains unconscious but gives rise to affect and action, which did not occur in the parent" (Balint 1990, 115). Until Kay could identify with her grandmother, she could not imaginatively perceive her nor her own mother, that figure who *had lost her* mother. Enid Balint writes,

> During the early years of analysis I did not grasp that the patient was living out, or demonstrating, her mother's catastrophe as well as her own. It was only when this became clear that real work started in the analysis.
> (Balint 1990, 115)

Enid Balint concluded that when working with patients, one always has to be aware of three generations.

Imaginative perception is an elaboration of Winnicott's term, "subjective phenomena". It is when the infant or patient "imagines what he perceives and thus creates his own partly imagined, partly perceived world" (Balint 1989,

103). The emerging infant lives in an alive space, not a void, where his perception of reality is discovered mutually with an other (mother), in a "space partly filled with the content of the unconscious internal world" (Ibid., 102) and the other, not yet perceived person. Enid Balint elaborates on Winnicott's often repeated truism, there is no infant without a mother, by adding "there can be no live breast, either biologically or psychologically with milk in it, without a live infant. The one creates the other" (Ibid., 102). An alive "space can be refound in analysis" (Ibid., 102). Enid Balint amplifies:

> My idea is that the first imaginative perception can only arise out of a state of eager aliveness in two people, the infant with the potential for life and the mother alive inside herself and tuning in to the emerging infant.
>
> (Ibid., 102)

Mr Smith

Enid Balint's ideas about imaginative perception came alive in the analytic process demonstrated to her by Mr Smith, the patient she writes about in 'Memory and Consciousness' and 'Creative Life'. For the first three-and-a-half years of the analysis she could not imaginatively perceive him, nor could he imaginatively perceive her. She felt frustrated, confused and out of touch with him, while also feeling there was a "him" somewhere to be found. She felt controlled by him to be there, but that she did not exist for him. He would enter the consulting room, fling himself on the couch, urgently demanding attention, making loud grunting and squeaky noises. She recognized that she was, most of the time, the non-existent mother to the non-existent 'I' or 'me' of her patient and was careful not to project any "false personality" into him that would misunderstand him (Balint 1987, 476–7). Mr Smith, though married and successful at business, had no close relationships. He had no memories that he could verbalize of any kind from before he was at public school nor from his last session or even from two previous analyses. The only thing he remembered was what happened at work. He felt he did not exist in childhood or infancy, and his mother did not exist for him; his father was more real to him.

After three years, Enid Balint registered a change, the beginning of consciousness. Mr Smith the baby was in the room; memory was emerging. She writes,

> He used the couch and the cushions ... as a baby might ... putting his face into the cushions and holding onto a corner ... His body was very much 'there' and he kicked and thrashed ... If I interpreted what I thought his baby body was feeling – for instance that he wanted something to hold onto but there was nothing ... he could not find what he was looking for – he would listen and ... then start to talk lucidly ... about work.
>
> (Ibid., 476)

Enid Balint had sensed that he was in a stage just prior to becoming 'there'. She had to remain in touch with the uncomfortable state of not under- standing him before he could tell her what it was like, which he began to do. He used a voice which he called the narrator's, the one who had a voice to speak about him to her. In the narrator's voice and words, the grown man and the muddled baby body very slowly began to come together, in words that he found. She writes, "the words … [were] sometimes relished … at those times the baby's mouth seemed to be tasting the words, eating words, and spitting them out of his mouth with pleasure" (Ibid., 477). The discoveries that Enid Balint made in the work with Mr Smith accentuated her profound conviction that,

> In my view the analyst has to be just as observant, perhaps even more so, about what he does not do as about what he does. What the analyst does not say must be remembered by him more carefully than what he does say, because the decision to leave it to the patient, or to wait for the right time, is a very important one. It is so much easier to say what comes to one's mind when a patient says something than to remember what one thought but did not say.
>
> (Balint 1993a, 126)

Enid hypothesized that Mr Smith's ability to perceive external reality had been lost around the time of the birth of his sister, when he was three, when the world felt totally unacceptable to him. He could not learn about it or play with it, which would have made him feel part of the world. "He had no sense of himself in a place" (Balint 1987, 481). One task of the analysis was to allow him a feeling of time for growth and development, time for him to find his own story, told in his own words, in order to be able to imagine his own existence. Enid Balint writes, "The recognition of patterns and similarities is essential if a baby is to build up a world in which he can live and locate himself. Presumably … the mother has to recognise her infant, make him feel he belongs" (Ibid., 482). Mr Smith's traumatic perceptions of his sister had been disavowed, leading to a loss of memory of the world in which the perception occurred, and a loss of an imaginative world of 'I' and 'other' in which he could play and find his way to understanding it. Mr Smith found with his analyst an unobtrusive other who could wait while Mr Smith discovered his language and could begin to tell his story. Juliet Mitchell summarized, "… in the context of a truly present 'other', the imaginative perception of reality can emerge and memory and consciousness become possible" (Mitchell 1993, 85).

Conclusion

Enid Balint named and elaborated the centrality of mutuality and mutual concern in healthy development, her concepts that join the two participants together. Mutuality and mutual concern set the infant, with (m)other, on the path towards imaginative perception and that in turn is integral to having an imaginative and creative life. Our enduring appreciation of Enid Balint is her clinical understanding of the significance of these in the analytic relationship. We end with her words: "I am ... interested in, and listening for, what is happening between two people, although I bear in mind that there may be three people, or no distinct person at all" (Balint 1993b, 225).

Note

1 See also Sklar 2017, 19.

Acknowledgements

First presented at Independent Psychoanalysis Trust Conference:
Independent Women Psychoanalysts of the British Psychoanalytical Society – 23 July 2019, London, England.

References

Antonis, B. & Wolf, E. (2008). 'Affect and Body: On the Contribution of Independent Women Psychoanalysts'. In: *Female Experience: Four Generations of British Women Psychoanalysts on Work with Women* Second Edition, Raphael-Leff, J. & Perelberg, R. (eds), London: Anna Freud Centre, 315–329.

Balint, E. (1963). 'On Being Empty of Oneself'. *International Journal of Psychoanalysis*, 44: 470–480.

Balint, E. (1968). 'The Mirror and the Receiver'. In: *Before I Was I: Psychoanalysis and the Imagination*, Mitchell, J. & Parsons, M. (eds), London: Free Association Books, 1993, 56–62.

Balint, E. (1973). 'Technical Problems found in the Analysis of Women by a Woman Analyst: A Contribution to the Question What Does a Woman Want?', *International Journal of Psychoanalysis*, 54: 195–201.

Balint, E. (1983). 'Memory and Consciousness'. Chapter 7 in: *Before I Was I: Psychoanalysis and the Imagination*, Mitchell, J. & Parsons, M. (eds), London: Free Association Books, 1993, 85–98.

Balint, E. (1989). 'Creative Life'. Chapter 8 in: Before I Was I: Psychoanalysis and the Imagination, Mitchell, J. & Parsons, M. (eds), London: Free Association Books, 1993, 99–108.

Balint, E. (1990). 'Unconscious Communication'. Chapter 9 in: *Before I Was I: Psychoanalysis and the Imagination*, Mitchell, J. & Parsons, M. (eds), London: Free Association Books, 1993, 109–118.

Balint, E. (1993a). 'One Analyst's Technique'. Chapter 10 in: *Before I Was I: Psychoanalysis and the Imagination*, Mitchell, J. & Parsons, M. (eds), London: Free Association Books, 1993, 119–129.

Balint, E. (1993b). 'Enid Balint Interviewed by Juliet Mitchell'. Chapter 18 in: *Before I Was I: Psychoanalysis and the Imagination*, Mitchell, J. & Parsons, M. (eds), London: Free Association Books, 1993, 221–236.

Mitchell, J. (1993). 'Introductions to Chapters in Part 1'. In: *Before I Was I: Psychoanalysis and the Imagination*, Mitchell, J. & Parsons, M. (eds), London: Free Association Books, 1993.

Parsons, M. (1993). 'Introduction'. In: *Before I Was I: Psychoanalysis and the Imagination*, Mitchell, J. & Parsons, M. (eds), London: Free Association Books, 1993, 1–7.

Parsons, M. (2021). 'Then and Now: Revisiting Enid Balint's *Before I Was I: Psychoanalysis and the Imagination*', *Journal of the American Psychoanalytic Association*, 69/6: 1199–1214.

Sklar, J. (2017). 'Regression and New Beginnings: Michael, Alice and Enid Balint, and the circulation of Ideas'. In: *Balint Matters: Psychosomatics and the Art of Assessment*, London: Karnac Books, 3–25.

Winnicott, D.W. (1963). 'The Development of the Capacity for Concern'. In: *The Collected Works of D.W. Winnicott*, Volume 6, 1960–1963, Caldwell, L. & Taylor Robinson, H., New York: Oxford University Press, 2017, 351–356.

Index

Note: Locators in *italic* indicate figures.

Abraham, K 18, 37
Abram, J 70–81, 150n4
affect, spontaneous and authentic 142–147
affect, theory of 31n15, 65, 71, 77–79, 80, 105–106, 107
affective response of the analyst 25, 63, 95, 124–126
'Affects in Theory and Practice' (Brierley) 71, 76, 77–79
aggression 6, 10, 22, 59, 61, 80, 89, 109, 164
alertness 64, 137
aliveness 65, 116, 148
Alster, E 13, 86–100
analyst's emotional response 78, 88, 92, 95, 98, 124, 145
analyst's hate 145–146
analyst's love 142–145, 152n25
analytic attitude 63, 86, 99
analytic courage 99, 100
analytic frame 110–111
analytic relationship 25–27, 125
analytical situation, 2-people relationship 25–26, 30n9, 90, 91–92; *see also* Heimann, P
Anna Freud National Centre for Children and Families 27
Answering Activity 113–115
antisemitism 18, 30n3, 38
Antonis, B 3–14, 75, 156–169
anxiety, separation 22, 23
Apostles, Cambridge Apostles Society 44
Ariadne thread 77–78
Armistice letter 13, 70, 73–74, 80, 82n5
art and sublimation 60–62, 63, 66

artist 60–62, 63, 107, 137, 150–151n7, 150n5
Association of Independent Psychoanalysts (AIP) 5, 12, 15n17
atmosphere, BPAS 4, 6, 9, 18, 40, 42, 43
atmosphere, clinical work 137–140
attunement 28, 71, 79
authentic self 3, 142
authentic voice 11, 13
authenticity 26, 135, 145
autonomy 20

Balint, E 14, 26, 156–169; biographical details 157; case studies: Mr Smith 167–169 / Mrs X 163 / Mrs Y 164–167 / Sarah 159–163; imaginative perception 111–112, 156, 159, 162, 166–167, 168–169; mutual concern 156, 162, 163, 164–166, 168–169; mutuality, mutual experience 143, 156, 159–161, 164–165, 166, 168–169
Balint, M 21, 24, 25, 151n9
Bare Attention 136, 137–138, 140, 145
Barnett, B 131
becoming a psychoanalyst 3–14, 128, 157
Bell, V 37
Berlin 18, 37, 53–54, 55, 72, 74, 88–89
Bion, W 79, 139–140, 143, 151n15, 151n17, 158
blind drawing 136–137
Bloomsbury Group, BPAS 3, 17, 35, 36; Adrian and Karin Stephen 37–38; concept of freedom 40–41; James and Alix Strachey 37
bodily experience 107, 114, 165
body 162, 165